FIN·DE·SIÈCLE
SOCIALISM

FIN·DE·SIÈCLE SOCIALISM

SOCIALISM

and other essays,

MARTIN JAY

ROUTLEDGE · NEW YORK & LONDON

For Cathy, again

First published in 1988 by
Routledge
An imprint of Routledge, Chapman and Hall, Inc.
29 West 35 Street
New York, NY 10001

Published in Great Britain by
Routledge
11 New Fetter Lane
London EC4P 4EE

Library of Congress Cataloging in Publication Data

Jay, Martin, 1944–
  Fin-de-siècle socialism.

  Includes bibliographies.
  1. Communism—1945–   . I. Title.
HX44.J324 1988   335.43′09   88–18460
ISBN 0–415–90007–7
ISBN 0–415–90008–5 (pbk.)

British Library Cataloguing in Publication Data

Jay, Martin, 1944–
  Fin-de-siècle socialism.
  1. Socialism
  I. Title
  335
  ISBN 0–415–90007–7
  ISBN 0–415–90008–5 (pbk.)

Contents

Contents

Acknowledgments

A collection of essays always has disparate roots and a wide variety of people who watered them. It is a genuine pleasure now to have a chance to express my gratitude for their acts of intellectual nurturance. Rather than discriminate among those who solicited, commented on or criticized each piece, let me simply name them all and assure them of my thanks for their different kinds of help: Russell Berman, Richard Bernstein, William Bouwsma, Jürgen Habermas, Geoffrey Hartman, Charles Lemert, Eugene Lunn, Steven Kaplan, Lolle Nauta, Paul Piccone, Avital Ronell, Ilya Sruber, Giorgio Tagliacozzo, David Wellbury and Jerry Zaslove. Special appreciation must be extended to Dominick LaCapra, who read the entire manuscript with his characteristic analytical acumen; Leo Lowenthal, who improved virtually all of the essays with his relentless critical scrutiny; and my wife, Catherine Gallagher, who once again proved to be my ideal reader, in more ways than one. Shana Gallagher and Rebecca Jay, who grew along with this collection, also deserve thanks for periodically reminding me that there is life away from the typewriter or under the glare of the reading lamp.

Let me also express my thanks to the journals where several of these pieces first found an audience: *History and Theory*, *Praxis International*, *Telos*, *Theory and Society* and *Stanford Literature Review*. I also owe a debt of gratitude to the presses that published anthologies where others initially appeared: Cornell University Press, Humanities Press, M.I.T. Press, Polity Press and the Suhrkamp Verlag. Finally, I want to acknowledge the efforts of my editor at Routledge, William P. Germano, who has once again helped me collect my thoughts; Diane Gibbons, who copyedited the manuscript, and Gerd Horten, who prepared the index.

1

Fin-de-siècle Socialism

At first glance, the title of this essay may seem perversely oxymoronic. The term *fin-de-siècle*, after all, normally conjures up the anxious and despairing mood associated with the decadents of late 19th-century bourgeois culture, while the socialism of that same era was still in the full flush of its exuberant youth. Although the now familiar notion of a "crisis in Marxism" was in fact first introduced by Thomas Masaryk in 1898,[1] the overwhelming majority of his contemporaries on the left looked confidently to the dawning new century for the realization of their hopes. Indeed, for many bourgeois intellectuals who sought a way out of the melancholic paralysis of *fin-de-siècle* culture, identification with the socialist movement was a frequent choice. Not surprisingly, many of these same intellectuals who later reflected on the phenomenon, such as Georg Lukács,[2] damned the *fin-de-siècle* literati as the self-pitying spokesmen of a moribund class class about to be swept off the historical stage. Socialism, they insisted, must look for its cultural models to the earlier period of a bourgeois culture on the ascendancy, when healthier models of organic wholeness were produced by a rising historical class. There was nothing positive, so they claimed, to be learned from dwelling on a backward-looking, nostalgic phenomenon with no relevance to an expected socialist future.

We are now, however, fast approaching the *fin* of another *siècle*, and one in which such glowing expectations seem further than ever from realization. It may, therefore, be instructive to consider the possible parallels between the late 19th century and the waning years of our own. For in so doing, we may find some suggestions for the socialism that is likely to develop in the 21st century. Bourgeois culture, like

1

bourgeois society, survived its apparent decadence and found new ways to invigorate itself. So too socialism, both as a theoretical tradition and a body of practices, may well find the means to transcend the current mood of what has appropriately been called "left melancholy"[3] in the century to come.

No better starting point for an analysis of the bourgeois *fin-de-siècle* can be found in the writings of that great diagnostician of decadence, Friedrich Nietzsche, whose ideas, not coincidentally, are no less current today than they were a century ago. "What is the sign of every literary decadence?," he asked in *The Case of Wagner*, and answered:

> That life no longer dwells in the whole. The word becomes sovereign and leaps out of the sentence, the sentence reaches out and obscures the meaning of the page, the page gains life at the expense of the whole—the whole is no longer a whole. But this is the simile of every style of *decadence*: every time, the anarchy of atoms, disaggregation of the will . . . .[4]

For many attracted to socialism in the wake of this disaggregation, it was precisely its promise to overcome such antinomian fragmentation and restore or construct for the first time a new whole that proved so alluring. In particular, as I have tried to demonstrate elsewhere,[5] the lure of totality as a normative goal was one of the defining characteristics of the tradition of Western Marxism, which began with Lukács, Karl Korsch, Ernst Bloch, and Antonio Gramsci in the years after the Russian Revolution. Often themselves survivors of youthful infatuations with bourgeois decadence, they came to argue that a new cultural harmony could only be forged on the basis of a genuine social community in which the multiple fractures of modern life were healed.

The history of Western Marxism is, however, the story of the progressive unravelling of that hope. For it became increasingly clear to most of its later adherents that normative totality as the perfectly harmonious community posited by Hegelian Marxism at its most utopian was neither a coherent nor a viable goal. And concomitantly, the attempt to employ a descriptive notion of totality to make sense of the longitudinal course of history or even the current synchronic whole also foundered. As a result, the spectre of detotalization and disintegration, which haunted the bourgeois *fin-de-siècle*, has returned to chill the socialist movement—if one can still speak of it in the singular—of our own day.

Of the many reasons for this displaced repetition of an earlier trajectory, let me single out only a few for special emphasis. To distinguish totality from either an infinity or an aggregate, it was necessary to specify its external boundaries or limits and identify the coherence of its internal structure. The former generally meant isolating something called "history" or "society" from something else called "nature," and then restricting the category of totality only to the former.[6] The process of totalization could thus be understood in part as emancipation from what Marx had called *Naturwüchsigkeit* or man's embeddedness in nature. Inspired in part by the methodological differentiation of the *Geistes-* from the *Naturwissenschaften* in the late 19th century and reacting against the invasion of Second International Marxism by Darwinian and other non-dialectical assumptions, the early Western Marxists sought to delimit the concept of totality by excluding the natural from it. Although the reified social relations of capitalism might be seen as functioning like a "second nature," which could be dissolved by de-reifying revolutionary praxis, there remained the thorny problem of the role "first" nature played in any society, even the most emancipated. When Western Marxists like the members of the Frankfurt School began seriously to consider the costs of excluding nature from the historical totality, they also began to question the self-sufficiency of a purely historicist notion of that whole. As Theodor Adorno noted as early as 1932, nature and history were best grasped as a chiasmic couplet in the idea of "natural history."[7] In other words, the domination of nature inherent in the species imperialism of an overly historicist view of the totality had to be resisted by giving the natural object its due, without however regressing to an equally one-sided naturalistic ontology.

Because socialist holism was based on a strongly humanist and productivist notion of totalization, it could easily become the target of an ecological alternative, which decentered "man" from "his" central expressivist role. Although certain ecologists have themselves argued for a holistic complementarity between man and nature, they have explicitly jettisoned the Promethean impulse of Marxism and other industrially fixated socialist theories with their celebration of *homo faber*. The new ecological activism is, paradoxically, directed against an exaggerated humanist confidence in our ability to remake the world in our own image. In some ways, it draws on an essentially passive notion of "letting-be" derived, consciously or not, more from writers like Martin Heidegger and late Maurice Merleau-Ponty than from traditional historical materialists.[8] Even when ecologists like the German Green theorists Thomas Ebermann and Rainer Trampert try to link their ideas to the socialist movement, they reinterpret radical needs in terms of a post-materialist notion of diminished productive development that smacks more of Charles Fourier than Marx.[9]

Not only did problems with the external natural frontier of the totality develop—so too did concerns with what might be called its internal frontier, when Marxists like Wilhelm Reich and Herbert Marcuse began to insist on the importance of psychology. For now the sufficiency of a purely social analysis, which reduced individual interiority to a reflex of social institutions, was called into question. The "over-socialized concept of man" criticized by non-Marxists was also implicitly challenged by Marxists as well. The relationship between psychology and sociology, like that between nature and history, was understood more in chiasmic than dialectical terms, with the result that no totalizing higher third could be invoked to synthesize their separate logics.[10]

If the external and internal boundaries of the totality have come to appear harder to grasp, so too has its coherent structure. To avoid the reduction of the whole to a mere aggregate of disparate and autonomous elements, Marxist holism necessarily sought to locate an essential level of determination within the whole. Although the simple base-superstructure economism of the Second International gave way to the Marxist Humanist alternative of a creative meta-subject, with the proletariat as the constitutive universal class of history, the basic model of a hierarchically determining, totalizing center was retained. Even when Louis Althusser attacked Hegelian Marxism for its expressivist notion of the totality, he held on doggedly to the belief in a dominant structure, an economic mode of production that was determinant in a last instance that paradoxically never came. With the collapse of the Althusserian project, manifested in such widely remarked apostasies as that of Barry Hindess and Paul Hirst,[11] the search for a privileged key to unlock the structural mechanism determining the whole has been all but abandoned. If, to borrow Claus Offe's phrase, we live in an era of "disorganized capitalism,"[12] it has seemed highly problematic to assume the existence of a coherent organizational principle.

This lesson has been widely absorbed by many of the theoreticians of *fin-de-siècle* socialism. Ernesto Laclau and Chantal Mouffe, lapsed Althusserians, are salient examples. In their recent *Hegemony and Socialist Strategy*, they explicitly attack all essentialist a priorism and with it the search for a viable notion of the social whole:

> The incomplete character of every totality necessarily leads us to abandon, as a terrain of analysis, the premise of "*Society*" as a sutured and self-defined totality. "Society" is not a valid object of discourse. There is no single underlying principle fixing—and hence constituting—the whole field of differences.[13]

Instead, they argue for a revised version of Gramsci's notion of hegemony filtered through a post-structuralist critique of the possibility of an identitarian subjectivity. An inevitable casualty of their alternative is a strong notion of a universal historical agent. And so with André Gorz and many others, they bid their *adieux au proletariat*.[14]

If, as Laclau and Mouffe conclude, a holistic view of society—indeed any generic notion of society—is no longer a valid object of discourse, one major reason for this contention derives from the now widespread hostility to any epistemological vantage point claiming totalistic knowledge. Marxism's more scientific adherents had implicitly assumed the God's eye view of a transcendental, monological meta-subject able to grasp the whole from a presumed point exterior to it. Their critical, neo-Hegelian competitors turned instead to the argument ultimately derived from Giambattista Vico's *verum-factum* principle, which claimed epistemological privilege stemmed from constitutive power.[15] That is, the proletariat as the maker of the social whole would come to recognize itself in the alienated and reified institutions of the capitalist world. This totalistic understanding would lead to a revolutionary reappropriation of the social world by the class ultimately responsible for its construction.

A host of trenchant criticisms have been raised in many quarters against both of these epistemological models, which I need not detail now. What might, however, be emphasized is the realization, perhaps most clearly expressed in the work of the late Alvin Gouldner, that the totalistic claims of Marxism, whether scientific or critical, were far less a reflection of the putative universality of the proletariat than that presumed by another group in society, the intellectuals.[16] Although Gouldner's contention that they constituted a new class of their own with their own universalist claims remains controversial, his injunction to examine the interests of theorists rather than the claims of theory has been difficult to ignore. Rather than articulating the needs and aspirations of others, the intellectuals—who have always played a vital role in any socialist discourse—must be understood as a social group (or a constellation of several groups) with their own agenda. Michel Foucault's well-known critique of the universalist intellectuals so often found in the socialist camp in the name of a more "specific" intellectual able to engage in far more limited struggles, expresses their new modesty about the totalizing pretensions of those who arrogate to themselves knowledge of the whole.[17]

Perhaps even more powerful than the critique of intellectual arrogance has been the effect of the feminist attack on the gender assumptions of the traditional Marxist humanist notion of subjectivity. The privileging of class as the determinant of meaningful social cohesion has meant marginalizing sexual difference. However fruitful it may be to compare the exchange of women with commodity exchange or situate the sexual division of labour in its economic counterpart, we now know that the politics of reproduction cannot be completely re-described in terms of the politics of production. As a result the social struggles around issues of patriarchy and misogyny are never subsumable under those dealing with economic issues, however much they may be intertwined. Despite the many attempts to articulate a coherent socialist feminism, it is difficult to avoid the conclusion that the relationship between the two movements is an uneasy articulation rather than a smoothly harmonious totalization.

The retreat of the intellectual from "his" putative role as spokesman for the whole and the feminist critique of an allegedly ungendered humanist collective subject suggests another dimension of *fin-de-siècle* socialism, which echoes its bourgeois predecessor. I refer to what might be called the crisis of representation, which is so widely remarked today. Here the domains of politics, culture, and language are intricately intertwined. One of the cliches of literary history is that decadence involved, among other things, an attenuation of the link between sign and referent, whose complete separation was then realized in certain forms of aesthetic modernism.[18] If there remained a mimetic or referential element in the *fin-de-siècle* aesthetic, it generally involved the interior state of the artist's sensibility rather than the external world of historical or social reality. But even here words were understood as scarcely adequate to the task of faithfully reproducing such internal experiences. Whatever confidence the earlier Romantics may have had in the expressive abilities of language or the earlier Realists in its mimetic capacities—and there is now a widespread suspicion that they were not as secure as we once assumed—it was severely undermined by the *fin-de-siècle*. Although it has recently been argued that the leaving behind of an expressivist or representational aesthetic made room for the productivist Marxist aesthetics of a Vladimir Tatlin or Bertolt Brecht,[19] the more immediate impact was to enable language to close in on itself and withdraw from external concerns almost entirely.

Ultimately, to be sure, it was not so much a belief in the inadequacy of language to represent its objective that blocked any easy notion of representation as its opposite. That is, the inability of language to avoid over-representation has been widely remarked in the wake of recent discussions of the excessive surplus of signification produced by linguistic performance. But whether the problem is understood in terms of under- or over-representation, the simple notion of congruence between word and thing assumed before the linguistic turn of 20th-century thought is no longer remotely defensible.

In our own era, the crisis of representation and mimesis has, of course, been extended beyond the sphere of aesthetics narrowly defined to embrace all language, including that which socialist theoreticians have used to conceptualize social relations. The implication has also been quickly drawn that representation is a political problem as well, and one especially acute for socialists in the face of the disastrous history of vanguard parties claiming to speak in the name of the proletariat.[20] A certain fit between advocating such representative politics and the aesthetics of representation in the work of such Marxist thinkers as Lukács has not escaped attention.

Interestingly, the traditional leftist antidote to the danger of indirect representation promoted by Jean-Jacques Rousseau and his progeny, that of direct democracy, has lost much of its allure in the aftermath of inconclusive attempts to realize it in the modern world, such as workers' self-management in Yugoslavia. An indication of this realization can be found in the continuing popularity of writers like Hannah Arendt, who scrupulously segregate the ideal of direct political democracy from any socio-economic entanglement. Even more tellingly, the post-structuralist critique of perfect transparency and immediacy has made the very idea of a totally unrepresented collective will itself problematic.[21] Instead, contemporary writers like Jacques Rancière have pondered the question "how can a social relation be represented in the political order"[22] when the proletariat has shown itself to be unrepresentable? Others like Claude Lefort have responded by questioning the very notion of a popular sovereign who can ever be positively represented. Perhaps instead, in modern, non-totalitarian societies, the site of power is best conceptualized as a space occupied by no identifiable force, a space which defies any coherent representation.[23] Accordingly, other commentators like Jean Cohen have contended that the very search for a revolutionary subject whose interests and will might be expressed in a unified way is an outmoded quest more likely to lead to oppression than emancipation.[24] For if no totality can be understood as the exfoliation of an expressivist subject, it is dangerous to posit the potential existence of such a subject in the future, which can be proleptically represented. As was the case with *fin-de-siècle* bourgeois culture, the crisis of representation and totality has been accompanied by a loss of faith in the strong, self-conscious subject, whether individual or collective.

Other parallels between the waning years of the 19th and the 20th centuries might be suggested, but before the pattern of repetition and displacement becomes too mechanically predictable, it is time to shift gears and examine some of the differences between *fin-de-siècle* socialism and its bourgeois predecessor. For, the new Nietzscheanism to the contrary notwithstanding, history has a way of defeating simple returns. Perhaps the most notable difference is the disparity between the original *fin-de-siècle*'s attitude towards politics itself and our own. Whereas one of the earmarks of 19th-century decadence was a retreat from the realm of politics into aesthetic or psychological pursuits,[25] *fin-de-siècle* socialism has in contrast rediscovered its value. There was, to be sure, a withdrawal from the often apocalyptic, expressivist politics of the New Left into personal, even narcissistic self-absorption during the 1970s. The so-called *neue Innerlichkeit* of the West German *Tendenzwende* is an obvious example. But the widely discussed new social movements of the 1980s have reignited an interest in political activism, different from the discredited version of the old and the new left. The terrain, of course, has shifted dramatically. For rather than focusing on toppling or seizing the bourgeois state, an impotent strategy which reflected the still totalistic impulses of an earlier era, the new politics has rediscovered the plural sites of civil society, now understood as far more than the economic market place. Rather than seeking a perfectly unitarian political identity, its practitioners are willing to play different roles in different contexts. Instead of challenging the system as a whole through what Marcuse made famous as the "great refusal," they have abandoned the very belief in an identifiable, coherent system to be overthrown. Rather than seeking an ultimate explanation for all oppression in economic, productivist, or class terms, they've sought to yoke together a series of relatively autonomous struggles in a loose and unhierarchical bloc or coalition. And without effacing entirely the boundaries between public and private, as the New Left tended to do in certain of its moods, they have come to acknowledge the shifting ways in which political activity can manifest itself in both. Here the importance of the ecological and feminist movements mentioned above must once again be emphasized.

Accompanying the new respect for the multiple sites of political practice has been a no less widespread reassessment of the value of bourgeois democracy as more than a mere ideological smokescreen. Typical of the new attitude is the work of the Italian political theorist Norberto Bobbio, who concludes a recent survey of the internal contradictions between democratic theory and practice with the affirmation that "unkept promises and unanticipated obstacles notwithstanding, they have not been such as to 'transform' democratic into autocratic regimes. The substantial difference between the two remains. The minimal content of the democratic state has not diminished."[26] Eschewing both the goal of direct democracy and the vanguardist notion of a representative elite speaking in the name of *the* subject of history, Bobbio and others have emphasized the ways in which liberal democratic forms, however imperfect, provide for the adjudication of the different claims coming from an inevitably pluralist civil society. Here politics is not conceptualized in terms of an absolutely expressive congruence between spheres, but rather as one element in a more decentered structural complex. Representation is thus conceived neither as an evil entirely to be distrusted—as in the direct democratic model—nor as a perfect embodiment of an objective universal interest—as in the Leninist model—but rather as an inevitably flawed, but nonetheless indispensible mechanism in a non-totalized world.

This new appreciation of the value of democratic politics is apparent in the work of many socialist theorists with a variety of different pedigrees. Former Budapest School follows of Lukács like Agnes Heller, Ferenc Fehér, and Mihaly Vajda have been joined by former Trotskyists like Cornelius Castoriadis and Claude Lefort; ex-Althusserians like Chantal Mouffe and Ernesto Laclau have converged with Frankfurt School devotees like Seyla Benhabib and Jean Cohen.[27] And even the *New Left Review* has muted much of its Leninist rhetoric and gingerly embraced some of the arguments of Jürgen Habermas.[28] In all of these writers, despite continuing differences of emphasis, there is a common recognition of the value of democratic politics in itself as something irreducible to socio-economic class struggle. And with that recognition has gone a new emphasis on the dangers of socialist traditions, like Leninism, that promised the end of politics in the name of a unified sovereign will.[29]

Here, to be sure, theory has been closely following practice, as the most laudable struggles of the recent past and present have been those (such as the anti-apartheid movement in South Africa, Solidarity in Poland, and Corey Aquino's overthrow of Ferdinand Marcos in the Phillipines) that focus more on demands for political democratization than for changes in the mode of production. Even in actually existing socialist states like China, a yearning for greater democratization appears to stir more political activism than any other goal. It may also be possible in the Soviet Union of Mikhail Gorbachev to see glimmers of a similar trend, even if it is by no means clear how far it can go.

Although it would be easy to dismiss this development as a mere echo of a shopworn ideology more often celebrated than realized in the capitalist West, it would be an enormous mistake to underplay its significance for the future of socialism. The checkered history of post-revolutionary socialist societies in our century strongly suggests that unless democratic institutions are safeguarded and expanded, there is a remarkable pressure to gravitate to other, far less savory political forms. It surely would have chagrined Marx—although perhaps not his more libertarian critics like Mikhail Bakunin—to see how comfortable socialism and political authoritarianism can be together. The bizarre

spectacle of autocratic rulers like Joseph Stalin, Josip Tito and Mao Tse-
tung holding on to power for life suggests, in fact, that monarchy is a
far more likely prototype for socialist politics in certain 20th-century
regimes than anything remotely derivable from the democratic
tradition—at least in its liberal and parliamentary forms.[30]

If *fin-de-siècle* socialist theory has come to value that tradition and fear
for its obliteration, this shift typifies another of its salient characteristics: its cautious willingness to defend, however selectively, the
achievements of bourgeois modernization, and not merely in terms of
technological progress. Here the abandonment of totalistic modes of
thought has meant a refusal to counterpose capitalism as a package,
with all of its contents equally tainted, to an alleged socialist alternative
understood as its radical negation. Habermas in particular has given
voice to this defensive dimension of *fin-de-siècle* socialism with his
widely discussed plea to continue supporting the "uncompleted project
of modernity."[31] As he recently told two Dutch interviewers:

> What constitutes the idea of socialism, for me, is the possibility of
> overcoming the onesidedness of the capitalist process of rationaliza-
> tion . . . in the sense of the rise to dominance of cognitive-
> instrumental aspects, which results in everything else being driven
> into the realm of apparent irrationality. . . . My criticism of Marx is
> that he failed to see that capitalist production methods ushered in not
> only a new apolitical form of class domination, but a new level of
> system differentiation (as Luhmann would say). This differentiation
> had enormous evolutionary advantages over the level reached in
> state-organized societies of pre-bourgeois periods.[32]

This clear-eyed, one might even say glowing, affirmation of differentiation is shared by Habermas with many other current socialist
theoreticians, who have been disabused of the goal of complete
normative totalization in the Hegelian Marxist mold. Even among the
leftist opposition in Eastern Europe, as Heller and Fehér have recently
noted,[33] the yearning for totality has been all but abandoned. This shift
suggests one final contrast between *fin-de-siècle* socialism and its
bourgeois prototype. For the loss of hope in so utopian an outcome has
meant a corresponding acceptance of the inevitable imperfections of
whatever social order humans might create. Despite the onset of "left
melancholy" in the wake of the New Left's collapse, there is little of
that desperate, lacerating cultural despair that marked the decadence
of the late 19th century. Even though in a nuclear age, there may well
be better grounds for apocalyptic nightmares, the mood of *fin-de-siècle*
socialism, if one can tentatively generalize about such things, is not as
self-indulgently hysterical as that of its bourgeois predecessor. Even

the radical foreboding that led earlier leftists like Rosa Luxemburg to posit a melodramatic choice between socialism and barbarism no longer seems very pervasive. We have survived too long in the midst of that "state of emergency"[34] Walter Benjamin called our permanent condition in 1940 to feel as compelled as earlier generations may have been to pull the emergency cord.

For as deeply problematic as contemporary society may be, as widespread as its injustices certainly still are, there is little appetite for its wholesale repudiation in the name of a highly uncertain alternative. Unlike the earlier radical intellectuals who welcomed the imminent collapse of a "botched civilization," as Ezra Pound put it, there are few socialists in our *fin-de-siècle* who have fantasies of purgation by fire. Only the scattered and deluded bands of terrorists who are in no meaningful sense on the left express a residual hope in this bankrupt scenario. Their desperado tactics, disruptive and costly as they may be, have utterly failed to ignite anything but an outrage that transcends virtually all political and social boundaries.

The successive disillusionments with various socialist experiments in this century have taken their toll. An overdue recognition of the failures of Second World Communism, so long denied by tortuous exercises in Orwellian double-speak, has been followed by the collapse of hopes in salvation from the Third World. A history of victimization can no longer be seen in itself as a source of privileged access to a superior future. In fact, the entire progressivist discourse in which certain classes or countries were understood as the cutting edge of a world-historical movement has been called deeply into question.

Once again an interesting difference can be discerned in relation to the 19th century *fin-de-siècle*. Whereas bourgeois decadence soon gave way to a militantly modernist aesthetic movement that saw itself as the vanguard of cultural vitalization, contemporary culture—whether it be called post-modernist or not—has given up the grandiose project of the avant-garde.[35] In fact, belief in the twin, often intertwined vanguards of the early 20th century, aesthetic and political, has been replaced by a general wariness about any group claiming to represent the onset of a future whose narrative only they can somehow foretell. Whatever one may feel about the ambiguous claims of the celebrants of post-modernism, their turn against the overblown rhetoric of cultural redemption once employed by many modernists resonates well with the mood of *fin-de-siècle* socialism. Even defenders of modernity like Habermas have resolutely jettisoned the vanguardist pretensions of political and aesthetic elites.

If one were to isolate perhaps the most striking difference between the original *fin-de-siècle* and our own, it would concern the question of redemption itself. For if the bourgeois decadents were wracked by a mood of cultural desperation, it was largely because of their still potent yearnings for messianic redemption of one sort or another.[36] Here the old trope of initial unity, then temporary disunity, and ultimate higher unity, a trope derived from religious roots and evident in Romantic and Idealist historiosophies in the 19th century,[37] was still powerfully effective. As has often been noted, the birth of Western Marxism at the end of the first world war and in the aftermath of the Bolshevik Revolution was deeply marked by messianic expectations. Figures like Lukács, Bloch, Benjamin, and Leo Lowenthal cannot be understood without reference to this highly charged context. As late as the 1940s, Adorno could still claim that decadence harbored within it an embryonic utopian impulse that could reverse the decline of the West.[38]

Such rhetoric, indeed the very concept of a redeemed social being, is largely absent from *fin-de-siècle* socialism. In the pages of journals like *Telos*, where it once reigned supreme, the politics of redemption has come under increasing fire by commentators like Joel Whitebook and Ferenc Fehér.[39] Attacking it as a residue of the Romantic counter-enlightenment, they have argued instead for a more sober politics of *Mündigkeit* or maturity, in which the utopian hope of perfect reconciliation and normative totality are quietly laid to rest. Here the guiding spirit is that of Habermas, who has become perhaps the exemplary socialist theoretician of the mood I have been claiming pervades the end of our century. Ironically, in the light of his well-known quarrels with post-structuralism, he shares with its advocates a fundamental distrust of a single meta-narrative of normative totalization. His stress on differentiation is not, to be sure the same as theirs on *différance*, but both express reservations about the nostalgic *cum* utopian hope for total dedifferentiation expressed in the socialism of redemption.

The lowering of expectations evident in the politics of *Mündigkeit* has not, to be sure, gone unchallenged by those who fear the watering down of *fin-de-siècle* socialism into little more than a radical democratic opposition in a still bourgeois world.[40] Optimistically believing in a counter-hegemonic block of disparate protest groups, they claim, fails to address the difficulty of coordinating their different agendas; rainbow coalitions, they worry, can be as ephemeral as the natural phenomenon for which they are named. Without a more all-embracing emancipatory project, what is to keep the different groups from working only for their selfish interests in a climate of *sauve qui peut*?

This anxiety has not gone unnoticed by advocates or the new post-redemptive socialism. Laclau and Mouffe, for example, agree that without "utopia," without the possibility of negating an order beyond the point that we are able to threaten it, there is no possibility at all of the constitution of a radical imaginary—whether democratic or of any other type. The presence of this imaginary as a set of symbolic meanings which totalize as negativity a certain social order is absolutely essential for the constitution of all left-wing thought.[41]

But then they remind us that there will always be a tension between this utopian imaginary and its realization. Thus, "every radical democratic politics should avoid the two extremes represented by the totalitarian myth of the Ideal City, and the positivist pragmatism of reformists without a project."[42]

Habermas also expresses a certain cautious insistence on the utopian moment in the emancipatory project, but he warns against trying to flesh it out in concrete terms, a mistake Marx made with his productivist belief in liberation through dominating nature. For Habermas instead, "the only utopian perspectives in social theory which we can straightforwardly maintain are of a procedural nature. For the utopian lineaments of any future emancipated society can be no more than necessary general conditions of it. They cannot be in the nature of a design for a form of life."[43]

For those who find this argument too bloodless and politically uninspiring—who, after all, would man the barricades for a utopia of procedures?—the importance of *fin-de-siècle* socialism's defense of the achievements of enlightenment emancipation should not be forgotten. If, as a number of observers have argued, new social movements can in large measure be understood as defensive reactions of a communicatively rationalized life-world against the incursions of an instrumentally rationalized state and market,[44] then we can understand the socialist imaginary—even in its utopian form—as much in terms of preserving and expanding historical gains as in those of dreaming of a redeemed future.

Fin-de-siècle socialism honors the memory of those who once had such dreams not by a doctrinaire retention of obsolete expectations, whose inevitable shipwreck could only lead to a paralyzing disillusionment. It does so instead by refashioning the best impulses of the socialist tradition for the challenges of a new century—or to be more precise, of a new millenium, in which the millennial hopes of the last are finally laid to rest. There is sufficient work to be done without being haunted by the need to measure what modest successes might be granted to us against the daunting model of a normatively totalized, fully redeemed social order. For such a utopia, we must finally admit, is a last instance that can never come.

FROM INTELLECTUAL HISTORY TO CULTURAL CRITICISM

2

Should Intellectual History Take a Linguistic Turn? Reflections on the Habermas–Gadamer Debate

When the intellectual historians of the next century come to write their accounts of our own, they will inevitably remark on the dramatic quickening of interest in virtually all disciplines in the question of language. Although anticipations of this change can be discerned in literature before 1900, an obvious example being the poetics of Stephane Mallarmé, the twentieth century dawned with the long-standing assumption still widely unshaken that language is an essentially transparent medium for the expression of ideas and emotions or the description of an external world. Private mental reflection was thus taken to be prior to public, intersubjective discourse. Generally accompanying the equally time-honored notion that truth is an adequate expression of objective reality, this concept of language can be traced at least as far back as Plato's denigration of Sophistic rhetoric and the poetical ambiguities of the Homeric epic.[1] Perhaps its most exaggerated manifestation in the Western philosophical tradition was Baruch Spinoza's attempt to negate linguistic mediation entirely by casting philosophy in the form of geometric proofs. In the early twentieth century, its greatest exemplar was Ludwig Wittgenstein's *Tractatus* with its contention that language provides *Bilder* (pictures or models) of a real external world.[2]

Although, to be sure, there were isolated exceptions, such as the antischolastic rhetoricians of the Italian Renaissance, most notably Lorenzo Valla and Mario Nizolio, and the later, relatively isolated figures of Giambattista Vico and Johann Georg Hamann, it was not really until our own century that mainstream Western philosophy took a decisive linguistic turn. Why this occurred, whether or not it was a product of the crisis in signification in later bourgeois culture, cannot concern us now. What is important to note instead is that the linguistic turn in philosophy affected many other disciplines and came in several different forms. It is now even threatening to penetrate the defenses of that most conservative of cultural enterprises, the study of history, through the opening provided by intellectual historians who have allowed what they examine to influence how they examine it.

Before speculating on the wisdom of following their example, one must determine which theory of language is being employed—for the rejection of the older descriptive model has taken several forms. Despite certain examples of cross-fertilization to be noted below, until very recently there has been a remarkable degree of insularity along national lines. In England, the linguistic turn was taken in the interwar era by Wittgenstein at Cambridge and J. L. Austin and Gilbert Ryle at Oxford.[3] Very schematically put and bracketing the differences among them, these philosophers understood language less as a neutral medium of expression or representation than as a complex human activity. Language was first of all speech, which was a central component of what Wittgenstein called a form of life. Accordingly, the philosopher's task was not to construct an ideal metalanguage neutralizing the concrete mediation of the speaker, but rather to examine and clarify ordinary language within specific social contexts. Understanding the meaning of a word as its specific use, the ordinary language philosopher directed his attention to the performative as well as descriptive function of language, at sentences as speech acts (promises, assertions, commands, questions, and so on) as well as propositions about the world. In Austin's terminology, such speech acts have three dimensions: a locutionary one, which conveys their propositional content; an illocutionary one, which conveys their force (the "I promise you that" or "I command you to"); and a perlocutionary one, which is actually what is done after the utterance is made. Because of their illocutionary force in particular, speech acts are to be understood essentially as communication between or among speakers, as intersubjective dialogues. In other words, language is an eminently social practice.

In France, linguistic philosophy has generally meant something very different than in England or Germany.[4] Here the turn came a generation later than in England. After the waning of existentialism, which at least in its Sartrean form paid little attention to language,[5] French culture discovered the revolution in linguistics begun by Ferdinand de Saussure before World War I and combined it with the ethnological speculations of Marcel Mauss to create the explosive movements that have become familiar to us as semiotics, structuralism, and post-structuralism. Abandoning the descriptive view of language, the proponents of these movements did not, however, embrace the English alternative of language as speech and intersubjective communication. Rather than focusing on meaning or intentionality, on the illocutionary dimension of utterances or speech acts, they explored what they saw as the deeper level of structural regularities that constitute language as an unintended and arbitrary system of diacritical signs—what in Saussure's now familiar terminology is the level of *langue* rather than *parole*. Interested less in the historical development of a linguistic system than in its synchronic relations, they tended to dismiss historical consciousness itself as a fictional construct no different from the other codes used in the present to order reality. The repetition of or transformations within a given set of relations interested them far more than change or process.

Although Saussure himself had seen speech as the basis of language, more recent post-structuralists, and here the obvious figure is Jacques Derrida, have emphasized the primacy or at least the equivalent status of writing. With its unspecified audience and absent author, writing suggests the autonomous nature of language as a system beyond human subjectivity. In the name of an impersonal play of intertextuality rather than intersubjectivity, they have systematically deconstructed all received notions of the subject, argued against reducing meaning to the intention of original authors, and inflated the role of the critic of philosopher into that of a godlike producer of new combinations of linguistic signs. Stressing the silences and absences in language, they have sought to unmask the ways language disingenuously hides from itself its inability to represent anything outside its own boundaries.

In the hands of the most historically concerned of the post-structuralists, Michel Foucault, intellectual history has been turned into an archaeology of past discourses whose diachronic transformation into each other is virtually ignored. Grounded in a view of language as more like an archive or library—impersonal, self-referential, and beyond subjective mastery—than an intersubjective dialogue, Foucault's alternative to traditional intellectual history eliminates concern over the issues of origin, cause, source, influence, and purpose. Instead, it concentrates on discontinuities and ruptures, remaining radically hostile to any teleological or causal view of the course of history. Although Foucault's position evolved somewhat over the years, some would say in a direction closer to hermeneutics,[6] and while he has by no means been universally accepted by all post-structuralists, as his widely discussed polemic with Derrida demonstrates,[7] his anti-subjectivist concept of language can be taken to represent the general French attitude of the past two decades.

In Germany, on the other hand, a very different linguistic turn occurred. To understand its roots would require a discussion of German cultural history as far back at least as the Reformation, when Protestants needed to find a way to interpret scripture once the authority of the Catholic Church was no longer binding. The resulting practice of biblical exegesis became known as hermeneutics in the middle of the seventeenth century, following J. C. Dannhauer's use of the word in a book title.[8] Originally a Greek term, it referred to the god Hermes, the sayer or announcer of divine messages—often, to be sure, in oracular and ambiguous form. Hermeneutics retained its early emphasis on saying as it accumulated other meanings such as interpreting, translating, and explaining. Christianity had, of course, long emphasized the importance of the Word, Saint Paul having claimed that salvation comes through the ears. The sacramental character of speech continued to inform later hermeneutic theory as it widened beyond biblical exegesis. The *Sturm und Drang* philosopher Johann Georg Hamann, who shared with Vico a belief in the priority of poetry over prose, saw nature as the embodiment of a divine word that spoke to man.[9] Language and thought, he claimed against Immanuel Kant and the Enlightenment, were one; abstractions violated the natural and sacramental character of the concrete word.

Although Kant and his successors in the idealist movement had little use for Hamann's irrational hermeneutics,[10] it was preserved and extended by the romantics, most notably the theologian Friedrich Schleiermacher. For Schleiermacher, all cultural creation and reception had to be understood as a process of continuous interpretation. His general hermeneutics went beyond the purely religious, legal, and philological uses to which it had previously been put. The understanding that marked everyday human interaction was hermeneutic in nature; all thought, Schleiermacher contended at an early stage in his career, was linguistic. Later he moved toward what might be called a more psychologistic version of hermeneutics in which the meaning to be recaptured was the original intention of a text's author, or even more fundamentally, his actual life experience. This latter assumption was also adopted later in the century by Wilhelm Dilthey in his attempt to ground the *Geisteswissenschaften* in a method of reexperiencing original intentionality. Under the impact of Edmund Husserl, Dilthey shifted away from a psychologistic version of hermeneutics in the last years of his life—but the concept of hermeneutics as the recovery of an original authorial intention of life experience has continued to influence later thinkers such as Emilo Betti, E. D. Hirsch, and, to some extent, Quentin Skinner.[11]

In certain circles, hermeneutics also preserved its links with its religious origins. Twentieth-century theologians like Martin Buber, Franz Rosenzweig, Friedrich Ebner, and Eugen Rosenstock-Huessy continued to share with Hamann a belief that divine revelation came through speech.[12] Committed to what the French post-structuralists would later damn as the "metaphysics of presence," they stressed the power of spoken language to unite subjects in a meaningful dialogue of common understanding—what Buber made famous as an "I-Thou" relationship. In Paul Ricoeur's well-known terms, they practiced hermeneutics as a recollection of primal meaning, a recognition of an original message, rather than as an exercise in suspicion to demystify illusion.[13] The latter, Ricoeur contended, was best exemplified by Karl Marx, Sigmund Freud, and Friedrich Nietzsche, none of whom is normally seen as primarily within the hermeneutics tradition.

Within the more secularized variants of modern German hermeneutics, however, it is possible to see the effects of both tendencies, often in uneasy tension within the same thinker's work. In two recent traditions particularly, that of *Existenzphilosophie* and Critical Theory, both impulses have been operative. Although Martin Heidegger's central preoccupation was the restoration of Being, his later work after his celebrated "turn" emphasized the extent to which language is prior to human intentionality and subjectivity.[14] The demystifying potential in this latter argument has been recognized by no less a deconstructionist than Derrida, who has turned it with Nietzschean ruthlessness against the nostalgic yearnings for wholeness in Heidegger's quest for Being.[15] In Critical Theory, similar yearnings can be discerned in Walter Benjamin's speculations on a primal *Ursprache* and Jürgen Habermas's notion of an ideal speech situation, to which we will return shortly. But insofar as Critical Theory has been concerned with the unmasking of ideology, carried to its extreme in the antinomian moments of Theodor Adorno's negative dialects, it must also be understood as practicing a hermeneutics of suspicion and demystification.

The tensions between the two impulses are in part responsible for the continued fecundity of the two traditions. Indeed, it might be said that the cutting edge of contemporary German hermeneutics is precisely where *Existenzphilosophie* and Critical Theory intersect, for it is here that the implications of the two types of hermeneutics have been most profoundly exposed. The central site of this intersection has been the ongoing debate between Habermas and the major disciple of Heideggerian hermeneutics, Hans-Georg Gadamer. Sparked in 1967 by Habermas's review of Gadamer's *magnum opus, Truth and Method*, the debate has gone through several cycles and generated a flood of secondary comment.[16] It is of particular importance for historians because Habermas specifically extended the scope of hermeneutics beyond philosophy and cultural criticism to the study of society itself. Like Peter Winch, A. R. Louch, and Hanna Pitkin in the ordinary language tradition,[17] and a host of authors in the structuralist and post-structuralist movement, he has speculated on the implications of a linguistic turn for social theory. Although the debate has not focused specifically on the issue of intellectual history, its implications are no less suggestive here than in other fields. Set against the hastily sketched backdrop of the other linguistic turns mentioned above, an examination of the confrontation between Habermas and Gadamer will help us to understand the opportunities and dangers latent in a basically linguistic approach to intellectual history.

Habermas's interest in hermeneutics was itself stimulated by Gadamer's work, so it is not surprising that they share a number of fundamental assumptions. Both reject the traditional philosophical view of language as a disinterested description of the real world, agreeing instead that it is a practical, intersubjective activity. Both see language, as Gadamer put it, as the "self-estrangement of speech," rather than a derivative of writing.[18] And both are interested more in the level of *parole* (or what the Germans call *Rede*) than *langue* (or *Sprache*). In Habermas's words,

> This abstraction of *language* from the use of language in *speech* (*langue* versus *parole*), which is made in both the logical and structuralist analysis of language, is meaningful. Nonetheless, this methodological step is not sufficient reason for the view that the pragmatic dimension of language from which one abstracts is beyond formal analysis . . . not only language but speech too—that is, the employment of sentences in utterances—is accessible to formal analysis.[19]

Although the precise nature of this formal analysis in Habermas's work is not equivalent to Gadamer's hermeneutics, both thinkers reject the view that linguistic philosophy should study only underlying structures as synchronic diacritical systems. By emphasizing the rhetorical and pragmatic dimension of language as communication, they introduce an inevitable historical moment into their theories, which sets them apart from their French counterparts.

Gadamer, however, was a student of Heidegger's in Marburg during the 1920s, and remains indebted to a number of his major premises. Many of these were anathema to Habermas's mentors in the Frankfurt School, and although he revised Critical Theory in several crucial ways,[20] Habermas inherited their distrust of Heidegger's project.[21] Gadamer's residual Heideggerianism has thus been at the heart of the debate. Following his teacher, Gadamer has extended the scope of hermeneutics beyond that of a method of the cultural sciences in Dilthey's sense. Endorsing Heidegger's celebrated contention that "language is the house of Being,"[22] Gadamer sees hermeneutics as fundamentally ontological. That is, all human reality is determined by its linguisticality (*Sprachlichkeit*). To understand any of it, therefore, is to engage in a process, an endless process, of interpretive reflection. Because human beings are thrown into a world already linguistically permeated, they do not invent language as a tool for their own purposes. It is not a technological instrument of manipulation. Rather, language is prior to humanity and speaks through it. Our finitude as human beings is encompassed by the infinity of language.

The second lesson Gadamer learned from Heidegger follows from this ontological premise. Because humans are always in the midst of a pregiven linguistic context, they can never achieve a transcendental vantage point outside it. There can be no presuppositionless knowledge, no point of absolute origin. Knowledge can be gained only experientially, through what Aristotle called *phronesis*, or practical wisdom. It cannot be achieved by adopting the method of the natural sciences in which a neutral observer confronts an objective world, which he passively records. Method (that is, scientific method) is not the way to truth. The "alienating distanciation"[23] of the sciences must be replaced by a participatory involvement in the dialectics of subject and subject and subject and object. Only by acknowledging one's place in an already given interpretative context, the so-called hermeneutic circle in which parts illuminate wholes and vice versa, can one correctly approach truth.

The third implication Gadamer drew from Heidegger's philosophy is that the scientific method was grounded in the untenable subjectivism that had dominated Western metaphysics since Plato. This subjectivism, which reached its apogee with René Descartes, assumed that the individual subject could gain knowledge of reality, either deductively or inductively, through a monological act of consciousness. Instead, Gadamer contends, understanding is inevitably an intersubjective process in which the participants carry out an endless dialogue, an infinite translation. Because each participant is thrown into this flux, he is never able to achieve knowledge totally by himself or without the cultural presuppositions that inform his thought.

Finally, Gadamer learned from Heidegger to repudiate the premise underlying hermeneutics from the later Schleiermacher to the early Dilthey, and revived in our own day by Betti, Hirsch, and Skinner, the premise that interpretation means recovering the intentionality of the original author of a cultural product. "The meaning of a text," he insists, "surpasses its author not occasionally, but always. Thus understanding is not a reproductive procedure, but rather always a productive one."[24] Because it is impossible to suspend one's own linguistic presuppositions and cancel out one's own historical context, it is equally impossible to enter into the mind of another human being, especially one from an earlier era. "The meaning of hermeneutical inquiry," Gadamer argues, "is to disclose the miracle of understanding texts or utterances and not the mysterious communication of souls. Understanding is participation in the common aim."[25] Dilthey's belief that total empathetic reexperiencing is possible in fact betrayed a subtle capitulation to the Cartesian subjectivism of the scientific method, because it showed that he felt the present situation of the historian could be bracketed and the distance between the past and present nullified.

That distance, Gadamer claims, is less a source of error than a ground of truthfulness. For truth can be achieved only through what Gadamer calls the "fusion of horizons" between the original thinkers or texts and their historical interpreters. Defining horizon as "the range of vision that includes everything that can be seen from a particular vantage point," he contends that individual horizons are always partial.[26] Like language itself, truth transcends the particular horizon of any one participant in the hermeneutic process. It is rather a mediation of past and present, an "application" of the text to the contemporary situation, never an allegedly objective view of the past "in itself." History is thus neither a Rankean recovery of the past "as it actually was," nor a Crocean reduction of the past to contemporary consciousness, but instead an integration of the two.

Here parenthetically, one might note an important parallel, not always acknowledged,[27] between Gadamer and the antipsychologistic structuralists and post-structuralists who also fulminate against the reduction of meaning to intention. In fact, one recent observer has argued that Derrida, whose debt to the later Heidegger I have already mentioned, complements rather than contradicts Gadamer because of their common denial of objective knowledge, disdain for authorial presence, rejection of totalized experiences, and Nietzschean love for interpretive play.[28] The essential differences, of course, are that Gadamer has not gone as far as the post-structuralists in decentering the subject or replacing intersubjectivity by intertextuality. Nor has he argued, as has Foucault, for radical discontinuities in history, preferring instead to emphasize the possibility of fusing past and present. The characteristic violent gesture of *découpage* or rupture, which Edward Said has identified as common to many structuralists and post-structuralists,[29] is totally absent from Gadamer's approach. Although he clearly rejects the traditional philosophical view of language as transparent, he avoids the other extreme of assuming its perfect opacity. Language, as Heidegger stressed, is the site of disclosure, of "unhiddenness." While meaning may exist where it is not intended, it also may appear where it is. Even the texts of the past should be treated as potential partners in a process of dialogic communication, not merely as dead things to be decoded. Hermeneutics, in short, need not be reduced to a process of infinite demystification; meaning, if not simply recovered, can be produced.

Gadamer's hermeneutics is even more obviously comparable to the ordinary language philosophy of the later Wittgenstein. Both share a view of language as a practice or a game whose rules and procedures can be learned only experientially. But whereas Wittgenstein isolates his language games from each other as distinct forms of life, Gadamer, more universalistic in his approach, argues for the potential translatability of one game into another. Similarly, he contends that hermeneutic interaction begins only between already mastered primary languages, while Wittgenstein focuses instead on the acquisition of language through a process of socialization into a form of life. For Gadamer, discourse is more like a dialogue or translation than a process of socialization; it is the fusion of already given horizons, rather than the achievement of an initial horizon *ex nihilo*.

But perhaps most important for our purposes, Gadamer, unlike Wittgenstein, contends that preconceptions, which he provocatively calls prejudices, play an inevitable role in the process of understanding. Indeed, he claims that it is only through our prejudices that our horizons are open to the past. Because Gadamer stresses the impossibility of presuppositionless knowledge, history plays a role in his hermeneutics that it never plays in English ordinary language philosophy. "Understanding," he argues, "is essentially, an effective-historical relation."[30] By "effective-historical" (*Wirkungsgeschichtliche*), Gadamer means that each text has accumulated a history of effects or interpretations that are a constituent part of its meaning for us. It is thus impossible to cancel out the intervening mediations, suspend our own historicity, and recuperate the initial meaning of a cultural phenomenon. The "correctness" of an interpretation is thus not a function of its fidelity to an imagined pure reading of a text; truth, as we have seen, is a historical fusion of horizons.

Moreover, Gadamer contends, an awareness of the effective-historical dimension of understanding helps to denaturalize our own given perspectives:

> Only by virtue of the phenomenon and clarified concept of "temporal distance" can the specifically *critical* task of hermeneutics be resolved,

that is, of knowing how to distinguish between blind prejudices and those which illuminate, between false prejudices and true prejudices. We must raise to a conscious level the prejudices which govern understanding and in this way realize the possibility that *"other* aims" emerge in their own right from tradition—which is nothing other than realizing the possibility that we can understand something in its *otherness.*[31]

Because of this avowed critical aim, Gadamer's position can be seen to have some resemblance to Ricoeur's hermeneutics of suspicion, for he distrusts both the text and the interpreter. At the same time, however, he is clearly concerned as much with the achievement of new truths as with the destruction of illusion, and is thus never as radically suspicious as Derrida.[32] Whether or not Gadamer provides a viable criterion by which to test true and false prejudices is a question to which we will return shortly.

Because Gadamer links truth and historicity so strongly, and argues for the dialectical overcoming of the gaps between language games, it is tempting to see an affinity to G. W. F. Hegel in his thought.[33] But in several crucial ways he remains closer to Heidegger. Although his view of the critic and philosopher is less passive than Heidegger's, he shares with his teacher an aversion to Hegel's metasubjectivism, preferring instead a concept of linguisticality that is prior to the distinction between subject and object. More important, he denies the Hegelian idea of an absolute, rational *logos* underlying the historical process as a whole. Stressing the finitude of human experience, he rejects the omniscient claims of Hegel's *Wissenschaft*. In fact, in Hegel's terms, Gadamer's untotalized infinity of perpetual translation would be called a "bad infinity" because of its resistance to closure. In opposition to Hegel, Gadamer elevates the power of authority and tradition to a place in knowledge denied them ever since the Enlightenment, except by romantics and conservatives. For Gadamer, tradition furnishes the flow of ideas and assumptions within which we must stand; even reason, he argues, is encompassed by tradition, rather than superior to it.

It was precisely on this issue that Habermas's quarrel with Gadamer was first joined in 1967. Although by no means a simple neo-Hegelian, Habermas was and remains anxious to retain Hegel's emphasis on rationality and his belief that history as a whole is potentially coherent. In fact, as Rüdiger Bubner has argued, Habermas was even closer to Hegel than were Adorno and Max Horkheimer because of his desire to construct the synthetic speculative system that negative dialectics had denied was possible.[34] Although a major component of the eclectic system that he has constructed is indebted to Gadamer's hermeneutics,

Habermas was compelled to challenge the ontological reading of hermeneutics Gadamer had derived from Heidegger. While agreeing that it had a practical dimension ignored by Dilthey, he nonetheless returned to the more modest Diltheyan notion of hermeneutics as a method of the cultural sciences. In somewhat traditional terms, he has argued that natural scientific knowledge is based on a nonhermeneutical, instrumental use of language, which is appropriate to the subjective domination of a natural object. More important, Habermas claims that in understanding society as well, hermeneutics can take us only so far. "This metainstitution of language as tradition," he writes, "is evidently dependent in turn on social processes that are not exhausted in normative relationships. Language is *also* a medium of domination and social power."[35] By grounding reflection entirely in the context-dependent understanding of the participants in the linguistic tradition, Gadamer had provided no way to go beyond their everyday consciousness. By stressing the prejudgmental nature of all understanding, he has proscribed calling into question the legitimacy of the conclusions reached by hermeneutical discourse. In other words, Gadamer lacks the means to uncover or criticize the socially determined distortions in communication which may produce an irrational or illegitimate consensus. What in the Marxist lexicon is commonly known as ideology critique is thus impossible on Gadamer's premises, because he fails to distinguish between authority and reason. Lacking a standard of criticism, he is too tolerant of and too receptive to the voices of the past. The emancipatory impulse of the Enlightenment, the generalizable interest in liberation from illegitimate structures of authority, is thus lost to Gadamer's theory, whose implications are inherently conservative.

It is perhaps indicative of Gadamer's impact on Habermas that in trying to overcome the weaknesses of a pure hermeneutics, Habermas resorts in large measure to a linguistic theory of his own.[36] But it is a theory tied less to the explication of the past than to the possibilities of the future. In ways that are too complicated to spell out now in any detail, Habermas argues for what he calls a "universal pragmatics" based on the implicit norm of perfect communication contained, to be sure counterfactually, in every intersubjective utterance.[37] Drawing on the Austinian distinction between the locutionary and illocutionary dimensions of speech acts, further developed in the work of John Searle,[38] Habermas contends that even without the idealist fiction of an a priori transcendental subject,[39] it is possible to isolate a normative telos in speech. In pragmatic terms, this telos is the rational testing of truth claims in an ongoing process of critical clarification. "*In the final analysis,*" he contends, "*the speaker can illocutionarily influence the hearer and vice versa, because speech-act-typical commitments are connected with cognitively testable validity claims*—that is, because the reciprocal bonds have a rational basis."[40]

Translated into social terms, this rational validity testing can take place only between or among equal subjects in nonhierarchical relationships. But because such social arrangements have rarely prevailed, the linguistic telos of undistorted communication has not hitherto been generally realized in history. Gadamer's purely linguistic focus cannot account for this situation for two reasons: first, because it lacks a criterion of rational discourse based on nonhierarchical relations; and second, because it cannot provide a causal analysis of social relations which emerge as much from the dialectic of instrumental reason, or labor, as from that of symbolically mediated interaction.[41] Thus, despite his anti-idealist intentions, Gadamer falls back into an idealized model of always possible perfect communicability. He has no sense of the need for an institutionally secured public sphere in which discourse can take place undistorted by inequalities of power.[42] As a result, he implicitly considers ideology to be caused merely by linguistic misunderstanding rather than by the interaction of linguistic, power, and economic factors.

In order to engage in an effective ideology critique, Habermas contends, it is necessary to employ both hermeneutic reflection and the type of scientific methodology used to examine natural phenomena. As Georg Lukács pointed out in *History and Class Consciousness*, society under capitalism is experienced as if it were a "second nature." Although on the deepest level this is an illusion because society is historically mutable, it is an illusion that can not simply be dispelled by seeing through it—for it is rooted in social institutions and relations. In Habermas's early work, especially *Knowledge and Human Interests*, psychoanalytic therapy was offered as a model for the kind of combined hermeneutic and explanatory method necessary to emancipate men from the thrall of illegitimate authority. The hermeneutic dimension of therapy is crucial in relieving the patient's neurotic symptoms, which are essentially forms of distorted communication within the psyche; nonetheless, the therapist has to draw upon a theoretical framework that transcends his or her interaction with the patient. Although the ultimate justification for that theory is the patient's emancipation from his or her discursive blockages, the theory itself is grounded in a nonhermeneutic explanatory epistemology.

While he does not completely abandon the psychoanalytic model in his more recent work, Habermas has turned more to the developmental theories of Jean Piaget and Lawrence Kohlberg, the systems theory of Talcott Parsons and Niklas Luhmann, and the theory of historical evolution in Marx—all to be sure with revisions—to provide the extrahermeneutic criteria by which social and linguistic distortion can be measured. Whether or not these theories are themselves valid or can be integrated in a fruitful way is, of course, highly problematic. What must, however, be understood is Habermas's continuing effort to find a critical vantage point outside the hermeneutic circle by which to avoid the conservative implications of Gadamer's position. If we are to be paroled—no pun intended—from what Nietzsche called the "prison-house of language,"[43] it is to such efforts that we must turn.

For Gadamer, however, Habermas's attempts to get outside the hermeneutic circle have been in vain. In several replies to his challenge, Gadamer asserted once again the ontological quality of linguisticality. "There is no societal reality," he contended, "with all its concrete forces that does not bring itself to representation in a consciousness that is linguistically articulated. Reality does not happen 'behind the back' of language."[44] In other words, the dialectics of instrumental reason, labor, and social institutions cannot be examined without the inevitable mediation of language. There is no way to find an Archimedean point outside the hermeneutic circle.

Moreover, Gadamer contended, Habermas too hastily equates openness to the authority of the past with blind, dogmatic submission to tradition. For authority, which is not automatically wrong, may be willingly accepted through increased insight into its validity. In fact, he argued, "authority can rule only because it is freely recognized or accepted. The obedience that belongs to true authority is neither blind nor slavish."[45] Nor is it possible to hold all of our opinions up to the test of rationality at once; there is inevitably a measure of rhetorical persuasion involved in any of our beliefs. To think that reason can be opposed to tradition in every case is to posit an "anarchistic utopia" or a Robespierrean dictatorship of the *soi-disant* rational.

Finally, Habermas's specific attempt to find an extrahermeneutic vantage point in Freudian theory is misleading. The psychoanalytic encounter is between two individuals who share an a priori interest in the resolution of the neurotic symptoms of one of them. The analyst is thus able, at least in theory, to bracket his or her own interests and work toward the common goal. Social interaction, in contrast, is among many different individuals or groups whose concrete, material interests may objectively clash. Possibly no amount of rational validity testing will lead to a perfect consensus. There is thus no necessary link between the ideal speech situation and the resolution of power-related material conflicts.

Recent defenders of Gadamer have added that his variety of hermeneutics is by no means as lacking in a critical dimension as

Habermas has charged. Hermeneutics aims at the exposure of preunderstandings and prejudices in order to denaturalize the given perspectives of nonreflective participants in the linguistic process. In David Hoy's words:

> Criticism implies distance, and the distance introduced by the generality of philosophical reflection makes possible the negative move essential to criticism. But criticism must also be able to return constructively, and here greater methodological self-awareness makes actual interpretations more self-consistent and hence more legitimate. Finally, hermeneutics also contributes a basis for arbitration between different interpretations by demanding that the extent to which the interpretation has clarified its own assumptions and scope—and has remained consistent with those assumptions and within that scope—be made a further test for the interpretation.[46]

All of these criteria—self consistency, clarification of assumptions, methodological self-awareness—are, however, internal to the interpretation itself and have little to say about the fit between the interpretation and its object, let alone the criterion of rationality. Even if one admits that the object of interpretation is a construct created by the fusion of horizons, there is still the problem of how one decides which fusion is superior. One possible answer, which is implied by Gadamer's undefended assumption of the universality of hermeneutic discourse, is that the more encompassing the interpretation, the better it is. But contained in this view is the harmonistic belief that horizons can be fused into bigger and better wholes, a notion that calls to mind Karl Mannheim's belief in a "relationist" totalization of conflicting views by the free-floating intelligentsia.[47] As the Frankfurt School showed in its frequent critiques of Mannheim, there may well be unharmonizable dissonances between different positions which resist fusion—at least until social conditions themselves are noncontradictory.[48] In other words, the reproach Gadamer made against Habermas's reliance on psychoanalysis as a model of social and linguistic totalization can be turned against his own optimistic assumption of fused horizons.

That Habermas's own notion of an undistorted speech situation may in general be open to this same charge is undeniable, but at least it is cast counterfactually as a future possibility, a kind of regulative ideal, rather than a present and past reality. Other questions about Habermas's own solutions may, of course, be easily raised, and they have been, especially by those beholden to other linguistic traditions. Aside from the objections made by contemporary defenders of a positivist view of language, such as Hans Albert, followers of French trends have introduced a number of troubling criticisms. Lacanians such as Samuel Weber, himself a former advocate of Critical Theory, have questioned the possibility of a fully rational discourse among subjects whose inherent capacity for reason can by no means be simply assumed.[49] Criticizing Habermas's reliance on an ego psychologistic reading of Freud, they have argued that the unconscious, understood in Lacanian terms as a perpetually decentering engine of desire, cannot allow the type of undistorted communicative discourse Habermas posits as the telos of language. The ideal speech situation is thus another form of that logocentric desire for perfect presence which dominated Western metaphysics for millennia. Derrideans like Dominick LaCapra have added that, lacking a concept of supplementarity, Habermas posits rigidly categorical distinctions that reproduce, against his intentions, a hierarchical structure of domination.[50] Defending the inevitability of ambiguity in terms Gadamer would approve, LaCapra suggests that "from the perspective of ordinary and literary language, the ideal speech situation might in one sense appear to be a technocratic fantasy."[51] Even those who generally support Habermas have acknowledged certain unresolved questions in his critique of Gadamer. As Thomas McCarthy concludes in his admirable summary of Habermas's work, "the shadow of the hermeneutic circle (in its Gadamerian, neo-Wittgensteinian, Kuhnian form) has by no means been finally dispelled,"[52] And Jack Mendelson, who is also a partisan of Habermas in the debate with Gadamer, follows Paul Ricoeur in arguing for at least a partial return to the earlier Frankfurt School's notion of an immanent critique in which the truth claims of a society's ideology are compared with its practice. This return is necessary, he contends, to avoid the overly abstract and ahistorical nature of the perfect speech situation:

> While in a sense the ideal of rational consensus may be immanent in language *per se* and not simply an external standard, in most societies it is bound to remain unarticulated in the actual culture. It becomes politically relevant as an ideal to be consciously striven for only in societies which have begun to approach it on the level of their own cultural traditions.[53]

Habermas's explication of his universal pragmatics is still very much in progress, so it is possible that he may yet meet some or all of these objections. In any event, it would be difficult to render a final judgment on the viability of his critique of Gadamer in the scope of this paper, even assuming I were fully equipped to do so. Instead, I would like to conclude with some observations about the relevance of the debate for the practice of intellectual history, in particular the issue of whether or not it should take a linguistic turn.

Most obviously, the Habermas-Gadamer debate reinforces the lesson learned from the ordinary language and structuralist critiques of the traditional notion of language as a transparent medium of expression and description. If language inevitably mediates meaning, indeed if it plays a constituent role in the creation of meaning, intellectual historians will have to pay some attention to the linguistic dimension of the texts they examine. How suggestive such an approach may be has already been shown by the pioneering efforts of Hayden White in *Metahistory* and *Tropics of Discourse*.[54] Although the boundaries between literary criticism and intellectual history need not be entirely dissolved, we have much to learn from our more theoretically self-conscious colleagues in that discipline.

The Habermas-Gadamer debate also draws our attention, however, to the fact that the intellectual historian who does want to incorporate linguistic insights into his work need not rely on only one paradigm of language to do so. Linguistic turns, as we have seen, may take very different directions. It may, in fact, be possible to integrate some of them, as Habermas's indebtedness to Austin and Searle and the common Heideggerian roots of Gadamer and Derrida suggest, but a fusion of the horizons of each is clearly no easy task. Choices, therefore, will have to be made. Because the tradition of hermeneutics has been most keenly interested in the question of history and has included historicity in its very definition of language, one can at least argue that it will be the most fruitful to follow. At the same time as it resists the naturalization of historical consciousness produced by a naively objectivist view of the past, it also avoids reducing history to an arbitrarily constructed fiction of the present.

Moreover, by jettisoning the earlier hermeneutic goal of perfect empathetic understanding of an authorial mind, Gadamerian hermeneutics frees us from the illusion that texts are merely congealed intentionalities waiting to be reexperienced at a later date. But at the same time, by resisting the radical antihumanism of structuralist and post-structuralist criticism, it reminds us that subjectivity, however that concept may be defined, can in fact be objectified, if in an inevitably mediated and imperfect way. Even if our intercourse with the past is through documents in the present, there is a dialogic component in that intercourse that cannot be put aside. Although it may well be that there is no perfectly centered subject lurking behind these texts, a subject which itself needs no further interpretation, it is nonetheless equally questionable to flatten out the distinction between subjectivity and objectivity to the point where no differences remain. Gadamerian hermeneutics, while avoiding what the New Critics W. K. Wimsatt and Monroe Beardsley called the "intentional fallacy," also resists what might be termed the "anti-intentional fallacy" of the structuralists and post-structuralists.

Another critical insight in Gadamer's account of interpretation arises from what he calls the effective-historical dimension of all understanding. The historical fate of a work should be included in the meaning of the work for us. What Gadamer's student Hans Robert Jauss calls a "reception aesthetics" suggests that the reproduction as well as the production of a text must be taken into account in its interpretation.[55] The history of a text's effects may well be more a chronicle of successive misunderstandings than perfect reproductions, that "map of misreadings" suggested by Harold Bloom,[56] but the potential for the specific distortions that do occur can be understood as latent in the original text. Thus, while it may be questionable to saddle Marx with responsibility for the Gulag Archipelago or blame Nietzsche for Auschwitz, it is nonetheless true that their writings could be misread as justifications for these horrors in a way that, say, those of John Stuart Mill or Alexis de Tocqueville could not.

One final implication of Gadamer's hermeneutics that merits comment concerns the notion of a fusion of horizons. Putting aside its problematic harmonistic implications, what this fusion suggests is, first, that historians themselves must be aware of their own historicity and, second, that they are themselves irrevocably changed by their reflective involvement with the past. Although it would be wrong to characterize this involvement simply as a form of surrender,[57] it is nonetheless more ambiguous in this regard than either the outmoded positivist objectification of the past or the more recent structuralist version of the historian as a detached decoder of the synchronic relations of the past preserved in the present.[58] Gadamer's defense of prejudice may well have conservative implications, but it reminds us that we delude ourselves if we think our present vantage point is somehow outside of history. Participation as well as distanciation is necessary to our understanding of the past. It is impossible, as some of the French post-structuralists seem to imply, to criticize the Western tradition from a position external to it.

Turning to Habermas's critique of Gadamer, there are two major lessons to be learned. First, Gadamer's Heideggerian ontologization of language need not be accepted without reservation.[59] As Ricoeur puts it in support of Habermas, "language is only the locus for the articulation of an experience which supports it . . . Everything consequently, does not arrive *in* language, but only comes *to* language."[60] Because certain social forms can be read as if they were languages, there is no reason to suppose their linguisticality exhausts their being. However one may wish to chastise Habermas for failing to see the supplementary ambiguities of his categorical distinctions, it is equally unwise to collapse the dialectic of labour completely into the dialectic of symbolically mediated interaction. Indeed, to understand and expose the distortions in the latter, one must have a grasp of the contradictions in the former. Intellectual historians must, therefore, continue to probe the interaction between texts and contexts through a combination of hermeneutic understanding and causal explanation. Even if the contexts themselves can be read as texts, as Ricoeur has suggestively argued,[61] here too a combination of *Verstehen* and *Erklärung* is necessary to make sense of the dynamics of their interaction with the texts themselves. Only by so doing will we be able to combine an effective hermeneutics of suspicion with one of recollected meaning, which seems to me the most fruitful way to enrich our intercourse with the past.

The second lesson suggested by Habermas's challenge to Gadamer concerns the critical implications of a method combining hermeneutic and nonhermeneutic insights. Habermas, as we have seen, faults Gadamer for his uncritical tolerance of tradition and prejudice as standards of judgment. Although Gadamer and his supporters have responded that hermeneutics does in fact contain critical standards by which to separate true from false prejudices, these have been relatively empty, imprecise, and self-referential. And as David Hoy has admitted, the central assumption of the universality of hermeneutic discourse, which separates Gadamer from Wittgenstein, is itself incapable of being grounded hermeneutically.[62] What, moreover, is the hermeneutic justification for that "anticipation of perfect coherence" which Gadamer insists is "always at work in achieving understanding"?[63] Habermas has confronted this problem with great candor and struggled to find more rational criteria linking language and society, without, however, falling back into a discredited transcendentalism. He has remained true to the classical Frankfurt School insight that critique and rationality are intimately linked. Whether or not he has fully succeeded in demonstrating the nature of that link, of course, is still very much in dispute.

But what does seem to me indisputable is the need to pursue such a search. There are, to be sure, some commentators who would equate rational criteria with the establishment of hierarchy, which in turn becomes an excuse for domination. Gadamer himself darkly warns against the Robespierrean danger in Habermas's fetish of reason.[64] To avoid this implication, it has sometimes seemed necessary to go to the opposite extreme of embracing what Edward Said has called the "nihilistic radicality" of Derrida's infinite play of dissemination and supplementarity.[65] It is, however, an illusion to think that in so doing, hierarchy is somehow avoided. For as Hayden White has acutely noted in his discussion of the "absurdist moment" in recent criticism, the result of so total a rejection of reason, totalization, and coherence is to privilege nature over culture, and in fact nature in its most demonic forms.[66] Habermas, to be sure, may have underestimated the costs of his own choice, as critics of his ego psychologistic model of the psyche have contended. The older Frankfurt School theme of the domination of nature has, in fact, been relatively muted in his revision of Critical Theory.[67] But he has certainly remained faithful to his mentors' concern for the dangers of an irrationalist celebration of the natural.

Intellectual history is, of course, filled with unattractive examples of rationally judgmental readings of the past—Georg Lukács's notorious *Die Zerstörung der Vernunft* comes to mind as a particularly insensitive case—and one would certainly not want a revival of Enlightenment historiography at its most naive. But in turning too eagerly to linguistic philosophy in any of its various guises and making it the sole or even primary source of our method, we risk losing the critical edge that rationalism, defended by Habermasian or other means, can provide. To avoid that risk, we must, to be sure, distinguish among various types of rationality—substantive, formal, objective, subjective, instrumental, technological, practical, and so on—in order to rebut the identification of reason with only one of its variants. Too often, in fact, such a reduction occurs, with the result that reason is rejected out of hand.

This sequence has perhaps been followed by certain contemporary linguistically inclined philosophers, Gadamer generally equating reason with the monological "subjectivism" of the scientific method and Derrida associating it with the logocentric desire for perfect presence underlying Western metaphysics. Because they are able to expose the vulnerabilities of these variants of reason, they move, perhaps too quickly, to a denigration of reason *per se*. Habermas's defense of reason as an intersubjectively generated quasi-regulative ideal entailed in discourse itself shows that these reductions of reason by no means exhaust its meaning. Indeed, the extraordinarily rich and fecund tradition of rationalism, in all its forms, is part of that "effective-historical consciousness" which constitutes the horizons of contemporary men and women. Intellectual historians ignore at their peril its power to give our intercourse with the past a valuable critical dimension.

To defend a rational moment in our method is not, however, to deny the importance of the recent turn in philosophy to linguistic issues. Just as the alternative between seeing language as either perfectly transparent or totally opaque is too rigidly posed, so too the opposition between a linguistically informed intellectual history and one indebted to traditional (or in Habermas's case, nontraditional) concepts of rationality is unnecessarily extreme. Whether the two horizons can be perfectly fused or must remain forever in a supplementary interaction is impossible to say. But without some dialogic play between them, our reading of the past will remain either anachronistic, in the sense of being indifferent to the liveliest philosophical currents of our day, or, what is worse, incapable of providing a critical perspective on the past and present in the name of a more attractive future.

3

Hierarchy and the Humanities:
The Radical Implications of
a Conservative Idea

It is customary to begin essays of this kind with an arresting quotation from an eminent source, a practice that both displays the author's ostensible erudition and covertly betrays his need to draw on an external authority to support the argument he is about to make. In order to remain true to this time honored convention, I have chosen as my opening text the following passage from Theodor Adorno's *Negative Dialectics*, written in 1966:

> All culture after Auschwitz, including its urgent critique, is garbage. In restoring itself after the things that happened without resistance in its own countryside, culture has turned entirely into the ideology it had been potentially—had been ever since it presumed, in opposition to material existence, to inspire that existence with the light denied it by the separation of the mind from manual labor. Whoever pleads for the maintenance of this radically culpable and shabby culture becomes its accomplice, while the man who says no to culture is directly furthering the barbarism which our culture showed itself to be.[1]

In short, to put it even more bluntly, the Holocaust has finally and irrevocably exposed the lie that supporters of culture and the humanities have promulgated for centuries in order to justify their existence: the claim that the pursuit of what we usually call "high culture" is somehow a humanizing endeavor, nurturing what R. S. Crane once called "the virtues and knowledge that separate men most sharply from the lower animals."[2] The harsh truth, acording to Adorno, is revealed instead in what he called a "magnificent line" of Bertolt Brecht's: "the mansion of culture is built of dogshit."[3]

If we unpack the implications of Adorno's bitter outburst, three specific points seem to me paramount. The first is his typically Marxist admonition to avoid separating culture from society, or what he calls mental from manual labor. No materialist theory can countenance the alleged superiority of the former over the latter. The ascetic, anti-hedonist moment in what his friend Max Horkheimer called "affirmative culture"[4] was in fact partly responsible for the life-denying practices of modern totalitarianism. Insofar as culture is still honored at the expense of gratifying man's material needs, it must be exposed as repressive.

The second point is more directly historical. For Adorno, whose philosophy of history had long since abandoned any Marxist or even liberal belief in progress, Auschwitz was the final confirmation of Western culture's failure to lead to genuine emancipation. Like George Steiner, who gave wide currency to the same idea in his *Language and Silence* of 1967, Adorno expressed not only the guilt of the survivor, but also the anguish of the mandarin whose faith in the saving powers of high culture had been irremediably shattered. The threat that had been latent in the claims of earlier defenders of humanism like Irving Babbitt, who boasted that what they were defending was not equivalent to "sentimental naturalism" or "humanitarianism,"[5] was thus now realized. For as Steiner put it in a well-known lament, "we know now that a man can read Goethe or Rilke in the evening, that he can play Bach and Schubert, and go to his day's work at Auschwitz in the morning."[6] Indeed, and this is perhaps an even more frightening thought, the tears spent weeping for fictional victims may diminish our capacity to react to the misfortune of real ones.

The third and most indirect implication of Adorno's argument concerns a more general issue, and the one on which I want to dwell today: the apparently sinister effect of cultural hierarchy. For it seems at first glance that Adorno is challenging the very claim culture and the humanities make to nurture an appreciation of truth, goodness, and beauty, an appreciation that separates humans at their best from what Crane and many others call "the lower animals." There is, Adorno seems to be suggesting, a covert complicity between the alleged superiority of mental over manual labor and society's collective domination over the natural world, that disastrous "dialectic of the enlightenment," he and Max Horkheimer traced in their most influential book.[7] To hold on to such an elevated view of culture, Adorno implies, is to be an accomplice of the barbarism it failed to prevent. The great chain of being thus turns out to be a shackles for those allegedly lower on the scale of virtue or worth. Only a total leveling of such a hierarchical vision of reality, Adorno seems to be saying, will prevent such a complicity from continuing.

And yet, as anyone familiar with Adorno's work will readily attest, he doggedly refused to eschew judgments of value in his criticism of both social and cultural phenomena. Certainly no friend of popular or mass culture, the "culture industry" as he scornfully called it, Adorno had little tolerance for those who retreated into a pseudo-democratic relativism in their eagerness to escape the guilt of high culture. Thus, as he insisted in the final line of the remarks I quoted a few moments ago, "the man who says no to culture is directly furthering the barbarism which our culture showed itself to be."

If Adorno seems to be contradicting himself, both attacking culture as garbage and rejecting the implications of that very attack, the explanation is that he was attempting to confront without flinching one of the thorniest aporias of the modern condition: the impossibility of finding a stance, on intellectual as well as political issues, that is free of some sort of self-contradiction. In particular, he wanted to remain true to the inherently ambiguous nature of high culture, at once a false consolation for real suffering and an embattled refuge of the utopian hopes for overcoming that very misery. He wanted, moreover, to avoid finding a conciliatory middle ground between these two incompatible truths, following instead his dictum in *Minima Moralia* that "the dialectic advances by way of extremes, driving thoughts with the utmost consequentiality to the point where they turn back on themselves, instead of qualifying them."[8]

Adorno's tormented attempt to hold on to both extremes without trying to forge a consistent position out of them offers an important lesson today when the delicate balance or, as he would call it, the negative dialectic of culture is threatened in new ways. If before Auschwitz, to use his shorthand expression, there was a general tendency to accept the elevating self-image of the humanities uncritically and thus ignore their covert complicity with barbarism, in the most recent period the opposite inclination seems to have gained the upper hand. From many sides, we are now constantly reminded that high culture does not save, indeed that it might do the opposite. Cultural elitism, we are insistently told, is the handmaiden of social elitism and thus has no place in a pluralist democracy, let alone in any more radically egalitarian polity. What hitherto had been the rallying cry of disgruntled populists and their unexpected allies among the more dadaist elements of the avant-garde has now become a widespread complaint.

The task today therefore is to make a case for the ambivalent virtues of hierarchy in order to redress the balance. In so doing, I will try to establish what can be seen as the covertly radical or at least critical dimensions of an idea that is normally considered conservative. Misunderstood, the argument I will make may appear to be a perverse plea to resist progressive change through a defense of tradition, a call to retreat from the "infinite universe" of modernity to the "closed world" of premodern hierarchical order.[9] To avoid this inference, let me stress my intention to "refunction," in Brecht's sense, rather than merely defend the value of cultural hierarchy. I am not, in other words, really trying to say that the mansion of culture is built of precious jewels and rare metals, and that as a result we would be unwise to try to disrupt its sturdy foundations.

In order to make my case, what must first be done is to establish the validity of my observation that there is a greater tendency today to denigrate than defend cultural hierarchy. To do so with any thoroughness would try your patience, however, as there has been a plethora of attacks launched by victims of the current version of that hierarchy. I am referring, of course, to the crescendo of criticism directed against "white, male, heterosexual" culture by those who fall outside those categories. It would be callous to deny the legitimacy of many of their complaints and condescending to advise them to be patient in trying to remedy them. What perhaps may be less out of order is a plea to examine more closely the ambiguities of the anti-hierarchical solution many of them propound. To defuse the inevitable suspicion that I may be doing so in order to protect my vested interest in the maintenance of Eurocentric, patriarchal culture, let me direct my remarks against two recent critics of hierarchy who cannot be construed as being among its most obvious victims. By focusing on their work, I hope to demonstrate two points: first, that the critique of hierarchy is now so widespread that it has permeated the ranks of those at the top and second, that the quarrel over its implications should not be construed as a mere class (or perhaps better put, status) struggle between the victims and victimizers of the current version of cultural inequality.

The two targets I have chosen are very different, one a distinguished senior historian rarely given to polemical bloodletting and the other a younger literary critic, who clearly often is. The former is William J. Bouwsma, recent president of the American Historical Association, currently Sather Professor and Chairman of the Department of History at the University of California, Berkeley, and a world-renowned scholar of the Renaissance and Reformation. He is also the author of a provocative essay in the *Journal of Interdisciplinary History* published in 1981 entitled "Intellectual History in the 1980s: From History of Ideas to History of Meaning." My second exemplar is Michael Ryan, who teaches English at Northeastern University and is the author of a book entitled *Marxism and Deconstruction*, published in 1982.[10] Taking these two scholars together is particularly instructive because they come from very different intellectual traditions, yet arrive at a similar destination in their attitude towards hierarchy. Bouwsma, from what might be called the perspective of a Christian anthropologist, and Ryan, who presents himself as a Marxist-feminist advocate of deconstruction, both vigorously denounce the evils of cultural elitism.

The stimulus to Bouwsma's reflections is what he sees as the current crisis of intellectual history, whose decline he calls "obvious and probably irreversible."[11] Rather than mourn this state of affairs, however, he celebrates it because he feels that the traditional basis of intellectual history was an idealist anthropology. "According to this view," he writes,

> the human personality consists of a hierarchy of discrete faculties, among which the intellect—more or less closely identified with reason—is highest. In the earlier stages of this tradition, the intellect was believed to constitute the divine element in man and so to distinguish him from the other animals . . . The association of the intellect with the brain gave the head ethical significance and converted it into a potent metaphor; the highest became best.[12]

Drawing on the lessons in humility taught recent mankind by Charles Darwin, Karl Marx, and Sigmund Freud, he concludes that it is no longer possible to define man as an essentially intellectual animal. This is not, however, to say that man is undifferentiated from other animals; his uniqueness, according to Bouwsma, lies in his capacity to invest the world in which he lives with meaning. But, he writes, "these efforts are not the work of the 'intellect' or of any particular area of the personality. They are rather a function of the human organism as a whole."[13] Contemporary cultural anthropologists are thus particularly useful for historians who want to construct what Clifford Geertz calls "thick descriptions"[14] of the webs of meanings in which we are suspended. They provide us with a model of the human condition, which "rejects the conception of man as a hierarchy of discrete faculties . . . [and] the assignment of privileged status a priori to one or another area of human activity. Since it conceives of the human personality as a mysterious whole, it is opposed to all reductionism."[15] In short, the traditional distinction between intellectual and other forms of history should be discarded, as must that between a privileged sphere of high culture and culture in the broader anthropological sense.

In this essay, Bouwsma's vantage point seems to be that of contemporary anthropology, but, as I mentioned a moment ago, there is a deeper, more religiously motivated premise underlying his argument. In an earlier essay to which Bouwsma kindly drew my attention, he probed the concept of "Christian Adulthood" for a

Daedalus volume on the theme of maturity.[16] In this piece, he defends the Christian ideal of adulthood against what he calls the alternative model of "manhood," which is derived largely from classical antiquity. In that latter view, whose gender connotation was by no means an accident, are embedded "both the metaphysical distinction between form and substance, with its hints of anthropological dualism, and a characteristic distinction, within man, among the several elements of the human personality: soul and body, or reason, will, and passion."[17] Manhood was associated closely with the domination of reason, which was absent in the child. Human rationality was a sign of man's participation in the divine, as well as a tool to order the chaotic ambiguities of the world.

Through a characteristically learned account of the Christian response to this legacy from the classical world, Bouwsma shows that alongside one tradition, which adopted the ideal of manhood and pitted man's allegedly higher soul against his baser passions, another tradition developed, which did not. This second Christian ideal was one of "adulthood," a term without the gender connotations of its classical predecessor. Rather than privileging sober maturity over playful childhood, this ideal recognizes the valuable residues of our pre-rational selves in our adult lives. Growth does not mean leaving our capacity for play behind, but rather remaining open to the possibility of divine foolishness. Nor does the Christian adult in this view place the soul above the body, whose ultimate resurrection is a sign of its value. "Adulthood," Bouwsma writes, "does not recognize real qualitative and hierarchical distinctions *within* the personality; it sees man, whether child or adult, as living whole."[18]

What is especially striking about Bouwsma's reconstruction of this holistic vision of Christian adulthood, at least for our purposes, is the use to which he implicitly puts it in his more recent essay on intellectual history and the history of meaning. In the original *Daedalus* article he admits that it is a normative view, which has found only occasional realization in history as an antidote to the classical ideal of manhood whose hierarchical discriminations were also embodied in social forms. In the second essay, however, he bases his argument for the obsolescence of intellectual history on the implicit assumption that something like Christian adulthood in fact describes the way we really are:

> We can hardly any longer define man as an intellectual animal. However we regard him, he is both less and more than this—and infinitely more interesting, which is the major explanation for the fact that an autonomous intellectual is now likely to seem, like the

discrete intellect of the old anthropology, at best an irrelevant abstraction from real life.[19]

Or in other words, our disciplinary distinctions need no longer be hierarchical because a holistic meaning-giving man has in fact replaced the hierarchically divided man of the classical ideology, at least in our self-understanding of the human condition. Thus, paradoxically, the blows to human pride in the work of Darwin, Marx, and Freud, with their anti-idealist debunking of rationality, has led to a less elitist vision of our status, which approaches the Christian model of adulthood.

Why this new vision should be extrapolated back into history is not, however, completely clear for two reasons. First, if the classical view held sway as long as Bouwsma concedes it did, historians cannot hope to understand the past unless we acknowledge its powerful formative effect on the cultural differentiations that were the lived experience of our ancestors. Second, and more important, the social hierarchy that in some sense was the underpinning of those distinctions must be taken into account in any attempt to reconstruct how meaning was made in history. As Antonio Gramsci once put it, "All men are intellectuals . . . but not all men have in society the function of intellectuals."[20] The same might be said of men as meaning-givers, which Geertz's "cultural idealism,"[21] as Marvin Harris has called it, often fails to register. To cite another critic of this position, Ronald Walters:

> Ideally, thick description says something about society. In practice, it often describes reality as a drama in which the focus is upon symbolic exchanges, not social consequences. Words like "class," "exploitation," and—most important—"power," recede, drop out of the analysis or take new, less strident meanings."[22]

It is, in fact, ironic to hear Bouwsma argue that "an autonomous intellectual is now likely to seem . . . at best an irrelevant abstraction from real life" just at the time when contemporary sociologists like Alvin Gouldner, George Konrád and Ivan Szelényi are presenting the intellectuals as a "new class" or on "the road to class power."[23] The point is not to return to an idealist defense of pure intellect above the fray or to construct watertight divisions between high and low culture, but rather to acknowledge that social differentiation has effected in the past and still continues to effect the means through which webs of meaning are created and sustained. As sociolinguists like Basil Bernstein and others have demonstrated,[24] the linguistic codes of different social groups are decisive in the ways in which they interpret and reproduce their cultural reality. That some, whom we call intellectuals, depend on what Gouldner terms a "culture of critical discourse," which is relatively more reflexive and context-independent than the discourse of non-intellectuals, means that we must still be aware of the ways in which the model of Christian adulthood is thwarted in the modern world. In fact, I would argue that pretending it is not is itself a contributing factor to the maintenance of the very hierarchical distinctions that it hopes to overcome.

Before commenting on the reasons I think this pretense functions in this way, let me turn to Michael Ryan's no less impassioned critique of hierarchy. Ryan would no doubt have little but scorn for Bouwsma's model of Christian adulthood as a holistically integrated personality. To the St. Augustine who cried "I want to be healed completely, for I am a complete whole,"[25] he would probably reply that the only thing from which you really suffer is the old logocentric myth of perfect presence. Relief can come only from a willingness to engage in the infinite, explosive, transgressive play that makes a mockery of any pretension to centered subjectivity, a play that is far more Dionysian than that envisaged in the Christian model by Bouwsma. And yet, tacitly in tandem with Bouwsma, Ryan is unremittingly hostile to the elitist privileging of reason or the soul over the other aspects of the human personality. Radical deconstruction and Christian anthropology thus both converge in their distaste for the evils of cultural hierarchy.

In *Marxism and Deconstruction*, Ryan's general intention is to present what he calls a "critical articulation" of these two traditions in order to fashion a libertarian intellectual and political position that will avoid the authoritarianism of earlier leftist efforts. In his eagerness to win the energies of deconstructionist intoxication for the revolution, as Walter Benjamin might have put it,[26] he tends to gloss over many of the very substantial differences that pit Jacques Derrida against Marx. It is difficult, for example, to know how to reconcile his typically Marxist Humanist call for a politics that treats people as "responsible and creative agents"[27] with the deconstructionist demolition of any self that could conceivably be the center of such agency. Nor is it very clear how Derrida's philosophy can really support the Marxist demand, which Ryan seems to champion, for a "full development of all human faculties,"[28] a slogan that recalls the very ideology of classical *Bildung* that deconstructionists have had so much fun debunking. Inconsistencies of this type abound in his argument,[29] which may trouble those of us still hung up on the virtues of logical coherence.

But rather than multiply examples of Ryan's questionable reasoning, I will return to the more basic animus that motivates his attempt to force the marriage of Derrida and Marx, an animus directed against hierarchy of any kind. What he finds most attractive in deconstruction is its resistance to a politics of exclusion, which he claims has a "necessary relationship"[30] with the hierarchical conceptual thinking Derrida has sought to undermine. Most important among such conceptual hierarchies are the distinctions between transcendence and immanence; consciousness and the body; mental and manual labor; theory and practice; reason and the irrational; efficiency and chaos; science and ideology; works of art and ordinary texts; and speech and writing. All of these privilege the first term over the second, which leads to the domination, marginalization, or exclusion of the latter. Deconstruction, as Ryan defends it, goes so far as to call into question all conceptual thinking as an essentialist suppression of difference and the non-identical; "in fact," he writes, "all knowledge operates through acts of exclusion and marginalization."[31]

Following Derrida's arguments in his essay, "The White Mythology,"[32] he further contends that the major victims of such hierarchically tainted knowledge have been women and third-world peoples who are excluded from the patriarchal version of rationality promoted by European men. So-called feminine hysteria, therefore, is a therapeutic corrective to male rationality, "a sign of moral and philosophical goodness"[33] which, to be sure, ought not to be enthroned in a new hierarchical position of domination. Any intellectual or cultural hierarchy, Ryan argues, is immediately complicitous with political repression. Thus, for example, "there is an analogy in Lenin between his practice of reading and theorizing—locating the center, the paradigm, the master theme, the essence through exclusion, manipulation and suppression—and his theory of socialist practice—order, discipline, central authority, exclusiveness."[34] The truly libertarian alternative, Ryan argues, is a politics of permanent revolution, which is analogous to the infinite, transgressive play supported by deconstruction.

Regardless of whether or not this vision should be denounced as an updated version of what Lenin damned as "infantile leftism," it is unlikely to appeal to many observers today, especially after the recent discrediting of the romantic image of the Chinese Cultural Revolution held in certain quarters a decade ago. Nor will it seem very attractive to those with longer memories who recall the disturbing links between a totally relativist cultural nihilism and the decisionist politics of will that contributed to fascism. In fact, one of the most influential interpretations of fascism, that of Ernst Nolte,[35] understands it precisely in terms of a reaction against the very same transcendence that Ryan also so despises.

What, however, seems even more fundamentally questionable in Ryan's argument—and here I think there is a parallel with a weakness in Bouwsma's—is the ultimately ahistorical assumption on which it is based. Perhaps because Ryan is so hostile to hierarchy of any kind, he refuses to privilege any historical cause in explaining the source of present inequalities. Instead he supports a holistic relationism in which nothing is prior to anything else. Although helping him to avoid the pitfalls of reductionism, this methodological bias makes it impossible for him to ask the difficult question: are some hierarchies more basic and irremediable than others? It also prevents him from acknowledging that merely seeing through the hierarchical distinctions of our cultural and social life as harmful illusions does little to dispel them in reality. Thus, he engages in a kind of magical thinking in which he contends that "mental labor is always manual,"[36] "theoretical knowledge is immediately practice,"[37] and "'the political' and 'the economic' cannot even be considered as separate categories for the sake of theoretical exposition."[38] In other words, in his haste to deconstruct the hierarchical distinctions he dislikes, he fails to grasp their tenacious rootedness in an objective world created over time and deeply resistant to change. Like Bouwsma's contention that the hierarchical separation between mind and body underlying the distinction between intellectual and other forms of history is no longer operative, Ryan's arguments present a desideratum as if it were already a fact. And in so doing, they occlude our understanding of why in reality it is not. In short, the obstinately real hierarchical differentiations produced by history cannot be undone by positing an egalitarian process of "differencing" that exposes their illusoriness. The Marxist in Ryan is; to be sure, aware of this dilemma, but too often the deconstructionist in him acts as if the only task were "showing how public institutions and public power are cultural conventions sustained by acculturated personal belief."[39]

Even if we share all of the radical egalitarianism of these critics of hierarchy, we cannot hope to realize their aims by short-circuiting the painstaking process through which the obstacles to that realization might be overcome. Interpreting social institutions, structures, and practices as mere texts to be decoded and then discarded is akin to the mistaken culturist view of reification that certain Hegelian Marxists like Georg Lukács sometimes held in their more idealistic moods. Although a de-naturalizing consciousness of the subjective origins of the social world may be a necessary moment in the struggle to change society, it is not a sufficient one. Indeed, paradoxically, by assuming that public institutions are merely "cultural conventions" that can be changed by exposing their artificiality, we may blind ourselves to the deeper, more varied sources that generated them and the still potent functions that they now serve.

In fact, any attempt to locate those sources is bound to be a daunting endeavor, which perhaps accounts for the self-protective deconstructionist dismissal of any search for origins. A wide variety of divergent hypotheses has, of course, been offered in the hope of accounting for social, cultural, political, and sexual inequality. The intellectual historian Arthur Lovejoy traced the great chain of being to Plato's denigration of the sensible world in favor of the intelligible.[40] Emile Durkheim sought an answer in the religious distinction between the sacred and the profane, which itself reflected the opposition between collective moral life and individual material existence.[41] Freud conjectured that when men stood erect and lost their ability to react positively to olfactory stimuli, they began to feel shame about their "baser" sexual and excretory functions.[42] Privileging the sense of sight over that of smell thus was congruent with the sexual repression that is the bedrock of cultural hierarchy. Jean-Jacques Rousseau, with his more primitive understanding of the psyche, blamed it on psychological proclivities towards pride and envy, while Marx pointed his finger at the division of labor and private property. A more recent Marxist, Alfred Sohn-Rethel, argued that the invention of an abstract money economy in classical Greece led to the distinction between pure, abstract thought and its impure concrete opposite.[43] This in turn created the fateful distinction between mental and manual labor, which still persists today. Michel Foucault claimed that it is our inevitable fall into language, which gives us the ability to say two things with the identical word and the same thing with different words, that makes hierarchical distinctions possible.[44] Louis Dumont, who self-consciously defends the *Home hierarchicus* he sees in Indian caste society over the *Home aequalis* of the West, traced hierarchy to what he calls the "encompassing of the contrary."[45] There is, he claimed, a necessarily hierarchical relationship between a whole or set and an element within it, which is expressed, for example, in the biblical myth of Eve created from Adam's rib. Hierarchy is thus not a chain of superimposed commands or even the ranking of different values, but rather an expression of a holistic unity of opposites that is as much a part of the structure of human thought as the binary oppositions posited by Claude Lévi-Strauss. And there is, of course, a plethora of explanations —biological, demographic, social—for the hierarchical relations between men and women that many feminists now claim is the fundamental inequality of civilization.

All of these explanations are, of course, highly speculative and I cannot pretend to offer any genuine guidance in choosing among them. What they suggest, however, is the extraordinary difficulty of overturning hierarchy, which, to put it mildly, is an overdetermined phenomenon derived from a vast number of possible sources. It may seem that unless we get down on all fours; give up language, private property, and the division of labor; undo all social abstractions like money; stop thinking in terms of parts and wholes; and overcome our biological differences, it is highly probable that hierarchy in one form or another will be around for some time to come. In fact, even its enemies tacitly fall back on hierarchical evaluative thinking. Thus, for example, Ryan claims that deconstruction shows that difference is "in fact more primordial and more general"[46] than the tradition of logocentric identity thinking that has tried to exclude it. From this priority, he implies, it then follows that privileging difference over sameness is somehow liberating.[47] This may be true, but it subtly restores the very type of hierarchical thinking that it is designed to overturn.

What may then be more useful—and is certainly less depressing—than speculating about the putative origins of hierarchy or struggling to find the perfectly consistent formula to express one's distaste for it is considering the present function or functions it fulfills. For, if the now celebrated genealogical method bequeathed to us by Friedrich Nietzsche is right, there may be no necessary connection between origins and current significance or function. In fact, if we take the general post-structuralist attack on the search for origins to heart, then it is really only the present function that matters. Such an attitude may go too far in severing that function entirely from its historical roots, but it is useful to remember if we are to avoid being paralyzed by the impossibility of reversing all of the possible sources I listed a few moments ago.

In probing the contemporary function of hierarchy, we are, however, confronted by the problem of bracketing or holding in abeyance our visceral egalitarian inclinations, which prevent us from acknowledging the ambiguous dialectic of culture suggested in the remarks of Adorno cited earlier. In particular, we have trouble avoiding the type of premature conflation of all types of hierarchy into variations on the theme of domination that Ryan, for all his stress on difference, exemplifies. For such an homogenization prevents us from considering the possibility that some may not work in tandem with others, but rather against them.[48] It is in fact precisely this possibility that brings us back to our initial question, the implications of Adorno's claim that all culture after Auschwitz is garbage. Taken at face value, this charge suggests that cultural hierarchy is indeed complicitous with the pervasive social domination that Adorno abhorred. But if we recall Adorno's contrary admonition that "the man who says no to culture is directly furthering the barbarism which our culture showed itself to be," it is clear that in his mind something potentially emancipatory was still preserved in elite culture despite its tainted status as false consolation. It is difficult, after all, to imagine Adorno, or anyone else for that matter, claiming that all garbage after Auschwitz is culture, a reversal whose absurdity is even more blatant if we apply it to Brecht's scatological observation about the mansion of culture.

What Adorno felt should be salvaged from the traditional elitist notion of high culture as superior to everyday life was evident in many places throughout his work, but perhaps nowhere as clearly as in his debate with Benjamin over the implications of Surrealism.[49] Without spelling out all its ramifications, the following points should be made. For Benjamin, Surrealism represented a revolutionary attempt to reintegrate radical art and life. Or to put it in terms of his now celebrated concept of the aura, the Surrealists tried to obliterate the cultic, ritually derived distance between unique works of art and prosaic reality in order to harness the emancipatory power of art to transform society. The de-auraticization of art, a process abetted by the technological innovations of the 20th century, was thus a healthy development, which would help bring about the overturning of both cultural and social hierarchy. Surrealism was the prototype of other similar modernist movements, like the *neue Sachlichkeit*, and of what we now sometimes call post-modernist ones, in its desire to collapse art back into the life-world from which it originally emerged.

Although sharing his friend's sensitivity to the de-auraticization of much recent art, Adorno was far less sanguine than Benjamin about its revolutionary potential. Instead, he championed that current in aesthetic modernism which remained esoteric rather than exoteric in its appeal. Figures like Arnold Schoenberg and Samuel Beckett, who resisted the demand to make their art immediately effective in political or social terms, were more genuinely revolutionary in the long run than those, like the Surrealists, who did not. There were, of course, costs in such a choice, as Adorno's more activist lefist critics never tired of reminding him. A totally inaccessible artistic elitism might never find the way to reunite its emancipatory potential with the social forces that could help realize it.

But at least in the years since their quarrel was first joined, I think it can be said that Adorno has gotten the better of the argument. For rather than leading to anything demonstrably revolutionary, the integration of de-auraticized art and life has led to the cooptation of artistic negativity by new variants of affirmative culture. The once disturbing techniques of movements like Surrealism have shown themselves to be easily adaptable to the demands of consumer advertising. In other words, the attempt to break down a hierarchical cultural relationship may unintentionally have contributed to the maintenance of a still hierarchical social one. What Herbert Marcuse once called "repressive desublimation"[50] in reference to the pseudo-liberation of sexuality in our seemingly hedonist culture has thus had its analogue in aesthetic terms. The conclusion that Adorno reached was that an art which resists reabsorption into everyday life in the short run may help prepare the way for a more genuinely liberating unification in the future. The same might perhaps be said of other variants of hierarchy that now pervade our cultural life, such as the distinction between intellectual and other forms of history which Bouwsma with his premature plea for an ecumenical history of meaning wants us to reject.

My point in conclusion is not that we should be simply complacent about the elitist aspects of the humanities as they are now conceived. Nor am I pleading for some timeless canon of great works existing in an ahistorical Arnoldian realm of the best and most beautiful. The exact content of what we privilege as higher than other aspects of our cultural experience must constantly be rethought and challenged. So-called high culture has been and will continue to be renewed from below, just as popular or even mass culture derives much of its energies from above. The boundaries shift and dissolve, the categories harden and soften, each era defines itself both through acceptance of and rebellion against the values of the past. No specific received hierarchy is immutable, nor should any be defended as such. Esoteric art is not forever superior to exoteric, whatever its present function may be.

What I would argue, however, is that the process of establishing new hierarchical evaluations itself remains, at least for the foreseeable future, inescapable and indeed worthy of our approbation. For all the efforts of anti-elitists of whatever kind, whether deconstructionist, feminist, populist, or even Christian anthropologist, to debunk it, there seems little likelihood of their success. Even the much ballyhooed demise of the avant-garde, which has led some critics to question Adorno's faith in esoteric modernism, has not really lead to the flattening out of all cultural inequalities. If there are genuine reasons to bemoan the specific implications of the types of hierarchy that now exist, and I think there are, there are also reasons to be thankful that we have not entirely lost our capacity to make distinctions of quality and rank. For as the Hungarian critic Sandor Radnoti recently put it, "The *revocation* of [the] alienation [of high art from society in general] is not only impossible in dynamic societies, but is not even desirable. It is not desirable because the exclusive character of a demand for recognition as belonging to the world would annihilate the criticism that the art work exercises over the world"[51] It is as the much-maligned guardians of this alienation that the humanities, not despite but because of their inevitable elitism, can justify whatever emancipatory role they may still play even in the grim aftermath of Auschwitz.

4

Two Cheers for Paraphrase:
The Confessions of a
Synoptic Intellectual Historian

> I strive *not* after exactness, but after a synoptic view.
>
> Ludwig Wittgenstein

It may be a truism, but is nonetheless often true, that we rarely know what we are actually doing until someone else tells us. So it was with a genuine sense of discovery that I found my work cited in Dominick LaCapra's penetrating essay "Rethinking Intellectual History and Reading Texts" as an example of what he calls "synoptic content analysis."[1] This method of reconstructing the past, he contends, adopts a "documentary approach" to texts rather than seeing them as "worklike" with all of the complexity we normally attribute to works of art. More specifically,

> the documentary situates the text in terms of factual or literal dimensions involving reference to empirical reality and conveying information about it. The worklike supplements empirical reality by adding to, and subtracting from, it. It thereby involves dimensions of the text not reducible to the documentary, prominently including the roles of commitment, interpretation, and imagination. The worklike is critical and transformative for it deconstructs and reconstructs the given, in a sense repeating it but also bringing into the world something that did not exist before in that significant variation, alteration, or transformation. (pp. 52–53)

Because most intellectual historians tend to be trained like historians in general rather than literary critics, they lean toward a documentary rather than worklike method, avoiding particularly complex literary texts in favor of ones more easily reduced to a paraphrasable core of meaning, those straightforward "ideas" so often the heroes of their narratives. Even if the synoptic intellectual historian wants to go outside ideas or mental structures to the context in which they are situated, problems remain if the texts to be contextualized are simply assumed to contain arguments that are easily paraphrased, messages that are wholly independent of the medium through which they are conveyed. Furthermore, as LaCapra argues elsewhere, the context which is itself adduced to explain these allegedly unproblematic ideas must also "be seen as a text of sorts. Its 'reading' and interpretation post problems as difficult as those posed by the most intricate written text."[2] The relationship between text and context ought, therefore, to be conceptualized as another form of intertextuality rather than a relationship between ideas or mind and world.

Such arguments will, of course, be familiar to every contemporary literary critic, but LaCapra is certainly correct to emphasize how rarely they are articulated by historians, intellectual or otherwise. Certainly, when I wrote the book he singles out as an example of synoptic content analysis back in the early 1970s, I was blissfully unaware of their existence. At the time, it seemed a sufficiently challenging task merely to reconstruct the demandingly difficult arguments of the Frankfurt School and relate them to the life histories of its members without then proceeding to deconstruct them as well. Nor apparently had I learned the lesson by 1980, when I delivered a paper on the Jürgen Habermas-Hans-Georg Gadamer debate to a conference in part organized by LaCapra at Cornell University on methods in intellectual history.[3] My failings in this regard were brought home a short time later when the literary critic Michael Ryan referred to the paper in his *Marxism and Deconstruction*.[4] Now, however, the ante was much higher, as Ryan focused on what he saw as the more sinister political implications of synoptic intellectual history. Reflecting on his experience in the audience, he wrote,

> I was struck by how faithfully the method of intellectual historiography followed the pattern of conceptualization as it is found in Western rationality. That method consists of giving a brief synopsis of the arguments of such thinkers. The synopsis in such historiography is analogous to a concept in that it abridges and reduces a complicated, heterogeneous mass to an abstract, homogeneous form. (p. 144)

What makes this method politically nefarious, Ryan argues, is its normative and hierarchical exclusion of everything that falls outside such a synopsis. Deconstruction, in contrast, valorizes heterogeneity and "criticizes the hubristic pretensions of reason to legislate the truth of the world as a synoptic rational concept that 'corresponds' 'adequately' to something in the world that has the same synoptic, abridged, isolated, crystallized, proper form" (p. 145).

Ryan then recalls that after the talk, he rose from the floor to ask me to comment on this fact, pointing out that my notion of rationality was probably connected to my being a first-world, white male—as was indeed virtually everyone else speaking at the conference. Reproducing his question, he continues,

> I suggested that if a third-world feminist attacked his rational assumptions and the institutional rationality of the conference, using nonacademic obscenity, she would have appeared irrational in relation to his universal reason, simply because such individualist, legislative reason, committed as it is in its very practice to a norm of homogeneous synoptic continuity, uncritical, nonanalytic academic male equanimity, and a well-balanced ratio, cannot tolerate the dissonance and heterogeneity which such deliberately disequilibrating deconstructive criticism introduces. (p. 145)

Then, to show how true this diagnosis was, he remembers that "fittingly enough, perhaps, the speaker cut me off before I could finish my remarks . . . I felt the touch of the iron fist beneath the urbane glove of while male liberalism" (p. 145).

Now, I must admit that I am still unconvinced by the logic of Ryan's argument—the thought of, say, Imelda Marcos running down the aisle shouting curses does not strike me as a model of emancipatory political practice. Indeed, the very assumption that all that third-world women can do to assert their otherness is to hurl "nonacademic obscenities" seems to me demeaning to those who can and do engage in rational dialogue. But Ryan's hyperbolic denunciation of the links between synoptic content analysis, reason, and the exclusion of difference does, I would concede, point to the deeper issues at stake in the debate over method raised with considerably more subtlety in LaCapra's essay. For it is true that in the paper that so outraged Ryan in his guise as *soi-disant* spokesperson for third-world women, I did essentially defend a Habermasian notion of communicative rationality as an antidote to what I saw as the uncritical and irrationalist implications of Gadamer's version of hermeneutics. Thus, there was perhaps a certain unintended fit between my synoptic method and what I was trying to defend in substantive terms, a fit which Ryan acutely noted.

Where, however, Ryan went astray was in his leap to the conclusion that my restricting his unlimited access to control the floor of the conference through an interminable "question" was a necessary effect of my bias for a reason that he claims must hierarchically exclude and marginalize what it cannot control. Here, ironically, his own recourse to a hasty synopsis of my method was the source of an unfortunate homogenization of different forms of reason. For communicative rationality, as Habermas describes it and as I was trying to explain, is an inherently intersubjective, symmetrically unhierarchical relationship. Under the conditions prevailing at a lecture, where it is assumed the audience has come to listen to and question the announced speaker rather than participate in a fully open discussion, communicative rationality is not really achieved. The public sphere in which it may perhaps be institutionalized cannot be understood on the essentially pedagogical model of the lecture hall, for as Habermas once put it, "in a process of enlightenment there can only be participants."[5] Nor is the rationality it hopes to realize comparable to the "individual, legislative reason" attacked by Ryan as necessarily exclusivist; it is instead based on the creation of ever-widening speech communities in which monological rationality is replaced by a dialogical discursive alternative.[6] Here too, of course, some exclusion may occur. In fact, it will necessarily be directed at those who claim a privileged right to suspend the procedures of the speech community in the name of a higher claim to truth, say that of nonacademic obscenity self-righteously defending itself as liberating otherness.

To pursue this point would, of course, take us too far afield from our more central concern with synoptic intellectual history. The slippage from one to the other is not, however, fortuitous, insofar as there are certain resonances in the very notion of synopsis that may account for the hostility it has aroused. Etymologically, the word derives from the image of a view of the whole, an image which implies a single, totalizing gaze that freezes what it sees into a synchronic and static picture. Like the panoptic gaze of the jailer in Jeremy Bentham's model prison, of which Michel Foucault has made us all so aware, it can be construed as a subtle tool of discipline and domination. Synoptic content analysis can thus be understood as akin to the technological perspective that Martin Heidegger in his influential essay "The Age of the World View" condemned for turning reality into a picture to be seen by an allegedly distanced spectator.[7] It is therefore not surprising to find that LaCapra acknowledges that his preference for a worklike rather than documentary approach to texts is explicitly indebted to Heidegger's discussion in another, but related, essay, "The Origin of the Work of Art."[8]

Now, this is not the place to launch a critical examination of the Heideggerian-Derridean distrust of monologic vision, which is now, and not without some justification, so widely shared. Nor can we probe the implications of Heidegger's alternative visual metaphor of *Umsicht* or circumspection, with its prereflexive, nonobjectifying, antirepresentational implications. Instead, it will be more useful to pose the simpler question: Must synoptic intellectual history always be understood as a variant of what might be called the monologic visual fallacy or the discipline of the totalizing gaze? Is the intellectual historian who practices it necessarily playing the questionable role of omniscient narrator who pretends to be above the fray, looking down with a God's-eye view on the events or their documentary residues he or she summarily records? And in so doing, does such a historian inevitably smooth over the tensions, iron out the contradictions, and reduce the complex play of the texts whose narrative relation to each other and to their contexts he or she synoptically reconstructs?

In certain respects, these questions lead back to the time-honored aesthetic problem of what might be called the paraphrasability of the poetic. In traditional romantic and idealist aesthetics, as well as in some versions of Anglo-American New Criticism, poetry was precisely that which defied reduction to a mere prosaic or conceptual summary of its content. Symbols, images, metaphors, and so on, were all understood to be too particularized and polysemic to be paraphrased in critical discourse. Instead, all that could be done was to appreciate their irreducible integrity, for not only do we murder when we dissect, we also do so by trying to distill content from form.

The most useful rebuttal of this position that I have encountered appears in the Italian Marxist Galvano Della Volpe's *Critique of Taste*, a work that seeks to demonstrate the inevitably conceptual dimension of art, even before the critic tries to analyze it. Against a long tradition of aesthetics that he sees stretching from Samuel Taylor Coleridge to Georg Lukács, Della Volpe contends that works of art are always "tauto-heterological identities," containing both imagistic and conceptual, material and ideal, sensual and mental dimensions. Poetic characters, he writes,

> are dianoetic or discursive universals: normal epistemological events which result, like any other concrete concept or universal, from an abstraction by genera based at one and the same time on the *categorical* nature of things and their *material* or empirical-perceptual being.[9]

The formal quality of poetry, moreover, is inevitably part of a conceptually mediated discourse that lifts it above the chaos of mere material, sensual stimulation. Although poetic texts are polysemic rather than univocal, paraphrase, which Della Volpe calls "the *regression* to current linguistic use" (p. 133), has an ultimately revalatory function in that it

> constitutes the premise of an internal *progression* of thought and *sèma* or truth, an internal variation and development of meanings, which

is disclosed or resolved precisely in a *critical* paraphrase or philological comparison (in the widest sense of "philological") of the paraphrase with that which is paraphrased. This comparison is the *beginning* and the *end* of a whole process (reconstitution of a dialectic) of truth. (p. 133)

Once we acknowledge its central role, Della Volpe continues, we liberate

the paraphrase of poetry from the disreputable features (superfluity, indeed harmfulness) attributed to it by traditional post-romantic and decadent taste, which elects to ignore the discursive and dialectical nature of poetic truth revealed by critical paraphrase, and to confer a mythical and dogmatic character on it by endowing it with "intuitive" immediacy. Our account also avoids the uncritical equation of the paraphrase and the paraphrased poetic text into which abstract aesthetic rationalism falls. (p. 133)

Della Volpe's argument is interesting for several reasons. First, it transcends the sterile alternative between those, on the one hand, who want to oppose original work and critical paraphrase as if they were totally antithetical and those, on the other hand, who naively assume an essential identity between the meaning of the first text, its univocal signification, and its paraphrastic double. The oxymoronic notion of a tauto-heterological unity, which Della Volpe uses throughout his work, captures the more complicated relationship between the text and its synopsis better than either of these extreme alternatives. His position is also suggestive because of its emphasis on what might be called the always already paraphrastic nature of the original texts. Thus, for example, when either the literary critic or the intellectual historian reads Johann Wolfgang von Goethe's *Faust* or G. W. F. Hegel's *Phenomenology*, he or she must acknowledge that for all the irreducible uniqueness of each text, the language they depend on necessarily invokes what Della Volpe calls "dianoetic or discursive universals," terms with the same homogenizing implications as those used later in second-order paraphrases. Or to put it in a way that reverses the now familiar deconstructionist argument that texts—whether literary or expository—are always calling themselves into question, both primary works and secondary accounts are alike in their reliance on signifiers that are, on at least one level, universalizing abstractions that inevitably yoke together heterogeneous particulars. The perpetual search by poets for a more imagistically concrete and nonconceptual language is thus always frustrated by the limits of language itself, at least insofar as it functions as a medium of intersubjective communication. The language terrorists, to use Jean Paulhan's familiar opposition, never fully win their battle against the rhetoricians without giving up the semantically meaningful dimension of their work. The attempt made by certain modernists, most notably the Symbolists, Imagists, and Surrealists, to write a poetry that would defy all paraphrase ultimately misfired, as language resisted the effort to be turned into nonreferential music or abstract painting. What this all suggests for intellectual history is that the synoptic method cannot be seen simply as the betrayal of the irreducibly complex and uniquely heterogeneous nature of the texts whose meaning they seek to paraphrase. For those texts themselves, however worklike in LaCapra's sense, *already* contain at least a moment of paraphrasis, which allows them to be used in a documentary way as evidence of the ideas or concepts they express.

This is not, however, to argue that the intellectual historian should rest content with merely presenting what seems to be the paraphrasable content of a text or a writer's more general *oeuvre*. To do so would be to endorse what might be called the naive synoptic approach, which its critics justly pillory as simplistic. For as Della Volpe points out, what is most valuable in critical paraphrase is the return move of comparing it with what it purports to reproduce. Even the enemies of paraphrase like the American New Critic John Crowe Ransom have admitted the usefulness of this approach. In his famous essay "Criticism, Inc.," Ransom first attacks synopsis and paraphrase by condescendingly noting that "high-school classes and the women's clubs delight in these procedures, which are easiest of all the systematic exercises possible in the discussion of literary objects."[10] But he then goes on to argue that even the sophisticated critic must analyze a poem into its paraphrasable and nonparaphrasable dimensions:

> However the critic may spell them, the two terms are in his mind: the prose core to which he can violently reduce the total object, and the differentia, residue, or tissue, which keeps the object poetical or entire. The character of the poem resides for the good critic in its way of exhibiting the residuary character. (p. 238)

Poetry is not, therefore, simply what is lost in the translation; it should be understood instead as the creative tension between what can be translated into a prose core and what cannot.

It might, of course, be argued that the very search for a prose core behind or beneath the actual text is to fall prey to a faulty metaphysics of presence that fails to acknowledge the infinite regress in such a procedure. For as Friedrich Nietzsche pointed out in that early essay now so incessantly quoted, "On Truth and Lie in an Extra-Moral

Sense," truth may well be a "mobile army of metaphors, metonymies, anthropomorphisms . . . illusions about which one has forgotten that this is what they are, metaphors which are worn out and without sensuous powers, coins which have lost their pictures and now matter only as metal, no longer as coins.[11] Whether or not this is a true statement about truth, an old problem that has been with us ever since the Greeks contemplated the propensity of all Cretans to lie, cannot concern us now.

What is, however, important to note is that even if we accept the notion that no text really contains an irreducible prose core of ideas that can be synoptically reproduced, the function of paraphrase is itself not therefore eliminated. For even a radically antiobjectivist theory like the affective stylistics of Stanley Fish accords it a central role. For Fish, all readers inevitably bring expectations to their reception of a text, which then may be realized or frustrated in the temporal process of reading. Understanding always therefore entails what might be called—the terms are mine not Fish's—proleptic paraphrase or anticipatory synopsis. As Fish writes,

> we comprehend not in terms of the deep structure alone but in terms of a *relationship* between the unfolding, in time, of the surface structure and a continual checking of it against our projection (always in terms of surface structure) of what the deep structure will reveal itself to be; and when the final discovery has been made and *the* deep structure is perceived, all the "mistakes"—the positing, on the basis of incomplete evidence, of deep structures that failed to materialize—will not be cancelled out. They have existed in the mental life of the reader; they *mean*.[12]

In other words, the very act of reading entails an anticipation of the pattern or structure that will appear when the entire work is finished. Whereas this anticipation is likely to produce mistakes in the first reading of a text, mistakes which are, as Fish contends, part of the meaningful experience of aesthetic reception, on subsequent readings, synoptic memories will function to weed out the most unsupportable of these false anticipations. They may, to be sure, themselves be undermined by those later readings and require further adjustment. But if anything, the role of anticipatory and retrospective synopsis will continue to grow as we return to the "same" text on different occasions. The same might be said, *a fortiori*, of even later attempts to reconstruct the text's meaning through a written account.

Even if we do not presuppose a fixed core of prosaic meaning in an original text or claim that such a meaning is the result of an authorial intention that can be recaptured whole, paraphrase is still, therefore, an essential part of our intercourse as historians or critics with cultural artifacts. Indeed, it might be argued that it is a central element in the hermeneutic process of dialogue that Gadamer persuasively claims is essential to historical self-consciousness itself. For it is the capacity of texts to be paraphrased and reparaphrased that allows what he calls the "fusion of horizon" between past and present, however provisional and open-ended, to occur.[13] Because of the dialogic nature of this process, the linguistic give and take between the original text and its parallel restatement in our terms, any purely visual and therefore monologic rendering of synopsis is misguided.[14]

Put even more strongly, what inclines it toward the kind of communicative rationality that is so different from the coercive, totalizing reason rejected by Ryan and other deconstructionists, is the telos of achieving an intersubjective consensus implied in the very act of seeking a common ground—or better put, arriving at a fused horizon—between past and present. That circular process of beginning with texts and returning to them after a mediating paraphrase, in Della Volpe's sense, or beginning with synoptic expectations and correcting them through new readings that return us again and again to a never-quite-the-same original, postulated by Fish, suggests a refinement of understanding that in some genuine sense can be called progressive. Without the paraphrastic moment in this hermeneutic process there can be no regulative ideal of perfect communicability, which Habermas sees as inherent in the illocutionary dimension of speech acts *per se*. The hope that at some state of the process the original author, were he still alive, might be able to say to the historian, "yes, that is exactly what I meant," is counterbalanced by the complementary hope that such an author might also be able to admit, after being presented with a new interpretative reconstruction of his work and its place in a larger pattern of meaning, "now I can see what my work really signifies." These are, to be sure, no more than regulative ideals, which provide a counterfactual standard by which we can imaginatively measure the inadequacies of our actual efforts. But as the unarticulated teleological premises of our synoptic reconstruction of the past, they function in a way that links paraphrastic intellectual history with communicative rationality.

The practical implications of all of this came home to me with special urgency when I was asked to write a short study of Theodor Adorno for Frank Kermode's Modern Masters series.[15] Adorno was himself an outspoken opponent of mere synopsis, often arguing that genuine philosophy is precisely that which eludes paraphrase. His emphasis on avoiding the tyranny of concepts by insisting on their nonidentity with the objects they purport to represent might easily be construed as compatible with the deconstructionist attack on logocentricity. In fact, in his *Marxism and Deconstruction*, Ryan claims that "the primary target of each is the logos or ratio, the principle of rational identity whose operation denies dialectical mediacy and differentiation" (p. 75). Although this homogenizing of their two positions underestimates the still powerful bias for reason in Adorno in comparison with Jacques Derrida—reason understood as more than merely conceptual identity —it correctly expresses the suspicion Adorno harbored toward any synthesizing, synoptic reproduction of his thought.

It was therefore obvious to me that trying to encompass that thought in the narrow confines of a series like the Modern Masters would be betraying one of Adorno's own deepest taboos. Although I found myself unable to avoid all of the guilt pangs engendered by this realization, I finally gained a measure of relief by trying to thematize the whole issue as explicitly as possible. Pointing out the taboo at the very beginning of my introduction, I defended the legitimacy of breaking it by invoking the now familiar argument that an author's intentionality is not the sole or even primary repository of his texts' meaning for his readers. Thus, although Adorno may have wanted to control the reception of his work by warning against paraphrasing its content, *any* reception must inevitably entail a certain amount of domestication and familiarization on the part of his readers and *a fortiori* of anyone who tries to write about it, paraphrastically or otherwise. There was therefore no difference in kind between the most faithful reproduction of the ideas in as close to their original form as possible and an exercise like mine, which made no pretense of doing so. If, as I have been arguing above, all readings contain a synoptic moment, then a frankly synoptic account such as that suitable for a Modern Masters volume was not so radically different from other types of reception, which self-consciously eschewed paraphrase. Or to put it in somewhat different terms, the transgression of Adorno's taboo was as necessary as it was inevitable in any reading—or, as Gadamer would put it, application—of his texts.

Beyond this general argument, I also attempted two other ploys that were designed to complicate the way in which my own particular reception would avoid the pitfalls of what I have called above naive paraphrase. First, I tried to apply Adorno's central idea of a force-field or constellation to his own intellectual career. Adorno had used these terms to indicate the kind of method that avoids reducing the tensions in a work or an *oeuvre* through an essentializing synopsis of their allegedly unified meaning. The force-field or constellation registered instead the untotalized, still conflicting energies that resisted such a reduction. Without falling back into a mere catalogue of unrelated elements or factors, such a method was true to the nonidentical impulse of negative dialectics. By turning it on Adorno's intellectual production and isolating what I saw as the five main forces in his own field or stars in his constellation—Western Marxism, aesthetic modernism, mandarin cultural despair, Jewish theology and, in a teleological rather than generative sense, proto-deconstructionism—I attempted what might be called a methodological or formal paraphrase of his work in order to illuminate its substantive tensions. In so doing, I hoped both to offer the reader a concrete illustration of Adorno's own approach and to go beyond his self-understanding by applying the approach, in ways he never did, back to his own work.

And secondly, I tried to employ different levels of paraphrase at different distances from his texts in separate chapters. In most cases, I drew on a wide variety of different texts from throughout his career to extract a coherent pattern that could be identified as Adorno's basic position on certain issues, a practice that was abetted by his frequent repetition of arguments in new contexts. In fact, at the end of the book, I invoked the observation made by several critics that Adorno's antisystematic intentions were belied by his tendency to make the same point again and again no matter the object of his scrutiny, a charge also often leveled at deconstructionists who homogenize every text they treat into an example of the same *différance*.

But against the assumption that all of his texts merely repeated the same pattern in a kind of infinite self-paraphrase, I reminded my readers of the detotalizing energies unleashed by the unreconciled tensions in his own force-field. These I tried to illustrate through a close examination of a single text in the chapter I devoted to the philosophical underpinnings of his general position, his negative dialectics. The text I chose was the fourteen-page essay he wrote shortly before his death on "Subject-Object."[16] Rather than offering a synoptic overview of his philosophy as a whole, I worked my way through this densely argued and often elliptical essay, deliberately following the paratactic and chiasmic logic of its organization as best as I could. But to illuminate rather than merely reproduce the often underdeveloped and cryptic arguments of "Subject-Object," I found it also necessary to depart from the text's own level of discourse and introduce explanations that drew on implicit paraphrases of Adorno's general position, as I understood it from reading his *oeuvre* as a whole. This was not so much an exercise in intertextuality in the manner of certain deconstructionist writings as an interplay of close reading and generalizing paraphrase, somewhat akin to what, as I mentioned above, Della Volpe argues is necessary even for understanding poetic texts.

In varying the types of approach I used in this little book, I sought to make as problematic as possible the naive paraphrastic assumptions that often underlie popularizations without, however, abandoning the necessary tool of synopsis in presenting Adorno to readers who may have little or no direct knowledge of his work. My hope, as I expressly emphasized in the book's introduction, was to induce my readers to turn to the original texts rather than to lull them into the false conclusion that now they really had Adorno's essential meaning and therefore could spare themselves the pain of finding it out for themselves. Whether or not the book will be successful in this regard remains, of course, very much to be seen.

Let me finish by returning to my point of origin with a consideration of LaCapra's critique of paraphrastic intellectual history. All along I have felt somewhat uneasy about caricaturing his position, especially by linking it associatively with Ryan's. For in the footnote in "Rethinking Intellectual History and Reading Texts" where LaCapra cites my work as an example of synoptic content analysis, he in fact calls that method "both necessary and limited as a method of analyzing complex texts" (p. 55). In my preceding remarks, I have been dwelling only on the necessity and indeed the virtues of that method, in its sophisticated rather than naive form, and thus have had little to say about its limitations. But I would now want to agree with LaCapra that even at its most sophisticated, paraphrase by itself is not enough. The great contribution of critics who have exhorted intellectual historians to pay more attention to the materiality of texts is to remind us of the inevitable obstacles in any attempt to render or reproduce a thought transparently without linguistic mediation. And by stressing the worklike rather than merely documentary quality of every written record of the past, they have alerted us to the active role we as historians must more self-consciously assume in our reconstruction of a lost reality that can never be simply repeated.

But having admitted this insufficiency, the reason for my raising only two cheers for paraphrase rather than the normal three, I want to emphasize nonetheless that to be insufficient does not mean to be unnecessary, as the more extreme deconstructionist position exemplified by Ryan implies. In fact, I want to go further and warn against the dangers latent in the wholesale abandonment of a method whose links with communicative rationality are, as I have tried briefly to demonstrate, so strong. In the past few years, we have become increasingly sensitive to the ways in which language erodes meaning, disperses intentionality, and frustrates understanding. It is perhaps time to be equally open to those aspects of it that preserve hope for a very different kind of human solidarity. In its very modest way, synoptic content analysis, in its sophisticated rather than naive form, may justifiably be defended as a prefiguration of such an outcome.

READING THE LEGACY
OF SOCIALISM

5

Vico and Western Marxism

In a work as celebrated and controversial as Karl Marx's *Das Kapital*, even the footnotes have generated substantial commentaries. Perhaps none has been as extensive as that sparked by the note Marx devoted to the then little-known 18th-century philosopher Giambattista Vico.[1] Until a recent critique by Eugene Kamenka,[2] it had been generally assumed that this note, the only reference to Vico in all of Marx's published writings, indicated an intellectual debt of considerable proportions. Although the size of that debt now seems somewhat smaller, thanks to Kamenka's arguments, it is nonetheless true that Marxists of a wide variety of persuasions have been eager to appropriate Vico's legacy for their own purposes. These purposes have not, however, always been alike and so, not surprisingly, Vico has meant different things to different Marxists. For the theoreticians of the Second International, such as Paul Lafargue and Antonio Labriola,[3] he was understood as the anticipator of Marx's objective laws of historical development. In particular, his belief in an "ideal eternal history" traversed by all peoples (with the exception of the Hebrews) was interpreted as a prefiguration of Marx's supposed assertion of an evolutionary path followed by all developing societies. Similarly, Vico's continued faith in providential intervention in the affairs of men was understood as a religious version of the Hegelian idea of "the cunning of Reason," which was itself secularized still further in Marx's idea of historical forces working behind the backs and against the wills of men. Based on similar parallels, the Austro-Marxist Max Adler claimed Vico as the father of scientific sociology, which in his eyes was the essence of Marxism.[4] For others, such as Georges Sorel,[5] who ultimately abandoned Marxism for Vico's notion of historical *corsi* and *recorsi*, Vico was understood as the anticipator of Marx's contention that ideas were the epiphenomena of material forces embodied in the mode of production. Still other commentators[6] found parallels in Vico's sensitivity to class struggle in history; or his general originality in valuing historical thinking in an era when it was almost universally disparaged; or his recognition that discrete historical epochs should be understood as coherently integrated totalities; or his critique of the individualist premises of social contract theory; or his contention that cultural products, such as the Homeric epics, were collective creations; or his equation of the human essence with the ensemble of social relations; and so on.

But perhaps the most widely discussed link between Vico and Marx, and the one which I want to treat in this paper, is that directly based on the famous footnote in *Capital*, which ends with the rhetorical question: "And would not such a history [of human technology] be easier [than one of natural technology] to compile, since, as Vico says, human history differs from natural history in this, that we have made the former, but not the latter?" Putting aside the issue of technology for a moment, what Marx was here acknowledging was Vico's now celebrated critique of René Descartes's defense of natural scientific knowledge as superior to humanistic knowledge. That defense was of course grounded in the assumption of a subjective observer having clear and distinct ideas of given objects outside of his consciousness. For Vico, to give the familiar argument in brief,[7] humanistic knowledge was more accurate than natural scientific knowledge because men have made culture and they can thus know what they have made, through an act of imaginative reconstruction, better than what is made by God or nature. Culture can be known from within, nature only from without. This was a humanization of an old Scholastic formula that was originally applied to God, the creator *ex nihilo*, whose knowledge was *per caussas* (or through causes). Vico generalized it in his most frequently quoted phrase, *verum et factum convertuntur*, which meant the true and the made are interchangeable.

By *verum* Vico meant a kind of *a priori* knowledge, which he called *scienza*, of a reality invented or constituted by men and therefore logically accessible to their recollection. Its opposite in his vocabulary was *certum*, which meant the imperfect, contingent knowledge of already-given objects or processes knowable only by external observation, which he called *conscienza*. These realities were knowable, but they were not intelligible, that is, charged with meaning. Intelligibility was a function of a participatory rather than spectatorial link with the object of cognition. Vico included mathematics in the category of *verum*, because he thought men imposed it on the world rather than discovering it already there, as the Cartesians had assumed. But more importantly, at least for the Marxist tradition, he included knowledge of history in the *verum* category as well. To understand man meant therefore to conceive him historically, to recognize human nature not as a static essence but rather as a process of anthropogenesis. Cognition was thus re-cognition as the process of knowing reversed and mirrored the process of genesis so that once again a unity of subject and object might be achieved.

Vico, to be sure, also acknowledged the role of Providence in history, which helped guide the course of human development along the lines of that "ideal eternal history" mentioned above. This complication in the *verum-factum* principle meant that the unintended as well as the intended consequences of human action all conspired together to make the story a meaningful one. Vico was still enough of a Christian to believe that men pursued ends ultimately initiated by God, but which they were the immediate means of realizing. Thus, although God was the only possible possessor of perfect knowledge, man as a microcosm of his creator had enough of the divine spark in him to make the *verum-factum* principle meaningful for him as well.

For many of the Second International theorists, as we have seen, the providential residue in Vico was an important one. But for those who came to repudiate the orthodox Dialectical Materialism of the pre-World War I era, the *verum-factum* principle was given a radically humanistic reading. The automatic working out of objective historical laws, a belief whose political consequences were disastrous, was jettisoned in the name of a more activist reinterpretation of the Marxist heritage. The new interpreters were the founders of what has become known as the "Western Marxist" tradition,[8] from a chapter title in Maurice Merleau-Ponty's *Advertures of the Dialectic* of 1955.[9] By "Western Marxism," Merleau-Ponty meant an open-ended, non-dogmatic, self-critical alternative to the stultifying Marxism-Leninism of the Soviet Union and its Communist followers abroad, as well as to the feckless revisionism of Social Democracy. Georg Lukács was the exemplary Western Marxist for Merleau-Ponty, although he could easily have included Antonio Gramsci and Karl Korsch among the founding fathers. Their lead was followed by a number of important subsequent thinkers, many of whom were given added inspiration by the recovery of Marx's early manuscripts in the late 1920s: Ernst Bloch, Max Horkheimer, Theodor W. Adorno, Herbert Marcuse, Jean-Paul Sartre, Lucien Goldmann, Henri Lefebvre, Walter Benjamin, Enzo Paci, Jürgen Habermas and Merleau-Ponty himself. What these often very different thinkers shared was a disdain for naturalist, objectivist, deterministic Marxism, and a stress on objective human consciousness, a strong interest in cultural, philosophical, and methodological questions, a certain indebtedness to the *Geisteswissenschaft* tradition, and a belief that *praxis* was perhaps the central category of any Marxist analysis. Although Lukács, Korsch, and Gramsci had complicated and often strained relationships with organized political parties, most of the other Western Marxists maintained a critical distance from official socialist organizations. Their ideas had the greatest impact in the late 1960s, especially on the events of May 1968 in Paris, the Prague Spring of that same year, and the New Left in America and Western Europe. The current attempt to differentiate Eurocommunism from Soviet Marxism also owes something to the Western Marxists.

An important starting point of their analysis, especially obvious in Lukács and Gramsci, was Vico's contention that truth and making were convertible. I deliberately say a "starting point," for what I hope to demonstrate in this paper is that Western Marxism began increasingly to recognize insurmountable difficulties in Vico's argument. This observation is obviously the case if one widens the definition of Western Marxism, as Perry Anderson has recently done in his *Considerations on Western Marxism*,[10] to include avowed anti-Hegelian, anti-humanist Marxists such as Louis Althusser, Galvano Della Volpe and Lucio Colletti, who have little use for Vico as a forerunner of their version of a more scientific Marxism. (Althusser in fact stresses his special debt to Baruch Spinoza, one of Vico's chief targets.)[11] But it is also valid if one examines the history of Western Marxism in its narrower sense as the neo-Hegelian followers of Lukács, Korsch, and Gramsci—the "warm" current of Marxism which Ernst Bloch once counterposed to the "cold" current he associated with orthodox Dialectical Materialism and its more recent off-shoots.

To make this development clear, I would like to begin with a brief analysis of the ways in which Georg Lukács used Vico in his early work, much of which he later recanted, and then pass on to the increasingly more radical criticisms of his analysis made by members of the Frankfurt School. As I have argued elsewhere,[12] an unexpected convergence can be found between certain of their conclusions and those of the non-Hegelian Marxists who more obviously rejected the Vichian legacy.

Although, as Fredric Jameson has argued,[13] the shadow of Vico passes over the final chapters of Lukács's last pre-Marxist work, *The Theory of the Novel*, it is not until 1923 and *History and Class Consciousness*, the collection of essays written after Lukács's sudden conversion to Marxism in December 1918, that Vico's presence is really felt. In his key chapter on "Reification and the Consciousness of the Proletariat," Lukács approvingly invokes Marx's famous footnote to

Vico.[14] The context is a discussion of what he calls the "antinomies of bourgeois thought," best expressed in Immanuel Kant's philosophy, which he argues reflect the unresolved contradictions of bourgeois society. Among the most important of these antinomies are first, that between phenomenal knowledge, or knowledge of the world of appearances, and noumenal knowledge, or knowledge of essential things-in-themselves; and second, that between descriptive and normative knowledge, or what might be called facts and values, the *is* and the *ought*. For Lukács, these distinctions were preserved in more recent neo-Kantian and positivist thought, although Kant was their *locus classicus*. Bourgeois philosophy of any variety, Lukács contended, was unable to overcome these antinomies and thus escape from the cognitive and normative relativism they inevitably entailed because of the bourgeoisie's inability to grasp the world in its totality. Instead, it was limited to the specific perspective produced by its class status. As merely one embattled class in a society split along class lines, it could not transcend its fragmented world view which absolutized the antimonies mentioned above into eternal characteristics of human thought. Lacking a sense of the historical genesis of these splits in consciousness, which were rooted in the contradictions of capitalist society, the bourgeoisie lost the capacity to set them in motion as part of a dynamic process, both cognitive and social. Instead, it rendered the living flux that was history into a dead naturalism that saw society erroneously as a kind of "second nature." This vision of the world Lukács called reification,[15] which combined elements of Marx's notion of the fetishism of commodities with Max Weber's idea of the bureaucratic rationalization of the world and Georg Simmel's thoughts on the objectification of culture.

Before 1918, Lukács's own work, in particular his 1911 collection of essays entitled *Soul and Form*,[16] had expressed a keen sense of anguish at this state of affairs, but failed to offer a way out. The epoch, he wrote in *The Theory of the Novel*, was one of "transcendental homelessness."[17] Now, however, with his conversion to Marxism and his new faith that the Russian Revolution was a harbinger of global change, Lukács's despair ended. The key argument that allowed him to think a solution to the antinomies of bourgeois thought had arrived was Vico's belief that *verum* and *factum*, truth and making, were convertible. Although filtered through his readings in G. W. F. Hegel and J. G. Fichte, the *verum-factum* principle was clearly at the root of his new confidence. The bourgeoisie, he now argued, was prevented from knowledge of the concrete historical totality because of its essentially parasitic role in the production of the historical world. Because it did not truly make that world out of itself through its labor, its consciousness was necessarily reified and fragmented. Thus, for example, as Marx had shown in his critique of political economy, bourgeois thought stopped with the circulation and exchange of commodities and failed to grasp the dynamics of the underlying labor process that produced the world of commodity exchange.

The proletariat, on the other hand, had the potential to know the world, which, after all, its labor had done most to produce. But it had been victimized by the dominant world view of the bourgeoisie which prevented it from seeing the social world as the result of its *praxis*. What Gramsci was to call "cultural hegemony" meant that bourgeois values and modes of cognition were accepted by the working class and its spokesmen to a large degree. Indeed, Lukács contended, the theoreticians of the Second International, whether orthodox like Karl Kautsky or revisionist like Eduard Bernstein, were themselves infected by the antinomies of bourgeois thought. Their reliance on a scientistic objectivism or a moralistic voluntarism bore witness to their dilemma. The ultimate reason, however, was not so much theoretical obtuseness as the actual condition of the working class, which had not yet begun the difficult process of transforming and thereby dereifying the institutions of capitalist society. The empirical consciousness of the working class before 1917 had itself been confused and underdeveloped; its spokesmen were only marginally more advanced. Indeed, in some cases, they lagged behind the unreflective *praxis* of their more militant followers.

The Russian Revolution, with its promise to spread elsewhere, meant to Lukács the opening of a new era in human history, in which mankind's homelessness would end. The proletariat was leaving its status—as merely one class in a class society—behind and emerging as the universal class Marx had predicted it could become in a classless society. In so doing, it was engaged in the crucial task of dereifying bourgeois institutions, seeing them as transient obstacles on the road to socialism, and at the same time learning in practice to overcome the antinomies of bourgeois thought. In Vico's terms, it was becoming the "man," the human subject, who made history and therefore could understand it. No longer spectatorial and passive, its knowledge was that of a true participant. Theory and practice were thus united. In the transitional period, to be sure, spokesmen for the working class organized in a vanguard party were necessary to articulate the "imputed class consciousness" and its objective position in history assigned to the proletariat as it shook off the aftereffects of bourgeois cultural hegemony. But this role was soon to be superfluous as the revolution matured and was globally successful. Or, more precisely put, as the social world became more transparently the product of conscious and deliberate proletarian *praxis*, those who collectively made history would increasingly come to recognize themselves in it, which is what coming home would mean. The characteristic bourgeois mystification of a phenomenal world amenable only to scientific explanation and a noumenal world of opaque and unknowable things-in-themselves would be overcome. So, too, would the problem of the legitimacy of values, which bourgeois thinkers with their increasing impotence in the face of relativism had been unable to resolve. Fears of arbitrariness and contingency would end, once unrealistic expectations of an immutable and absolute moral system were replaced by an understanding of ethics as the given values of a concrete totality. The social world would be charged with meanings and values invested in it by its creators who would recognize their intentions in their creation. Obedience to self-imposed values would finally become a reality once the collective assertion of those values by a universal class replaced the traditional standards imposed by an elite, standards which bourgeois philosophy no longer knew how to justify. In the neo-Hegelian language of *History and Class Consciousness*, the subject of history, the proletariat as a universal class, would become identical with the object of history, the social world which it had created. The alienation of subject from object characteristic of capitalist society, indeed of all previous societies, would finally be transcended, and with it the antinomies of bourgeois thought.

Although much compressed, this, then, was the essence of Lukács's argument in the work which more than any other launched the Western Marxist tradition. Although in later years, Lukács specifically repudiated the Idealist elements in *History and Class Consciousness*, he never reversed his positive opinion of Vico's seminal importance for Marxist theory—as his glowing references in *The Young Hegel*, written in 1938, demonstrates.[18] This general assessment was shared by others in the Marxist Humanist camp. Antonio Gramsci's "philosophy of *praxis*" was deeply indebted to the major Italian exponent of Vico, Benedetto Croce, whose 1911 study of the *New Science* was as important to the 20th-century reception of Vico as Jules Michelet's had been to the 19th.[19] The result, as even the skeptical Kamenka admits, was that Gramsci frequently drew on Vico's legacy to help justify a number of his arguments.[20] The same might be said for the early Max Horkheimer, whose 1930 study of *The Origins of Bourgeois Philosophy of History*[21] ends with an accolade to Vico for having transcended the scientific limitations of Cartesian and Machiavellian theory and recognized the pivotal role of *praxis* in the construction of history. As late as the 1960s and early 1970s, Marxists still in the neo-Hegelian camp such as Ernst Bloch[22] and the Czech philosopher influential in the Prague Spring, Karel Kosik, paid homage to Vico's "seminal discovery of the historical nature of human nature."[23] The *New Science* is clearly apparent in Kosik's *Dialectic of the Concrete*, an example being the remarks: "In its essence and generality, *praxis* is the exposure of the mystery of man as an onto-formative being, as a being that *forms* the (socio-human) reality and therefore also grasps and interprets it (i.e., reality both human and extra-human, reality in its totality)."[24]

Nevertheless, as I intimated earlier, a growing challenge to the implications of Vico's legacy can also be discerned within the Western Marxist tradition. The clearest disillusionment appears in the writings of the Frankfurt School, in particular those of Horkheimer, Adorno, and Habermas. Although Vico was the hero of Horkheimer's 1930 work on the origins of the bourgeois philosophy of history, three years later he published a short piece entitled "On the Problems of Prediction in the Social Sciences,"[25] which expressed certain qualms about the *verum-factum* principle applied, as Lukács had, to the present and future rather than, as Vico had, merely to the past. Marxists, of course, had traditionally been anxious to understand the past in order to act effectively in the present. Lukács's use of Vico in *History and Class Consciousness* had assumed that the *verum-factum* principle could be applied not merely retroactively, but to the transformation of society that was in progress as well. Indeed, his argument implied that it could be *better* used for the present and future than for the past. For like Hegel (although unlike Vico),[26] he had assumed that the intelligibility of history was a function of its rationality. Insofar as a collective subject was embarked on the rational totalization of the world, the symmetry of action and knowledge that underlay the *verum-factum* principle was now in the process of being achieved.

In his 1933 article, Horkheimer started from the same rationalistic premise as had Lukács and Hegel. A "new science" of history would emerge once the object of that science, the social world, was constituted by men rationally and deliberately. Then the scientific goal of prediction, which had been validated in the natural world, would be possible as well for society. But in assessing the immediacy of that emergency Horkheimer parted company with Lukács. Not surprisingly, a German Jew writing in the fateful year of 1933 had a very different view of the imminence of a collective, rational subject of history than had Lukács a decade earlier. By expressing his doubts about the chances for revolutionary change, Horkheimer also voiced serious reservations about the applicability of the *verum-factum* principle as the cornerstone of a Marxist epistemology in a non-revolutionary age.

In attempting to understand the sources of the revolution's failure, Horkheimer and his colleagues at the Institute of Social Research raised questions which implicitly challenged the *verum-factum* principle on even more fundamental grounds. They began to search out the flaws in the equation of intelligibility and rationality assumed by the Hegelian-Marxist tradition that culminated in Lukács. Although conceding that Western Society had in a way been rationalized, they contended that the type of rationality involved was very different from that envisaged by Hegel, Marx, and Lukács when they spoke optimistically of the unity of reason and the world. Instead of the substantive rationality traditionally known as *Vernunft*, formal and instrumental rationality of the kind the classical German Idealists had associated with *Verstand* (intellect or understanding) was now dominant. Paradoxically, this rationalization of the world led to a decrease in intelligibility; the world was still alien, opaque, and reified, even though on one level it was increasingly rational. Although "made" by men and women, the "administered world" of the present did not return their gaze in an act of recognition.

In their joint work of 1944, *Dialectic of Enlightenment*, Horkheimer and Adorno traced the origins of this state of affairs. And in so doing, as previous observers have noted,[27] they indirectly formulated an even more serious critique of the *verum-factum* principle than that presented in their earlier work. Their basic argument was implicitly directed against the link Marx had made so casually in his footnote to Vico in *Das Kapital*, that between technology and the making of the human world. For Horkheimer and Adorno, the implications of this link were extremely important. First, knowledge of a world of objects constructed technologically could not conform perfectly to the model of making *ex nihilo* underlying the *verum-factum* principle. Technology, after all, entails an interaction between a human subject and a natural object which it transforms. Insofar as that object exists prior to its technological transformation, it cannot be understood totally through an act of subjective recognition. Natural objects could never become solely objects for, of, and by men; the dialectic of technology, indeed of labor *per se*, was thus a non-identical dialectic.

Second and perhaps even more important, the choice of technology as the model for all human *praxis* was a very dangerous one. Although it was true that the domination of nature through the use of technical, instrumental reason had led to advances in material comfort, it also had its hidden costs. The exploitation of external nature could lead to the type of ecological disasters we have become all too familiar with in the past few years. The "making" implicit in technology involved the control and manipulation of nature, which ought not to be seen as the prototype of all human history. Indeed, insofar as it had served as such a model, it led to the type of exploitative interaction between men that grew out of subjects mastering objects that appeared inanimate. Instead of the intricate dialectic of recognition Hegel had seen in the master-slave relationship he described in his *Phenomenology of the Spirit*, this technologically inspired master-slave interaction could not lead beyond domination. A further danger, which Horkheimer and Adorno evoked in their discussion of fascism, was the revenge of repressed nature in violent and irrational forms, which resulted from the prolonged stifling of natural impulses within man as well as without. Clearly, any version of the "making" of human history based on the technological domination of nature could not lead to true emancipation. In ways Horkheimer and Adorno did not spell out, another relationship between man and nature would have to be constructed before socialism could be said to be a reality. In this relationship the integrity of nature as something more than an object to be dominated would have to be preserved. Implicitly, this meant that the social world, which after all was the product of a complex dialectic of human and natural interaction, could not be merely reduced to the invention of a creator subject. And so the *verum-factum* principle could not be the simple way out of the antinomies of bourgeois thought.

In Adorno's *Negative Dialectics*, his intellectual testament of 1966, the distance between his position and Vico's was made even clearer. On the question of the collective creation of history, Adorno wrote, "To this day history lacks any total subject, however construable. Its substrate is the functional connection of real individual subjects."[28] As for deriving values and constituting meaning through the acts of creating and then recognizing one's creation, he argued, "The concept of sense involves an objectivity beyond all 'making.' A sense that is 'made' is already fictitious. It duplicates the subject, however collective, and defrauds it of what is seemingly granted."[29] And as for the belief that history was a realm utterly different from nature, Adorno invoked the category of "natural history," by which he meant the regrettable fact that hitherto the "objectivity of historic life is that of natural history,"[30] or what Lukács had called "second nature." Although Marxism might hope for the construction of a purely human history in which the natural law-like constraints of reified subjectivity no longer prevailed, it was vain to hope for the complete disentanglement of the historical from the natural. Thus the *verum-factum* principle could never be applied in the totally humanist way Lukács had in *History and Class Consciousness*, although one might hope for a possible increase in the relative weight of human subjectivity if such an increase did not entail the domination of nature.

Finally, in the writings of one last member of the Frankfurt School, Jürgen Habermas, the implications of this critique of the technological model for human *praxis* were spelled out more clearly, and still other reservations about Vico's legacy were voiced. For Habermas, there are three basic human interests that underlie historical development: an instrumental interest in the mastery of nature, a hermeneutic interest in the furtherance of undistorted intersubjective communication, and an emancipatory interest in the overthrowing of illegitimate authority structures. The ways in which Habermas defended and elaborated this argument are too intricate to be discussed now. Suffice it to say that in so doing, he too subtly distanced himself from the Vichian legacy in Marxism. In one of his earliest works, *Theory and Practice*,[31] published in 1963, Habermas acknowledged Vico's importance in inaugurating the philosophy of history with the *verum-factum* principle. But he then went on to suggest certain reservations about Vico's ideas, some of which we have already encountered.

First, he noted that historical knowledge, as Vico understood it, could only be a retrospective, backward-looking action after the making had occurred. Like Hegel's famous Owl of Minerva, who flies only at dusk, mankind can know its products only after they have been produced. For Vico with his cyclical view of history as a series of *corsi* and *ricorsi*, this fact created no problems. But once history was seen as progressing in an upward direction—a belief introduced into the Idealist tradition and, ultimately, into Marxism, by Kant's *Idea of a Universal History from a Cosmopolitan Point of View* of 1784—the epistemological consequences were profoundly troubling. For what, after all, was the final vantage point from which a retrospective view of the made historical reality could be achieved by its makers? Even Horkheimer's early hope that once history were made rationally and deliberately men would be able to know a future they were in the process of making, did not really save the *verum-factum* principle. For there was no necessary symmetry between a past already completed and a future which of necessity was always open. The only possible way to salvage the *verum-factum* principle once this was acknowledged would be to introduce, whether implicitly or explicitly, a theological assumption. This, in fact, was of course what Vico had done when he compared human knowledge of history with God's knowledge of His creation and designated Providence as the ultimate, if mediated, motor of history. From the divine vantage point, history can be grasped as a unity in which the beginning and end are seen as origin and goal. "In this construction," Habermas wrote, "there is only one single philosopher of history, and for him Vico's definitions are indeed appropriate: God himself."[32] Vico had therefore been wise in recognizing that man could not be a perfect surrogate for God. Providence was thus more than a mere residue of Vico's Christian upbringing which could be dispensed with in the name of a purely humanistic reading of the *verum-factum* principle, as Lukács had assumed in *History and Class Consciousness*. "Vico," Habermas remarked, "stretches providence as though it were a net under the trapeze of history, so that the nations are always caught by it again, as long as they still do not control history with their will and consciousness, even though, in themselves, they are the subjects of history."[33] This net, however, could not be used in a secular world in which faith in providential intervention, or in such surrogates for Providence as the inevitable laws of historical development, was no longer possible. "The framework which philosophy has taken over from theology, of history as totality, becomes questionable."[34]

In the first edition of *Theory and Practice*, Habermas finished his discussion of Vico's legacy with the guarded hope that the *verum-factum* principle, for all its faults, might nonetheless prove heuristically useful. "The philosophy of history," he wrote

> creates the fiction of historical subjects as the possible subject of history, as though objective tendencies of development, which actually are equivocal, were comprehended with will and consciousness by those who act politically and were decided by them for their own benefit. From the lofty observation post of this fiction the situation is revealed in its ambivalences, which are susceptible to practical intervention, so that an enlightened mankind can elevate itself then to become what up to that point it was only fictitiously.[35]

This conclusion, however, was not Habermas's last word on the subject, for appended to later editions of *Theory and Practice* is a footnote which takes back much of his optimism. Having begun our discussion of Vico's contribution to Western Marxism with a footnote, it is only fitting that we conclude it with another. It reads:

> I myself have often made uncritical use of the idea of a human species which constitutes itself as the subject of world-history in this book as well as in subsequent writings. It was not until I began my preliminary work on a communicative theory of society that the import and implications of the hypostatizing generation of subjectivity on the higher levels became clear to me.[36]

One of these implications, which he discusses in a later preface to the book, is that a vanguard party can easily assume it speaks for all of mankind on the basis of this hypostatization . Lukács's Leninism was thus of a piece with his humanistic rendering of the *verum-factum* principle. The alternative Habermas proposes, his communicative theory of society, cannot be elaborated here. But its general tendency is to confirm Adorno's remarks, quoted above from *Negative Dialectics*, about the real substrate of history being concrete individuals whose intersubjectivity cannot be correctly understood by equating it with a super-subject such as "mankind" or a "universal class."

Even more significantly, Habermas's new perspective draws upon a distinction between sub-variants of action reminiscent of that proposed by Hannah Arendt in *The Human Condition*.[37] For Habermas, following Arendt, all action is not synonymous with "making." There is an alternative activity which produces no product nor leaves behind an object which can be said to have been made. It is what he calls "symbolically mediated interaction," which he differentiates from the labor process with its construction of a world of use objects. Instead, it is the construction of a world of shared meanings and values through language. Its inherent *telos* is an undistorted speech situation in which a normative consensus is reached. Insofar as language cannot be reduced to a process of conscious making, however much it may be construed as a quintessential human activity, the *verum-factum* principle is ultimately inadequate as a guide to the mystery of human culture, especially as it might be conceived in some future emancipated state. Thus, even though recent critics may be correct in contending that Habermas too quickly and irrevocably divorces symbolically mediated interaction from the dialectic of labor,[38] his introduction of the communicative dimension into Marxist theory renders the *verum-factum* principle inoperable as the sole ground of a defensible Marxist epistemology. *Praxis* is more a pluralistic phenomenon than was generally understood earlier, an insight that curiously is shared by the Althusserian branch of the Western Marxist tradition whose utter repudiation of the *verum-factum* principle needs no further comment.

With Habermas's revisionary footnote, it seems to me that Vico's legacy to Marxism has been essentially exhausted. The result is that many of the epistemological problems it had been evoked to resolve remain still a source of considerable difficulty for Western Marxists unwilling to return to some new version of the Second International's scientism. In summary, I would like to recall the criticisms of the *verum-factum* principle that have led me to this gloomy conclusion:

1) Lukács's expectation of an imminent revolution that would bring to power a universal subject, both the subject and object of history, was obviously premature. The true makers of history were not yet in control of their production. When they might be was difficult to say, but until that was the case, how could they know what they had made? In other words, reification and alienation were still barriers to totalistic cognition. Lukács's stopgap measure of a vanguard party which merely expressed the imputed class consciousness of the

proletariat soon showed itself to be utterly without justification when that party developed into a Stalinist nightmare.

2) The *verum-factum* principle, based as it was on the theological notion that Providence used men's actions to make history, did not distinguish sufficiently between history intentionally made and history unintentionally made. Only the former could be known in any complete sense by its maker; thus, past history could only be imperfectly known and the future was still uncertain. The *verum-factum* principle could not be used to justify prediction until society was rationally planned. Furthermore, the rationalism informing the planning would have to break with the instrumental, formal variant now dominant.

3) The *verum-factum* principle was valid only for retrospective knowledge. But Marxism was supremely interested in finding a theoretical explanation of and justification for present *praxis* and future action.[39] Only if one made the theological assumption of some vantage point in the distant future and called it the "end of history" could the present and future be retrospectively viewed. This might be plausible for a God for whom history was a coherent totality with a beginning, middle, and end, but for man no such divine vantage point was possible.

4) The notion of a collective or transindividual historical subject who made history in the way a single artisan made, say, a pair of shoes illegitimately hypostatized a meta-subject which was simply an individual writ large. Here, too, the aftereffects of theology were evident, for the obvious prototype of such a meta-subject was God. A more promising approach would investigate the possibility for the uncoerced, intersubjective construction of a cultural and social consensus that would avoid the mystification accompanying notions of super-subjects of whatever kind.

5) The extreme separation of a history made entirely by men and a nature outside of human control was fraught with enormous dangers. The belief that history was made solely by the human objectification of subjectivity ignored the role of the interpenetration of the human and the natural that was the essence of the labor process. It, furthermore, veiled the fact that the dialectic of man and nature contained a crucial moment of domination that had affected relations between men as well. It also mystified the fact that all previous history was like "natural history" because of the role of reification and alienation. This meant that no full recognition could be reasonably expected from glances cast backward at a history that was also, in important ways, "natural." The expectation that some future history could be understood entirely as the product of human creation, without any natural element, carried

with it the threat of the continued domination of the natural with all the consequences outlined earlier. In short, it was vain to hope that humans would ever find themselves completely at home in the world, a world utterly of their own creation. The non-identity of the human and the natural, however dialectically they may be interpenetrated, could not be ended so easily, nor was it self-evident that such a fusion was without its costs. For on whose terms would the union be carried? If mankind were naturalized, wouldn't this mean the possible perpetuation of the mystification of society as "second nature," which had so restricted mankind in the past? If nature were humanized, might this not mean a perpetuation of the domination of nature that had so plagued Western history for millennia? And even if the perfect balance could be found, would the *verum-factum* principle, based as it was on the absolute separation of historical from natural knowledge, still be of use to us?

6) Finally, the reduction of *praxis* to making oversimplifies the complex ways in which men are active in the world. In particular, the creation of a commonly shared symbolic universe should not be understood in the same way that the creation of a world of artifacts normally is. Man is more than *homo faber*, and the *verum-factum* principle cannot account for the actions that are beyond that image of the human condition.

For these and possibly other reasons that might be introduced, Vico's legacy to the Marxist tradition, as fertile as it was in liberating that tradition from the scientistic delusions of the Second International, now appears to be entirely spent. But the thorny problems that it was introduced to resolve are still very much alive. Until they are solved, Marxism cannot claim to have overcome the antinomies of bourgeois thought, let alone to have ended the contradictions of bourgeois society.

6

Mass Culture and Aesthetic Redemption: The Debate Between Max Horkheimer and Siegfried Kracauer

One of the most persistent images in the now extensive literature on the intellectual migration is that of a group of elitist cultural mandarins who were shocked and appalled by the banality, vulgarity, and emptiness of the mass culture they first encountered in exile. Even leftist émigrés, so the conventional wisdom has it, were often extremely hostile to what a recent historian of the migration calls "the new opiates of the people."[1] There can, of course, be little doubt that many German intellectuals, whatever their political inclinations, did find American mass culture abhorrent, especially when they found themselves in such egregious centers of it as southern California.[2] And it is no less true, as the famous analysis of "one-dimensional man" by Herbert Marcuse demonstrates,[3] that Marxists often considered what they saw as pseudo-popular culture to be an obstacle to class struggle in their adopted country.

But what can, however, be questioned is the assumption that such critiques derived from a prior ignorance of or distaste for mass culture and a corresponding reverential attitude towards its presumed opposite, the high *Kultur* identified with German *Bildung*. For, as several recent historians of the Weimar Republic have demonstrated,[4] a vigorous debate over mass culture was already well underway in the immediate post-World War I period, if not before. And what is even more important, many Weimar leftists, future émigrés among them, welcomed the crisis of high culture that accompanied the end of the Second Reich and cheered the new democratic, technological, modernist mass art they hoped would replace it. Although generally hostile to the popular *völkisch* art of nostalgia that competed with this modernist alternative, they by no means rejected the possibility of a progressive version of mass culture. Inspired in part by the experiments of the Soviet avant-garde, and in part by the American cultural innovations in movies, sports, and jazz that flooded Germany after 1918, many Weimar leftists sought to combine the best of both egalitarian cultures to create what one historian of their efforts calls "simultaneous futures" for Germany.[5]

Moreover, the social underpinnings of the traditional concept of culture were called into question as many Weimar intellectuals reflected on the change in their own conditions hastened by the inflation of the early post-war years. No longer able to envisage themselves as members of an elite *Bildungsbürgertum* above the social fray, they sought ways to reconceptualize their role as active participants in the creation of a modern mass culture commensurate with or even in advance of the new political regime. Unlike the cultural spokesmen of the Wilhelmian Social Democratic Party, who tended to support traditional high culture and merely advocated its extension to the proletariat,[6] they recognized that a radically new culture had to be created to replace its exhausted predecessor.

What form that creation was to take, however, became a bone of vigorous contention on the Weimar left. And it remained one even under the changed conditions produced by the emigration. By that time official communist cultural policy, both in the Soviet Union and among its followers, had taken a drastically conservative turn with the coming of socialist realism as the party line in aesthetic matters.[7] As a result, the most innovative contributors to the ongoing debate came from the ranks of the unaffiliated, "homeless" left of Weimar, who were even more isolated from working-class politics after migrating to America.

Two of the most representative figures in that discussion were Max Horkheimer and Siegfried Kracauer, whose work, however, has never been systematically compared.[8] Because what each represented is so different, contrasting them now will help us grasp the full range of attitudes in the migration towards the issue of mass culture. Although many in their circle of friends and acquaintances, such as Theodor W. Adorno, Leo Lowenthal, Ernst Bloch, Walter Benjamin and Bertolt Brecht, also wrote extensively on the same questions, Horkheimer and Kracauer are particularly interesting to contrast in the light of a recent dichotomy introduced by the German literary critic Peter Bürger in his *Theory of the Avant-Garde*.[9] For they are almost perfect embodiments of the opposition Bürger posits between the normally synonymous terms modernism and the avant-garde.

Modernism, for Bürger, emerged out of the aestheticism of the late 19th century, which radically separated art from life. *L'art pour l'art* meant that the institution of art was to be contrasted with other social and cultural practices by its utter indifference to ethical, instrumental, utilitarian, or political concerns. Although modernism called into question the traditional image of the coherent, closed organic work of art by problematizing its formal and linguistic assumptions, it nonetheless remained wedded to the model of aesthetic autonomy underlying that tradition. The avant-garde, in contrast, attacked the very institution of art itself, challenging its alleged differentiation from the larger life world out of which it arose. Rather then resting content with a work-immanent approach that radicalized only artistic technique, such avant-garde movements as Dadaism, Surrealism, and Constructivism sought to subvert the assumption that art was an independent sub-system of the social and cultural whole. In so doing, especially in its more explicitly political moments, the avant-garde hoped to harness the utopian energies of art to revolutionize life, thus overcoming the pernicious division of labor characteristic of bourgeois modernization.

Without turning Bürger's suggestive dichotomy into too rigid an opposition, it is nonetheless very helpful in making sense of the differences between Horkheimer and Kracauer, in particular of their respective attitudes towards mass culture. And by following out the contrasting implications of their positions, we can also better understand their potential pitfalls after their importation to America. For it was in the émigré context that the optimistic expectations of the Weimar left, both modernist and avant-garde, were ultimately dashed.

Unlike the more celebrated aesthetic debates of their contemporaries,[10] the implicit quarrel between Horkheimer and Kracauer has never been treated because it left behind so few obvious residues. Despite their common friendships with Lowenthal and Adorno, the two men were on cool personal terms ever since the late 1920s. Kracauer, in his capacity as the *feuilleton* editor of the prestigious *Frankfurter Zeitung*, declined Horkheimer's request to write an article defending the Institute of Social Research from the charge that it was controlled by Communists.[11] Later, after their respective power statuses were reversed during the migration, Horkheimer was reluctant to forget this slight, and others like it.[12] Although Kracauer's desperate financial situation during his exile first in Paris and then in New York meant he was compelled to swallow his pride and appeal to the Institute for support, he never received enough to make him overcome the bitterness he felt towards Horkheimer. Tensions were increased by the way in which the work he submitted to the Institute was treated, in particular by Adorno.[13] Although the Institute was instrumental in helping him acquire the precious affidavit that allowed him to leave

France for America, Horkheimer, contrary to one historian's account, did not play any role in the process.[14]

But beyond these personal and at times petty reasons, the tensions between the two men had more substantive sources. As Wolfgang Schivelbusch has noted,[15] even in Weimar their contrasting intellectual situations had an impact. Kracauer, trained as an architect rather than an academic and, after 1920, employed as a journalist, was much more personally involved with the phenomenon of mass culture than Horkheimer, who remained within the mandarin university world, even if in a heterodox enclave. Moreover, as a journalist in the volatile economic atmosphere of the Weimar Republic, Kracauer did not have the financial security assured Horkheimer by his parents' wealth and the Institute's private endowment. In an essay entitled "On the Writer," published in the *Frankfurter Zeitung* in 1931,[16] Kracauer contended that all unaffiliated writers felt economic pressures to become like journalists and thus abandon transcendent, absolute questions in favor of more timely and mundane ones. Horkheimer, to be sure, was also drawn to problems in everyday life, as the aphorisms he pseudonymously published under the title *Dämmerung* in 1934 illustrate.[17] But if a number of these do discuss issues too trivial for traditional philosophers, with few exceptions mass culture is ignored. And elsewhere in his writings, Horkheimer was able to focus at length on the larger problems Kracauer's *feuilletons* could only glancingly address.

Kracauer, to be sure, was himself schooled in philosophy and social theory, well enough, in fact, to instruct the young Adorno in Kant shortly after the end of the war. But the theorists who most influenced him, Georg Simmel and Max Scheler, only reinforced his fascination with the surface manifestations of reality, which might be read phenomenologically to reveal their meaning. His hostility towards the more totalizing or dialectical thinkers to whom Horkheimer was attracted was sufficiently strong to allow Benjamin to call him "an enemy of philosophy" in 1923.[18] Whereas Horkheimer's fascination with Arthur Schopenhauer and G. W. F. Hegel meant that he was drawn away from the phenomenal world to the allegedly more essential realities beneath, which he then interpreted in increasingly Marxist terms, Kracauer, even when he too was influenced by Marxism, preferred to search for meaning on the level of appearances.

But perhaps the most fundamental source of their disagreement over mass culture was their different susceptibility to its lures. Many years later, Adorno would remember that "Kracauer's interest in the mass psychology of film was never merely critical. He had in himself some of the naive visual delight (*Sehlust*) of the movie-goer; even as he makes fun of the 'little shop girl,' he sees in her a form of his own reaction."[19] In contrast, Horkheimer, like Adorno himself, rarely showed anything but visceral distaste for all variants of mass culture, as least in his published writings both before and after his migration to America.

The perspective from which that animus came was not, however, that of a mandarin defender of elite culture, who spurns its antithesis because it provides mere entertainment to the uneducated. Like Kracauer, Horkheimer had little use for the idealist defense of *Bildung* per se, with its tendentious opposition between culture and civilization and its ascetic disdain for sensual gratification. In his seminal essay of 1936, "Egoism and the Freedom Movement: On the Anthropology of the Bourgeois Era," he coined the phrase, "the affirmative character of culture"[20] to describe its essentially conservative function as a consolation for actual suffering. Warnings against the Social Democratic contention that its benefits should be spread to the masses, he wrote:

> This undialectical view, which adopts the whole cultural concept of the bourgeoisie, its ascetic scale of priorities, and its concept of morality, but remains ignorant of its great artistic achievements, has dominated the reform strivings even of progressive nineteenth-century political parties down to this day, made thinking shallow and finally also contributed to defeat.[21]

Marcuse's influential essay "The Affirmative Character of Culture," which appeared in the *Zeitschrift für Sozialforschung* the following year, spelled out the implications of this argument in greater detail.[22] Although even affirmative high culture preserved a moment of protest by maintaining the utopian impulse in art, it turned it in the direction of compensation for the very non-utopian conditions of everyday life by restricting culture to a sphere above material reality. Like religion in Marx's celebrated analysis, high culture was a distorted expression of protest, which nonetheless functioned as a kind of opiate to dull the pain of class society.

Or rather, high culture in its traditional forms functioned in this way, according to Horkheimer, Marcuse, and their Frankfurt School colleagues. Hence they preferred its modernist successor, which was less "affirmative" than traditional culture, even if it too failed to find an immediate link between art and life. The modernist dissolution of the organic, holistic work of art—its self-conscious baring of the devices that such works had drawn on to create their illusions—meant such art could no longer function as a positive model of harmony into which the aesthetic consumer could escape as a refuge from his or her unhappiness in the real world. By its still dogged insistence on the possibility of art, even in this anti-organic form, modernism did maintain some hope for a different social reality in the future, but it did so only by denying the comforting belief that harmony, if only on the level of art, was possible today.

The modernist movement to which Horkheimer himself was initially drawn was the expressionism of the 1910s, in particular the ethical-libertarian version of it represented by such journals as Franz Pfemfert's *Die Aktion*.[23] Like Adorno, whose debt to the same source has recently been emphasized by Eugene Lunn,[24] Horkheimer was especially sensitive to the crisis of individual subjectivity registered by the Expressionists. About later movements like the Neue Sachlichkeit, Surrealism, or Constructivism—the movements Bürger identifies with the avant-garde rather than modernism—Horkheimer had certain reservations because he saw them cheerfully accepting the demise of the subject in the name of an allegedly collective successor. In *Dämmerung*, one of his harshest aphorisms was directed against the Neue Sachlichkeit of the mid-1920s, whose championing of the concrete he linked to the philosophical flight from relational thinking of the same years in the work of Scheler and others.[25] Both movements neglected the social and historical context of the isolated objects they sought to valorize.

Horkheimer was no less suspicious in *Dämmerung* of attempts to create a politically charged popular art, such as the revolutionary theater of Erwin Piscator and Bertolt Brecht. "The reason the theater cannot have a lasting revolutionary effect," he argued, "is that it turns the problems of the class struggle into objects of shared contemplation and discussion. It thus creates harmony in the aesthetic sphere. But proletarian consciousness must break through that harmony; that is one of the principal tasks of political activity."[26] When such plays really pose a political threat, he concluded, they will no longer be allowed to be performed. Until then, they merely provide a way for well-intentioned bourgeois audiences to salve their consciences.

As for the cinema, which held so much promise for Kracauer, the only aphorism in *Dämmerung* dealing with it stressed its compensatory function as a way to avoid confronting real suffering. "Of course, there are people that shed tears over 'Sunny Boy' at the movies," Horkheimer wrote: "And they do that at the very moment that, in the service of their own interests, real persons are slowly being tortured to death, simply because they were suspected of fighting for the liberation of mankind. Photography, telegraphy and the radio have shrunk the world. The populations of the cities witness the misery of the entire earth. One would think that this might prompt them to demand its abolition. But simultaneously, what is close has become the far-away. Now, the horror of one's own city is submerged in the general suffering, and people turn their attention to the marital problems of movie stars."[27] Thus, even the documentary potential of the film, its ability to record the actual misery of the world, could have a counterproductive impact. Like Georg Lukács with his distaste for mere reportage in the proletarian novels of the 1920s,[28] Horkheimer was suspicious of any attempt to combine political tendentiousness with a fetishistic emphasis on the unmediated "facts" of the world as it was.

Horkheimer's own aesthetic alternative did not become fully apparent until after his migration to America, by which time his collaboration with Adorno began to bear real fruit.[29] The essay entitled "Art and Mass Culture," published in the last volume of the Institute's journal in 1941,[30] shows his solidarity with Adorno's thinking on these subjects and his distance from Kracauer's. Written as a critique of the American philosopher Mortimer Adler's lame attempt to elevate the film into the pantheon of transhistorical artforms, the essay begins by noting the historical differentiation of "pure" art from the life world. The social basis of this split, according to Horkheimer, was "the private atomic subject"[31] who had not yet been reduced to a cog in the economic or technological machine. The aesthetic judgment made by such a subject, as Immanuel Kant had noted, contained a moment of genuinely disinterested humanism, which pointed towards a possible future of human solidarity. Thus, "an element of resistance is inherent in the most aloof art. . . . Art, since it became autonomous, has preserved the utopia that evaporated from religion."[32]

But the private realm that sustained such aesthetic judgments and the very existence of autonomous art, Horkheimer then warned, has been increasingly underminded, especially because of the crisis of the family. As he frequently lamented throughout this period, the family no longer functioned as "a kind of second womb, in whose warmth the individual gathered the strength necessary to stand alone outside it."[33] Instead of being socialized by the family, the child is directly manipulated by mass culture, whose effect is to bring about the "disappearance of the inner life."[34] As a result of these changes, Horkheimer concluded, "man has lost his power to conceive of a world different from that in which he lives. This other world was that of art. Today it survives only in those works which uncompromisingly express the gulf between the monadic individual and his barbarous surroundings—prose like Joyce's and paintings like Picasso's *Guernica*."[35]

Here the examples Horkheimer chose demonstrate his bias for

modernist rather than avant-garde works, in Bürger's sense. For such works as Joyce's and Picasso's, he contended, have given up the communicative function of art and express instead the isolation of the bourgeois subject in crisis. Rather than vainly trying to build a new social order like certain avant-garde experiments, they "abandon the idea that real community exists; they are the monuments of a solitary and despairing life that finds no bridge to any other or even to its own consciousness. . . . The work of art is the only adequate objectification of the individual's deserted state and despair."[36] In other words, only culture in its negative rather than affirmative state can sustain the utopian impulse in art.

As for the pseudo-populist attempts of Adler to celebrate film as the mass art of the present, comparable to the great art of the past, Horkheimer had only contempt. Introducing the phrase that was to become so central in his collaborative project with Adorno, *Dialectic of Enlightenment*, he scornfully wrote, "what today is called popular entertainment is actually demands evoked, manipulated and by implication deteriorated by the cultural industries. It has little to do with art, least of all where it pretends to be such."[37] No less questionable, Horkheimer continued, was Adler's neo-Aristotelian praise for the imitative function of film, for all it reproduces is the bad reality of the present. The same attitude was expressed in *Dialectic of Enlightenment* a few years later, where he and Adorno contended,

> Real life is becoming indistinguishable from the movies. The sound film, far surpassing the theater of illusion, leaves no room for imagination or reflection on the part of the spectator, who is unable to remain within the structure of the film, and yet ruminate uncontrolled by the exact details without losing the thread of the story: hence the film forces its victims to equate it directly with reality.[38]

Although Adorno seems to have moderated his hostility to films somewhat in his last years,[39] there is no evidence to suggest that Horkheimer ever did. In the posthumously published aphorisms entitled *Notizen*, he continued to argue that "all art has the quality of affording pleasure without first referring men to reality, as does the modern cinema. This draws interest only from real life and thus becomes its instrument."[40]

In so arguing, Horkheimer demonstrated how distant he always remained from Kracauer's view of mass culture in general and the cinema in particular. For unlike Horkheimer, Kracauer was optimistic about the disruptive, oppositional potential in film, whose realistic capacities he particularly praised. As an avant-gardist in Bürger's sense, he was highly sympathetic to the threat this new mass medium posed to the aesthetic hierarchies of traditional culture. Interestingly, his appreciation of this challenge was shared by the authorities in Wilhelmian Germany, where the film first appeared as a mass entertainment in 1895. As Gary Stark has recently demonstrated,[41] the German government quickly acted to regulate and censor what it saw as an inflammatory stimulus to lower-class unrest. No less anxious were the guardians of German *Bildung*, who assailed the cinema as a particular threat to that paragon of high culture, the theater. In fact, it was not until the first world war that the German authorities began to recognize another potential in films, the manipulative one that the Nazis were to bring to perfection a generation later.

Kracauer, to be sure, was himself aware of the cinema's ambiguous implications. In the celebrated and controversial discussion of the Weimar cinema written in his American exile, *From Caligari to Hitler*,[42] Kracauer showed himself keenly sensitive to the sinister potential of film, which he believed could be seen in German cinema even before it was taken over by the Leni Riefenstahls of the Nazi era. Here, in fact, he explicitly drew on much of the same social and psychological analysis that had motivated the Frankfurt School's work on authority and the family in the 1930s. Both Horkheimer and Erich Fromm, formerly an Institute figure, were cited by Kracauer as sources for his interpretative content analysis of the Weimer cinema.[43]

But Kracauer's other major exile reflection on cinema, his *Theory of Film: The Redemption of Physical Reality*, published in 1960, demonstrated his allegiance to an alternative vision of films that directly contradicted Horkheimer's. For it was precisely the reflective, mirroring quality of cinema that he found most compelling. Stressing its kinship with photography, he insisted that "films cling to the surface of things. They seem to be the more cinematic the less they focus directly on inward life, ideology, and spiritual concerns. This explains why many people with strong cultural leanings scorn the cinema. . . . Plausible as this verdict sounds, it strikes me as unhistorical and superficial because it fails to do justice to the human condition in our time. Perhaps our condition is such that we cannot gain access to the elusive essentials of life unless we assimilate the seemingly non-essential?"[44] It was for this reason that the film's "redemption of physical reality" was more progressive than its attempts to ape the high art of the past, in particular the theater. Indeed, as he had argued in *From Caligari to Hitler*,[45] it was only when the cinema began to abandon its true vocation and tried to "elevate" itself to the level of art that its potential for abuse was first opened.

In 1960, when *Theory of Film* appeared, Kracauer had long since abandoned his radical inclinations. But even during his most leftist period, during the waning years of the Weimar Republic, he staunchly defended the emancipatory effect of the cinema's revelation of surface realities. Unlike Horkheimer and other more Hegelian Marxists such as Lukács, he never employed a concept of reification to condemn appearances as distorted, fragmentary, and static misrepresentations of the deeper, more dialectical realities beneath. Hostile to the category of totality so crucial to Hegelian Marxism, he went so far as to claim in his study of Jacques Offenbach, written in the 1930s, that surfaces are the "place where petrifaction least occurs."[46] Even Adorno, who came to have his own suspicions about Hegelian Marxist notions of totality and reification, chastized Kracauer for his utter indifference to their importance.[47] Although he may have emphasized that film in a capitalist world had to be understood as a commodity and therefore drew the conclusion that film criticism must also be social criticism,[48] Kracauer never lost his faith in the truth-telling potential of film per se.

In fact, his optimism about the nature of the cinema spilled over as well to his social analyses, however much they may have been influenced by his leftist sympathies. In the Weimar period, he was most concerned with the new audience for the film, which he noted was especially attractive to the growing group known as the *Angestellten*, the white-collar workers whose susceptibility to right-wing irrationalism he probed in one his most telling works.[49] But elsewhere, he jettisoned the class-specific nature of his analysis and spoke more generally of the "homogeneous metropolitan public"[50] who went to the movies. In the eyes of later, more orthodox Marxist commentators like Helmut Lethen,[51] this loss of specificity meant an unfortunate neglect of the still potent difference between the proletariat and other groups in society, whose goals and social functions were by no means identical. *Die Angestellten* were not, after all, the real producers in society and therefore could not be counted on to revolutionize it in the way the working class might.

Whether or not Kracauer ever really thought the new homogeneous public for films would be radicalized by them or merely believed, in ways that Marxists like Lethen did not, that mass culture was effacing class differences is uncertain. But it is clear that he found much to praise in the ways audiences reacted to the films they saw. In a 1926 essay entitled "Cult of Distraction: On Berlin Movie Theaters,"[52] he defended *Zerstreuung*, diversion or distraction, as a healthy mode of perception in the modern world. As Simmel had argued, the typical experience of the urban dweller was that of discontinuous sense impressions, which flickered across the consciousness of the passive subject. Films, Kracauer contended, were the appropriate medium to register that experience. As such, they gave the lie to the traditional notions of artworks as organically closed totalities.

In so arguing, as Miriam Hansen has recently pointed out,[53] Kracauer was anticipating the argument of Walter Benjamin in his widely discussed essay on "The Work of Art in the Age of Mechanical Reproduction," an essay whose similar defense of distraction aroused the ire of Adorno.[54] Both Benjamin and Kracauer were hopeful about the political implications of the decline of the traditional aura around the work of art and welcomed its reintegration with the life world. Kracauer, in fact, seems to have had even less nostalgia for the lost aura than Benjamin in certain of his moods. The two friends were also closer to each other than to either Adorno or Horkheimer in their praise for the révolutionary Soviet filmmakers of the 1920s—especially Vsevolod Pudovkin and Sergei Eisenstein—whose collective rather than individualist view of the new medium they applauded.[55] And finally, like Benjamin, Kracauer was immensely impressed by the arguments of the Soviet playwright Sergei Tretjakov, who visited Berlin in 1931. As Hugh Ridley has argued, Kracauer's "On the Writer" and Benjamin's "Author as Producer," written three years later, both show the impact of Tretjakov's emphasis on the new role of the intellectual as a participant in the class struggle rather than an aloof observer of it.[56]

Tretjakov, a former Futurist turned Marxist, was a perfect embodiment of what Bürger has called the avant-garde rather than modernism. Kracauer's enthusiasm for him demonstrates how much he, too, can be situated in the same camp. Although Kracauer did not write extensively on the avant-garde movements of his day, the influence of Surrealism in certain of his writings has been detected by Benjamin and other commentators.[57] And despite his explicit distaste for the disillusioned and cynical qualities of the Neue Sachlichkeit,[58] there were echoes of its objectivist sobriety in such works as his novel *Ginster*.[59] Kracauer spoke truer than he knew when he referred to himself jokingly to Adorno as the "derrière-garde of the avant-garde"[60] in the 1920s.

No better testimony of the affinity can be offered than his celebrated essay on the Tiller Girls, a group of precision dancers from America, who toured Germany in 1927. "The Mass Ornament" begins with a characteristic plea for the value of investigating the "simple surface manifestations of an epoch."[61] As trivial as the Tiller Girls may seem, Kracauer argued, they reveal two fundamental aspects of contemporary reality. First, in their capacity as de-individualized, ornamental cogs in a cultural machine, they bear witness to the transformation of a people or a community into a mass. For, according to Kracauer, "only as parts of a mass, not as individuals who believe themselves to be formed from within, are human beings components of a pattern."[62] As such, the Tiller Girls express a sinister potential in modern life, whose implications Kracauer himself would later spell out in an unpublished essay on fascist propaganda he submitted to the *Zeitschrift* and in his supplement to *From Caligari to Hitler* on "Propaganda and the Nazi War Film."[63] What Benjamin later made famous as the "aestheticization of politics" was adumbrated in the aesthetic transformation of individuals into parts of a technological mechanism.[64]

But secondly, the Tiller Girls also expressed for Kracauer a potentially progressive tendency in modern life, which paradoxically derived from their relation to the process of capitalist modernization. With specific reference to the Taylorist methods of organizing labor that were so controversial in the 1920s, Kracauer contended that "the mass ornament is the aesthetic reflex of the rationality aspired to by the prevailing economic system."[65] Although at first glance, such an observation might appear congruent with his initial argument about the negative implications of the Tiller Girls, which would put him in the same camp as Horkheimer and the Frankfurt School, Kracauer took it in the opposite direction. "Certain intellectuals," he wrote, "have taken offense at the emergency of the Tiller Girls and the image created by the stadium pageants. Whatever amuses the masses, they judge as a diversion of the masses. Contrary to such opinion, I would argue that the *aesthetic* pleasure gained from the ornamental mass movements is *legitimate*."[66] The source of that legitimacy, he continued, is its mimetic content, even if the reality it imitates may in some sense be impoverished. Thus, "no matter how low one rates the value of the mass ornament, its level of reality is still above that of artistic productions which cultivate obsolete noble sentiments in withered forms—even when they have no further significance."[67]

What made this mimesis potentially progressive for Kracauer was his surprisingly positive attitude towards the larger process of rationalization itself, a process whose demythologizing and disenchanting effects he welcomed. "The kind of thinking which is associated with the present economic system," he argued, "has made possible a domination and use of self-contained nature which was not granted to any earlier epoch. The fact that this thinking makes the exploitation of nature possible is not decisive here—if human beings were merely exploiters of nature then nature would have triumphed over nature— but what is decisive here is that this process allows for greater independence from natural conditions and in this way makes room for the interjection of reason. We owe the bourgeois revolutions of the last hundred and fifty years precisely to this kind of *rationality*."[68]

Capitalism, to be sure, is only a stage in the process that will have to be surpassed. For, "the rationale of the capitalist system is not reason itself but obscured reason."[69] But there is no going back to mythical thinking or a lost oneness with nature; indeed, the problem is that "capitalism does not rationalize too much, but *too little*."[70]

The mass ornament, Kracauer then contended, is itself problematic not because it is a rationalization of life, but rather because it still retains certain mythological features. Most importantly, its human components are unable to express themselves, remaining instead mute and passive. But it would be wrong to try to remedy this deficiency by holding on to an outmoded notion of private expression, the traditional idea of high culture with its myth of the artistic genius. For it is no longer possible to reconstitute the social conditions that would allow such individualized art to be viable. "The privileged individuals, who do not accept the fact that they are an appendage to the prevailing economic system, have not even understood the mass ornament as a sign of this system. They dismiss the phenomenon while continuing to edify themselves at fine arts events, untouched by the reality present in the stadium pattern. The masses, who so spontaneously took to the pattern in openly acknowledging facts in their rough form, are superior to those intellectuals who despise it."[71] But what remains mythological about even this superior understanding, Kracauer had to admit, is the ultimately meaningless quality of the abstract rationality of both capitalism and the mass ornament, which opens the way to an irrational manipulation of the masses. "Reason," he wrote, "is impeded when the masses into which it should penetrate yield to emotions provided by the godless mythological cult. Its social meaning is much like that of the Roman *circus games* sponsored by tyrants."[72]

But if an "unobscured" reason is to be achieved in the future, Kracauer concluded, the only hope is to carry through the process of rationalization of which capitalism and mass art are a necessary stage. The esoteric work of art cannot provide a refuge for utopian hopes; only the exoteric work—in Bürger's sense, the avant-garde work—is the artwork of the future. Turning back to discredited elite versions of art is merely "a flight from reality. The process leads directly through the mass ornament, not away from it. It can move forward when thinking sets limits to nature and produces human beings in a way reason would produce them. Then society will change. Then, too, the mass ornament will vanish and human life itself will assume the traits of that ornament which expresses itself in the folk tales, face to face with truth."[73]

From the perspective of Horkheimer's later work, with its defense of esoteric modernism rather than exoteric avant-gardism, it is easy to see certain problems in Kracauer's argument. Not only did he fail to appreciate sufficiently the costs in the rationalist domination of nature, which were spelled out in *Dialectic of Enlightenment*, so too was his linear notion of capitalist rationality as a necessary stage in the transition to a genuinely rational future highly questionable. Indeed, it smacked of the orthodox Marxist philosophy of history which Kracauer in so many other respects found troubling.

When Kracauer lost the vestiges of his earlier radicalism during his exile in America, the defiantly optimistic note in such essays as "The Mass Ornament" was also jettisoned. What remained, however, was Kracauer's insistence on the importance of surface realities and the mass cultural redemption of them. In *Theory of Film* in particular, this emphasis was powerfully present, although now expressed in an elegiac, even melancholic mood noted by many commentators.[74] As I have argued elsewhere,[75] Kracauer began to adopt the disillusioned, even cynical attitude of the Neue Sachlichkeit at its most apolitical, the very attitude he had condemned in the 1920s. Now the collapse of art into life produced nothing utopian at all; or more precisely put, the redemption of physical reality led nowhere in social terms.

In the larger perspective provided by Peter Bürger, we can understand Kracauer's development as a striking example of the miscarriage of the avant-garde project to realize the critical potential in art by destroying its autonomy and reuniting it with the life world. The most compelling current version of that failure is the postmodernist art that is fully at peace with late capitalist society.[76] Despite the hopes of Kracauer and others like him, the de-institutionalization of art has meant a false sublation or *Aufhebung* of its negative and critical potential. Distraction has shown itself to be far more conformist in implication than either Kracauer or Benjamin had hoped.

Can, however, Horkheimer's modernist alternative, which was shared by most other members of the Frankfurt School,[77] be said to have fared any better? As the work of art progressively deconstructs itself as a coherent, integral whole, is there anything left which can function as even the negative placeholder of utopian impulses? Adorno himself, who is often criticized for clinging to a modernist aesthetic in the face of its decay, was forced to acknowledge the aging of the "new music" of the Arnold Schoenberg School, which had served as his model of critical art.[78] Near the end of his life, Horkheimer seems to have also understood the problem. In an aphorism published in his *Notizen*, he concluded "Today abstract art is to surrealism as positivism is to the Enlightenment. It no longer has any enemies."[79] Even the most intransigently non-communicative modernist art, he came to realize, was not immune to being integrated into affirmative culture by the market place. It was thus perhaps why he turned in his last years, after his return to Germany, to another possible locus of negation, religion.[80] If in 1941, he could write "art, since it became autonomous, has preserved the utopia that evaporated from religion," his controversial ruminations on theology suggest that he may ultimately have reversed the formula.

In any event, it is clear that Horkheimer's modernist reliance on autonomous art as a reliable counterweight to mass culture has shown itself to be as historically limited as Kracauer's avant-garde belief that the collapse of art into the life world would be a way-station to a rational future. The possible alternatives to these positions are not themselves very promising. One might still call for a deliberately engaged political art of the kind that Brecht or Hanns Eisler advocated, but the meager impact of attempts to apply their ideas in the 1960s suggest the limits of this approach. Or one might insist on covert utopian impulses latent even in the most seemingly conformist mass culture, as have more recent leftist critics like Fredric Jameson, Stanley Aronowitz, and Douglas Kellner.[81] The culture industry may well be not as totalitarian as Horkheimer and Adorno in their bleaker moments assumed. But whether or not it allows more than pockets of what a recent commentator has called "artificial negativity"[82] remains very much to be seen. Or one might follow Habermas and combine a Horkheimer-like contention that aesthetic rationalization is part of a more global process of social rationalization, which will preserve some differentiation rather than try to end it prematurely. But here too, problems remain with the relationship between the still disparate spheres of the modern totality, as well as with the nature of rationalization in each sphere.[83]

However one assesses the promise of these attempts, it is difficult to quell the doubt that we may have recently come to the end of an epoch in Western cultural history, an epoch in which art was assigned a privileged function as a radical, even utopian force capable of playing a leading role in changing society. Its inaugural document may have been Friedrich Schiller's *Letters on the Aesthetic Education of Man* in 1795, whereas Adorno's *Aesthetic Theory* of 1970 possibly served as its unintended epitaph. Whatever the final verdict on this enormously ambitious project may be, it is I think clear that the implicit debate between Horkheimer and Kracauer, whose outlines this paper has tried to trace, must be read as an important chapter in the story as a whole. The sobering lessons provided by their very different attempts to harness art for radical purposes make it difficult not to wonder if its end may be near.

7

For Gouldner:
Reflections on an Outlaw Marxist

In his Althusserian history of the origins of sociology, *Science, Class and Society*, Göran Therborn includes Alvin Gouldner with C. Wright Mills, Talcott Parsons, and Robert Friedrichs as leading exponents of what he calls "the American Ideology."[1] Finding common ground between Gouldner and Parsons is no easy task, but Therborn claims that they, like Mills and Friedrichs, shared an indifference to the scientificity of social theory properly understood and an unfortunate reluctance to focus on society as the central object of that theory. Instead, "the American Ideology" exhibits a "tendency to present social revolutions as sociological revolutions, to turn economic and political struggles and transformations into questions of culture and morality."[2] In the specific case of Gouldner, Therborn disapprovingly quotes his advice in *The Coming Crisis of Western Sociology* to focus on "those parts of the social world closest to the sociologist . . . rather than toward only the remote parts of his social surround,"[3] and concludes that Gouldner's "Reflexive Sociology is more concerned with guiding the personal morality of the social scientist than with the social contradictions and forces of social change he discerns."[4]

Whether or not Therborn's characterization of a specifically American ideology in sociology is accurate need not concern us now, although it might be noted in passing that he explicitly models it on what Karl Marx had called "the German Ideology" a century before and elsewhere in his book argues that sociology as a whole focuses on values and norms rather than social structures.[5] Nor need we pause with the accuracy of this still larger claim, which Gouldner himself critically addressed in *The Two Marxisms* and persuasively refuted.[6] What is interesting for our purposes instead is the light shed by

Therborn's argument, which was directed against Gouldner's earlier critique of sociology, on his later treatment of Marxism. For it is, I think, arguable that one can understand Gouldner's complicated relationship to the Marxist tradition be both defended and undermined only by grasping the special situation in which he found himself as a radical social theorist in America. Indeed, it may help us make more sense of his place in the Marxist tradition than in the sociological. For in the latter, as he once remarked with reference to his major domestic hero, his own position was "more 'European' and less 'wholesomely' American than Mill's."[7] But when he spoke as a Marxist, it was clearly in the accents of his native land. However often he may have fled to Europe for intellectual stimulation, Gouldner always remained profoundly indebted to the society that initially nurtured him. To point this out, I hasten to add, is only to apply one of the essential lessons Gouldner taught us so well, that behind every theory is a theorist whose own unique social situation helped shape and limit his thought.

"The American Ideology," as we have seen Therborn characterize it, lacks two things: a belief in theory as scientific and a focus on society as the central object of that theory. Both were indeed absent in Gouldner's engagement with Marxism. To the extent that he employed Marxism as his own method, Gouldner resisted draping himself in the mantle of science; although, as we will note shortly, he was not entirely hostile to the scientific strain in Marxism, he saw himself as a "reflexive Marxist," not a scientific one. And whereas on occasion he did attempt a Marxist analysis of a social object, an obvious example being his striking discussion of Stalinism as a variant of internal colonialism,[8] his primary focus remained on the development of Marxist theory itself and the conditions out of which it arose.

But the most fundamental and typically American absence at the heart of Gouldner's Marxism was his lack of faith in a concrete class, movement, or party capable of revolutionizing society. After a brief and unhappy involvement in Communist politics in the 1940s, he never again became politically active. All of his subsequent work assumed the nonexistence of a militant American working-class movement. Rather than pretending such a movement existed or thrashing about for an existing surrogate,[9] he acknowledged that he was an isolated and peripheral figure. "I am all too keenly aware," he once wrote, "that if I am a Marxist at all, I belong to no Marxist *community*, and certainly to no Marxist establishment. If my own view is solicited, I would have to label myself as a—Marxist *outlaw*."[10] Rather than apologizing for this status, Gouldner defiantly turned it into a virtue. Like the members of the Frankfurt School, on whose projects he worked during their American exile and for whose achievement he always had the highest praise,[11] Gouldner insisted on the creative effect of the disjuncture between theory and practice, at least in the present. Although it earned him the enmity of more militant New Leftists in the 1960s,[12] he steadfastly refused to politicize his intellectual work. His defense of that decision took two separate forms. In his controversial 1972 essay on "The Politics of the Mind," published in expanded form in *For Sociology*, he distinguished between partisanship, defined as "attachment to a *party* or 'part' of the larger interest," and commitment, which meant "an attachment to the larger interest itself."[13] "It is my general view," he wrote,

> that the theoretical and intellectual creativity of Marxists increase, other things equal, if they have made commitments rather than partisan attachments, if their primary commitment is to values rather than factions, to the broader Movement rather than to sectarian Party, if they have attached themselves to certain larger social strata, such as the working class or peasantry, to whose interests and whose "Movement" they are primarily committed, and if they do not submit to the discipline of a particular party, sect or organization, *in arriving at a definition of what the common interest of this social stratum* is.[14]

Here the obvious target was Leninism in any of its varieties, but Gouldner insisted that such a stance was fully compatible with the practice of Marx and Friedrich Engels. Elsewhere in his work,[15] Gouldner challenged the unification of theory and practice on broader grounds. Arguing that by the concept of "theory," Marx and his followers actually meant intellectuals and by "practice," they meant the proletariat, he contended that an inevitable tension existed between the two groups because of their asymmetrical relationship. Although in his more optimistic moments, he claimed that the opposition between the two need not be what Mao Tse-tung would have called an "antagonistic" contradiction,[16] by and large he recognized that the pedagogical way in which "theory" guided "practice" could easily become tyrannical. Traditional Marxism, he claimed, had passed over this potential conflict in silence by objectifying agents into abstractions to unify on the level of thought what in society was still split, a false solution that demonstrated Marxism's continuing debt to Idealism.

If, on the one hand, Gouldner defended the relative autonomy of radical theory, he was no less willing on the other to grant a certain legitimacy to the actions of the proletariat, even when it failed to live up to the expectations of its theoretical tutors. Unlike many frustrated Marxists in our era of betrayed hopes, he felt no compulsion to condemn the working class for failing to fulfill its historical role. In fact, he insisted that "much of the proletariat's accommodation to the present is, given its alternatives, rational. It is intellectual arrogance—the arrogance of some intellectuals—to suppose that the accommodation of the proletariat is merely an expression of their "false consciousness" or their political gullibility".[17] For all his apparent confidence in the leadership function of the intellectuals as a "New Class" in contemporary society, Gouldner recognized the authoritarian and elitist potential in their tutelary role. Within the Marxist tradition, paradoxically, it was the allegedly more emancipatory Hegelian strain that was most prone to this abuse. In terms that echoed Theodor Adorno's critique of Georg Lukács, Gouldner contended that the elitist potential in Marxism

> is grounded in the importance attributed to consciousness, an emphasis controlled, repressed, yet active even in orthodox Marxism, but salient and unbridled in its Hegelian formulation. It is this exaltation of consciousness that tends to transform the proletariat into political raw material, to be assembled and reprocessed by the Party organization, which justifies its leadership precisely in the name of its possession of theory and consciousness. . . . What the Hegelianizers want is a world in which men will control and indeed dominate the universe. They are, in short, the proponents of a humanistic imperialism; they must therefore be the foe of the natural even in man.[18]

Although Gouldner always warned against any form of anti-intellectualism, there was a streak of characteristic American populist wariness about intellectual pretension in his work. The guarded distance he maintained between his own position and that of Jürgen Habermas,[19] with whom in so many ways he was compatible, can be understood in part as an expression of that distrust. Echoing Hans-Georg Gadamer's critique of Habermas, he insisted on the limits of a "Culture of Critical Discourse":

> Rationality, like theory, then, is also in part always something of a false consciousness, pretending to know the rules it follows, pretending it has only followed rules it can and has spoken, when it must always follow other unspeakable rules as well.[20]

Even the ruthless self-reflexivity for which he so eloquently pleaded thus had its limits. For although the background assumptions of a theory could be thematically examined, the ground of *that* examination remained still to be problematized. The infinite regress such a step would set in motion demonstrated the inevitable irrationality in any theoretical endeavor. Gouldner, to be sure, wanted to minimize the sway of that irrationality through a process of sustained, if nonetheless finite, reflexivity. It was, in fact, because Marxism failed to go as far in this direction as he thought it should that Gouldner refused to identify himself completely with it. The figure of Henry Demuth, Marx's illegitimate son long repressed and denied by Marx himself and the movement he fostered, symbolized for Gouldner what he liked to call "the dark side of the dialectic."[21] Because he was so sensitive to this nether side, Gouldner refused to place that decisionist wager Lucien Goldmann had once admitted was the ground of his (and one might add, many other intellectuals') embrace of Marxism. Instead, Gouldner played Marxism off against the more academic tradition of sociology that dominated American mainstream social theory. Always insisting that sociology and socialism were Siamese twins tracing their common paternity back to Claude Saint-Simon, Gouldner argued against the frequently held view[22] that sociology was inherently counterrevolutionary in origin. Instead, he contended that sociology, properly understood, could be rescued from its conservative appropriation. If in *The Coming Crisis* he demonstrated how pervasive that appropriation had been, in *For Sociology* and *The Two Marxisms* he showed that nonetheless mainstream sociology could be used to expose the unarticulated premises of Marxism. There was also, he insisted, a rational core in sociology that should not be forgotten by those who strive to demystify its ideological function in contemporary Western society.

Gouldner was drawn to three figures in the sociological tradition in particular, although, as we will see shortly, there was a fourth who played a subterranean role in his thinking as well. From Karl Mannheim, whom he once acknowledged as "the father of us all,"[23] Gouldner absorbed the lesson that Marxism was itself only a partial ideology with its own roots in a specific segment of society. Although he differed from Mannheim in identifying that segment with the radical intelligentsia rather than the working class, he nonetheless praised him for "seeing that Marxism resisted efforts to see *itself* as a speech produced by speakers, who may also be limited by their own social context."[24] From Emile Durkheim, whom he wanted to rescue from the charge of Therborn and others that he put moral community *before* society,[25] Gouldner got reinforcement for his belief that economism neglected the cultural and ideological dimension of the social whole. In fact, so Gouldner argued, Durkheim's methodological holism, however much it may have reified society in opposition to the individual, was comparable to Lukács's concept of totality as a potent antidote to the reductive tendencies in traditional Marxism. Finally, from Max Weber Gouldner took an analysis of bureaucracy that could be applied fruitfully to twentieth-century distortions of socialism. He was always impatient with those recent discoverers of the problem of bureaucracy on the left, who failed to appreciate the value of "bourgeois" scholarship on the subject.[26] Weber's critique of bureaucracy was also at the heart of Gouldner's complicated and nuanced defense of Maoism in the 1960s and early 1970s; the cultural revolution, he argued, was an attempt by the Chinese leadership, which he called a "charismatic cohort,"[27] to forestall the sclerotic bureaucratization that befell the Soviet Union.

In addition to invoking traditional sociological theory as a corrective to Marxism, Gouldner drew as well on more recent work in sociolinguistics, most notably Basil Bernstein's distinction between "restricted" and "elaborated" codes and Lev Semonovich Vygotsky's notion of "inner speech."[28] Besides being the expression of a certain social stratum, every discourse, he contended, was also grounded in an unarticulated metaphoric code, which he called its paleosymbolic level.[29] Emotionally charged because of its association with authority figures during the initial stages of socialization into language, the paleosymbolic was exempt from the type of discursive justification that characterized consciously held ideologies. At times, it was consonant with those ideologies and helped reinforce them; but at other moments, it might be at odds with an articulated ideology and help undermine it.

Understanding the power of this paleosymbolic level, Gouldner argued, helped make sense of the curious ability of Marxism to transcend repeated "refutations" and thrive in so many seemingly incompatible contexts. "It is precisely because Marxism is grounded in this deeper paleosymbolic structure," Gouldner contended, "that its manifest, technical, upper level can survive contradiction; that it is able to accommodate to false predictions, without being demoralized by defeat."[30] The immanent code of Marxism, he claimed, was the dialectic of subject and object. Liberating the subject from domination by the "other" was its inherent goal; "Marxist socialism," he wrote with obvious reference to Lukács's interpretation, "is the political economy of the 'identical Subject—Object'."[31] The flexibility of Marxism in different circumstances resulted from the metaphoric openness of the two poles of the relationship. What constituted the dominated "subject" could change depending on the context. The proletariat, the peasantry, the people, the masses, the oppressed, the plebes, the damned of the earth, the slaves—all of these and more were possible metaphors for the subjective pole of the paleosymblic code of Marxism. Because of its extreme flexibility, Marxism could thus become a generalized theory of revolution applicable outside of the sphere for which it originally had been intended, the advanced industrial societies of the capitalist West. Drawing on the emotional energies that had once nurtured religion, Marxism could thus become the most potent contemporary protest against suffering of any kind. As a result, "whatever the defects of its intellectual edifice, its human roots go deep."[32]

Paradoxically, however, the paleosymbolic level of Marxism also might account for its unwitting contribution to new suffering. That tension between intellectuals and workers, "theory" and "practice," which Gouldner stressed as an unacknowledged contradiction in Marxism, could be understood as the identification of the subject with the allegedly rational intelligentsia and the proletariat with the "passive element" in the revolutionary process. Leninism, with its contention that class consciousness could only be brought to the proletariat from without, was thus not a completely illegitimate reading of Marxism, for it was in accord with a possible expression of its paleosymbolic code. Indeed, even Stalinism, so Gouldner averred, was not a total aberration without any roots in Marx's thought.[33] If the implications of the paleosymbolic level of Marxism were so fundamentally contradictory, it is not surprising that Gouldner came to emphasize the essentially antagonistic quality of the Marxist tradition as a whole. His last work was devoted to an exploration of its inherent and irreducible contradictions. *The Two Marxisms,* the first of a planned four-part investigation of the entire history of Marxism, dealt with the sources of those anomalies in the work of Marx and Engels themselves. Its prime targets were those interpreters of Marx, such as Norman Levine, George Lichtheim, Richard Bernstein, Melvin Rader, and Shlomo Avineri, who claimed that his work represented an essentially coherent unity. Based on a close reading of Marx's texts and a careful analysis of their internal tensions, Gouldner showed that from the very beginning of his career, Marx's work contained an unresolved "nuclear contradiction."[34] Under the pressure of unexpected events or because of new research conducted by Marx and his followers, the latent incompatibilities in his initial vision were transformed into outright anomalies. Marx, to be sure, had tried to paper over these inconsistencies, as he had his responsibility for Henry Demuth. Engels also contributed to what Gouldner called the "normalization" of the Marxist paradigm. But in time, the inherent contradictions in Marxism, which were aspects of the dialectic's "dark side," came fully to light.

The most characteristic defensive response to their appearance, Gouldner argued, was to assign one term of the contradiction to Marx and the other to Engels.[35] Through a process akin to psychological splitting, in which good traits were projected onto an idealized positive figure and bad ones onto a demonized antipode, many of his followers "saved" Marx from his inconsistencies by attributing all of his less attractive ideas to the hapless Engels. This illegitimate dichotomizing of Marx and Engels, no less questionable than the older assumption of their complete agreement on every issue, was abetted, Gouldner pointed out, by an ideological notion of literary property. Assuming that ideas and texts originate in the minds of single authors, this view of intellectual production was complicitous with the bourgeois transformation of collectively generated culture into privately owned goods, the very ideology Marxism set out to debunk.[36]

One of the most arresting by-products of this analysis was Gouldner's qualified rehabilitation of Engels, whose alleged deformation of Marx he showed to be latent in Marx himself. Moreover, insofar as one could legitimately assign certain ideas primarily to Engels rather than Marx, a number of his vices turned out to have hidden virtues. Thus, for example, his interest in a dialectics of nature, however naive philosophically, could be construed as a protest against the species imperialism in Marx's Promethean attitude towards nature, which Hegelian Marxists such as Lukács had developed even further. Although Gouldner never went as far as that other recent rehabilitator of Engels, the Italian Marxist Sebastiano Timpanaro, in calling for the consolidation of the historical and natural sciences,[37] he nonetheless argued that the absolute separation of history from nature had, as Engels had sensed, its price. "Let us not, however, flatter ourselves too much upon our human victories over nature," Engels had warned in terms that anticipated Max Horkheimer and Theodor Adorno's *Dialectic of Enlightenment*, "For every such victory it revenges itself upon us."[38] As for Engel's alleged overemphasis on technology as the determining factor in social development, Gouldner argued that Marx himself based much of his optimism about the future on the power of technological progress. But he had failed to confront the implications of that progress for the ending of alienation, which was predicated on overcoming the very division of labor that technology intensified. Although Engels had no real solution to this problem, his forthright stress on the inevitability of technological development under socialism had the virtue, so Gouldner contended, of bringing this crucial problem to light. Rather than "normalizing" the Marxist paradigm, in this case, Engels ultimately, if inadvertently, helped to highlight its internal tensions.

That such tensions existed, even though they could not simply be personified in the figures of Marx and Engels, was Gouldner's central point. At times, he conceptualized them under the rubric of romantic versus classical elements in Marxism,[39] or as the conflict between "theory" (the intellectuals) and "practice" (the proletariat), or as the clash between the surface level of Marxist ideology and the paleosymbolic code of its deep structure. But the primary contradiction he chose to emphasize as the essence of "the two Marxisms" was between what he called "the boundaried subsystems of elaborated theory"[40] that were Scientific and Critical Marxism. Always stressing that these were ideal types or analytic constructs and not descriptions of specific figures or camps in the history of Marxism, he contended they were tendencies in Marxism from its very inception that perpetually warred, like those two famous souls in Faust's breast, for domination of the whole. To schematize still further Gouldner's schema, the antithesis might be summarized as follows: Critical Marxism, stressing the "self-groundedness of men," privileged voluntarism, subjectivism, political activism, and methodological holism; whereas Scientific Marxism, believing in the "other-groundedness of men," emphasized determinism, objectivism, political quietism, and methodological reductionism. Critical Marxism interpreted Marxism in philosophical terms, usually Hegelian, and focused on superstructural issues, whereas Scientific Marxism stressed its affinities with the natural sciences and centered its analysis on the socioeconomic substructure. The general cognitive style of Critical Marxism was more soft-edged and ambiguous, in contrast with the brittler and more hard-edged style of its Scientific alternative. Latent in Critical Marxism was a certain pessimistic streak, because it lacked faith in the inevitability of socialism as the automatic outcome of history. It was thus prone to an apocalyptic revolutionary politics, a politics of catastrophic discontinuities, whereas Scientific Marxism, with its roots in a religious millennialism that guaranteed the coming of utopia,[41] tended towards a more optimistic and evolutionary political vision.

Gouldner's general attitude towards these two currents was by no means without its ambiguities. Although he was obviously more comfortable with Critical than Scientific Marxism, he did not simply endorse it in all respects, as some of his commentators have hastily assumed.[42] For reasons we have already noted, he pointed out that "It is a central contradiction of Critical Marxism, then, that while it has a potentiality for rationality and populism, it is also vulnerable to an authoritarian voluntarism, irrationality, and elitist terror."[43] Moreover, as we have seen, his defense of Engels on nature and his critique of species imperialism was directed more against Critical than Scientific Marxism. Gouldner, to be sure, had no use for the economistic bias of Scientific Marxism, which he blamed for its tendency to devalue the autonomy of mediating social structures between the state and the individual. In fact, neither Marxism dealt satisfactorily with the realm of civil society, whose preservation, albeit in a transformed way, would be a bulwark against the totalitarian potential that Marxism in practice clearly betrayed. Here was the main source of Gouldner's defense of the continued relevance of the sociological tradition, which, contrary to Therborn's claim, he saw as concerned with more than moral community alone. "Essentially," he wrote,

> sociology's traditions—precisely because they have been *conservative* —have centered on the problems connected with developing a *self*-maintaining civil society, social organizations, and social systems. Deepened knowledge of this is certainly indispensable for any social movement, such as Marxism, which seeks workers' control (when this is not equivalent to nationalization), or which seeks a responsible and competent citizenry, and hopes to develop persons capable of mutual aid and independence, and to retain a viable "public" sphere.[44]

As a result, so Gouldner concluded, any truly emancipatory theory would have to draw from sociology, as well as both Marxisms, using the insights of each to correct the defects of the others. There was as yet no way to construct a totalized general theory that could preserve those insights and avoid the defects, for there was still no social vantage point from which the whole could be known. No "outlaw Marxist" situated in the unfriendly context of American society could argue otherwise.

Such were the major lessons and implications of Gouldner's work on Marxism, lamentably abbreviated by his premature death. As a stimulus to future scholarship, not only on the Marxist tradition but on the history of theory production in general, they will surely prove immensely powerful. Indeed, as a demonstration of this claim, it may well be fitting to conclude our consideration of Gouldner's contribution by applying his own methodology reflexively to uncover the premises and possible problems in his own paradigm. By searching for the paleosymbolic level of Gouldner's own discourse, we may be able to discern the potential anomalies that will surface in the wake of future research or unexpected events. In the spirit of Gouldner's call for a "Marxist critique of Marxism,"[45] we might begin a Gouldnerian critique of Gouldner.

If, as we have seen, Gouldner identified the paleosymbolic code of Marxism as a dialectic of subject and object whose telos was their ultimate unity, the comparable code underlying his own work can, I think, be equated with a similar dialectic in which that synthesis was denied. As we have noted in examining his thoughts on the irreducible tensions between theory and practice, his warnings against the potential for authoritarian elitism on the part of intellectuals, and his reservations about the limits of the discourse of critical rationality, Gouldner's dialectic was inherently a negative one. In fact, in his essay on "The Dark Side of the Dialectic: Toward a New Objectivity," Gouldner made this immanent code manifest and, with veiled reference to the Frankfurt School, distinguished his own position from what he saw as a "bitter negative dialectic"[46] that led only to an indiscriminate "great refusal" denying all hope. His alternative, which he preferred to call a "dark dialectic," had no illusions about overcoming contradictions in the present, but resisted allowing that realization to degenerate into complete despair. One must both struggle and accept the limits of that struggle, Gouldner counseled; one must resist and yet be reconciled to the improbability of radical change, work for emancipation, but sometimes be willing to "surrender,"[47] in Kurt Wolff's terms, to the world rather than try to master it.

Such a qualified acceptance of contradiction, for all of Gouldner's rage against unnecessary injustice and suffering, ran like a leitmotif throughout his work. It was thus not surprising that he took such pleasure in exposing the "nuclear contradiction" in Marxism and scorned attempts to resolve it as ideological special pleading. Valorizing contradiction also allowed him to play Marxism off against sociology without reaching for a grand synthesis that would harmonize them in a noncontradictory manner. And in particular cases, such as his surprising endorsement of Louis Althusser's argument that ideology would persist even under socialism,[48] it provided him with a rationale for resisting the blandishments of utopianism, which he attacked as an ahistorical absolutization of norms that was paradoxically a form of anomie.[49] Because the immanent code of Gouldner's work was this "dark dialectic" of unreconciled contradictions, he often conceptualized issues in dichotomous terms. In *The Coming Crisis*, for example, he wrote, "After the sprawling genius of Saint-Simon, Western Sociology underwent a kind of 'binary fission' into two sociologies, each differentiated from the other both theoretically and institutionally, and each the reverse mirror image of the other."[50] The fission in question here was between the Academic sociology begun by Auguste Comte and the Party sociology of the radical intellectuals that was Marxism. Elsewhere in his work he pointed to another critical binary opposition that cut across the one mentioned above: the deep structures of Romanticism and Classicism.[51] And of course, as we have seen, he postulated that within Marxism there was fundamental opposition between a Critical and Scientific impulse.

At times, Gouldner acknowledged the merging of these dichotomies in specific cases, but he generally insisted on the importance of keeping them distinct for analytic purposes. In fact, it is arguable that because his paleosymbolic code valorized contradiction so strongly, he tended on occasion to defend his binary oppositions with more emotional force than was warranted. In so doing, he opened the door to those anomalies whose existence in other theories he had been so skillful in exposing. One might make this case by questioning Gouldner's contention that Marxism and sociology were mirror images of each other as twin descendants of Saint-Simon. The role of eighteenth-century political economy and nineteenth-century German philosophy in the origins of Marxism might be introduced to disrupt the apparent symmetry of the two "sociologies." Indeed, Gouldner's own reflections on the origins of Critical Marxism call into question his binary dichotomization of Marxism *per se* and sociology. A still more interesting anomaly can be discerned if we examine the central binary opposition within Marxism posited by Gouldner, that between its Scientific and Critical impulses. His deep emotional investment in this distinction can be seen in *The Two Marxisms* in a number of places, but perhaps nowhere as blatantly as in his critique of Perry Anderson's account of Western Marxism. According to Gouldner, Anderson refused to acknowledge the perpetual conflict between the two tendencies in Marxism and insisted instead on generational alternations. He thus viewed Western Marxism as a heterogeneous, but still essentially coherent phenomenon that resisted any reduction into Critical and Scientific wings. Gouldner's scorn for this obtuseness expressed itself in an *ad hominem* dismissal of Anderson as an unreconstructed English positivist:

> This is the authentic but archaic voice of "public school" British empiricism and comes with the porridge. The intellectual Ulysses has wandered home from his adventures abroad, settling snugly into his hearth after wenching with foreign theories, and returns to the sound ways of his fathers, his old dog Empiricism at his feet.[52]

Aside from the issue of whether or not Anderson can legitimately be called an empiricist,[52] Gouldner's defense of his categories raises two important questions. First, what is the role of empirical evidence in modifying, refining, or even refuting analytic generalizations? This is not the place to launch a serious discussion of this hoary question, but two remarks of Gouldner himself may be introduced as provisional answers. As he wrote in his defense of sociology against Marxism,

> In conceiving itself as an *empirical* science devoid of metaphysical presuppositions, in this most dubious expression of sociology's false consciousness, there is nonetheless an important way in which

sociology contributed to human emancipation and continues to have a liberative potential. For now, with the emphasis on the empirical, the self-understanding of all societies (including their elites) was in principle made problematic; it could now be subject to systematic question, to examination, and to a demand for justification. . . . Sociology's sheer empiricism, then, necessarily creates tensions for all authoritative definitions of social reality . . . [54]

And as he claimed in his critique of Lukács's fetish of method in *History and Class Consciousness,*

To reduce Marxism to a method is, in effect, to deprecate, if not to eliminate, questions of observation, statistics, data, fact; it is a surrender of the empirical, a willing surrender, because the empirical is after all the manifestation of concern for the "other," for alienness, for nature in its own autonomy. The young Lukács's methodological Marxism tables empirical interests precisely because he was a consciousness-enthralled Hegelian . . . [55]

Gouldner may well have been more of a Weberian than a "consciousness-enthralled Hegelian" in describing his binary opposition only as an ideal type, but his defensive resistance to modifications of that opposition suggest a closer similarity to Lukács than he would have wanted to admit. To put this issue in more concrete terms, if we find that a number, perhaps even a majority, of Western Marxists gravitate towards the ambiguous center of a continuum whose ends are the ideal types of Critical and Scientific Marxism, then we may well be justified in questioning the sufficiency of the categorical distinction. There is, in fact, surprising evidence, as I have argued elsewhere in defense of Anderson,[56] of similarities between "Critical" Marxists such as Adorno and "Scientific" ones such as Althusser and Lucio Colletti on certain issues, in particular the abandonment of Lukács's expressive holism. Although I certainly would not want to deny that Gouldner's distinction explains many of the tensions in Western Marxism, it would be incorrect to claim that all of them could be accommodated to his binary scheme. In fact, the second question his critique of Anderson raises is precisely how adequate such a dichotomous opposition really is in analyzing the material at hand. Does the bias towards binary contradictions at the paleosymbolic level of Gouldner's thought force him to impose too simple a pattern on the historical realities he tries to understand? Might it not be more useful, say, to introduce a second axis to bisect that created by Gouldner's dichotomy, an axis whose poles are Western and Eastern Marxism? In so doing, we might resolve what may well be called an anomaly in Gouldner's paradigm: its problematic inclusion of such Western Marxist academics as Horkheimer and Adorno with such Eastern Marxist political activists as V. I. Lenin and Leon Trotsky in the same Critical Marxist camp.

That Gouldner himself may have felt uneasy with the crudeness of his categories can perhaps be discerned in his struggle to get the formula right for the origins of Critical Marxism. On page 143 of *The Two Marxisms* he writes, "The advent of Critical Marxism represents a specific conjuncture: the pursuit of revolutionary socialism in industrially backward societies led by a very culturally advanced elite." On page 153 he nuances this further: "Critical Marxism was the product of an intellectual elite with *advanced education and considerable familiarity with science and technology,* either through their studies or from first-hand travels in industrial societies." But then on page 165 he writes that

> Critical Marxism emerged following World War I, the October Revolution and the German Revolution's failure. Its character is partly an effect of a prior domination of Scientific Marxism in the Second International . . . Critical Marxism is *not* to be understood as the ideology generated *by* (however serviceable it is *in*) the industrially backward areas of the world; it is, rather, the newer Marxism of a younger generation of Marxists, whose cohort developed in opposition to the Marxist establishment-in-being around the turn of the century.

If Gouldner had distinguished between an Eastern Critical Marxism represented by the Bolsheviks (and perhaps including such Third World revolutionaries as Mao and Fidel Castro) and a Western Critical Marxism exemplified by Karl Korsch, Ernst Bloch, Lukács, and others, then the obvious difficulty he had in finding a single formula to characterize its origins might have been avoided.

There is, to be sure, a grain of truth in his unwillingness to do so insofar as Lenin was the *practical* inspiration for both Eastern Critical Marxism and the initial generation of their Western counterparts. But theoretically, the latter were nurtured in a very different environment. Moreover, they quickly absorbed the lessons of the defeats of the postwar era in a way that Eastern or Third World Critical Marxism did not. And when Western Marxism finally found an audience in the 1960s, it was the students and disaffected professionals of advanced industrial societies rather than the peasantry of backward parts of the world. Although one can certainly find instances of sympathies between Western Critical Marxists and Third World revolutionaries— one thinks of Jean-Paul Sartre's fondness for Castro and Franz Fanon or Herbert Marcuse's support of the Viet Cong—by and large they were deeply alienated from the non-European descendants of Lenin. If anything, it was the more scientific Marxists in the Western camp, such as Althusser with his enthusiasm for Maoist thought, who felt more comfortable with their still Leninist politics.

One way to formulate the difference between Western and Eastern Critical Marxism is to examine somewhat more closely than did Gouldner the nature of their respective voluntarisms. Although he did posit a difference between what he called the "genteel voluntarism" of Bernstein and the Revisionists and the "Promethean voluntarism" of the Bolsheviks,[57] he missed an equally vital distinction between what might be termed vanguardist and mass voluntarism. Because Gouldner stressed the authoritarian and elitist potential in Critical Marxism as a whole, he tended to blur this opposition. But to the extent that certain Western Marxists drew on the anti-elitist heritage of Rosa Luxemburg or were impressed by council communist rather than party models of socialist organization or were sensitive to the need for a universally accessible public sphere, they very self-consciously fought the vanguardist voluntarism from above that degenerated into the bureaucratic voluntarism of the Stalin era. Although many Western Marxists such as members of the Frankfurt School shared Lenin's skepticism about spontaneous working-class consciousness (a skepticism, by the way, that can be traced back to the Scientific Marxism of Karl Kautsky), they were not prepared to endorse his coercive corrective. Intellectual elitism need not breed political authoritarianism, for as Habermas put it, in a passage that Gouldner (and his student Cornelis Disco) tended to forget, "the vindicating superiority of those who do the enlightening over those who are to be enlightened is theoretically unavoidable, but at the same time it is fictive and requires self-correction: in the process of enlightenment there can only be participants."[58]

The opposition between Western and Eastern Marxism can also be profitably applied to Gouldner's Scientific Marxist category. Maurice Merleau-Ponty's use of the Western Marxist rubric to mean Lukács and his heirs need not be allowed to occlude the continuities between their position and that of their Second International forebears in the West. In fact, one eminent commentator has argued that Western Marxism properly understood meant the Second International rather than the Hegelian Marxists because of its greater distance from Communism.[59] Although this latter claim is surely questionable, it does draw attention to certain similarities between Critical and Scientific Marxism in the West. For example, both tended to argue that socialism should build on the cultural and political legacy of liberal, democratic society rather than utterly repudiate it. Both, moreover, continued to insist that socialism could be initially constructed only where Marx thought it should, in the advanced industrial societies of the West rather than the backward premodern societies of the East. Both were also far truer to Marx's original cosmopolitanism than were their Eastern counterparts, who, beginning with Joseph Stalin's "socialism in one country," drew on the power of nationalism to bolster their revolutionary hopes.[60] And finally, both Critical and Scientific Marxism in the West were intellectually more flexible, open-ended, and undogmatic than either variety of Eastern Marxism, which transformed Marxism-Leninism into a doctrinaire metaphysics of legitimation.

One explanation of the similarities between Critical and Scientific Marxism in the West may be that both were oppositional movements never actually in positions of power. It is thus possibly less the political and cultural traditions of the West that account for their relatively supple and nonauthoritarian qualities than the luxury of never having to preside over an attempted transition to socialism. Be that as it may, the analytic dichotomy of Western and Eastern Marxism might profitably be superimposed over Gouldner's binary opposition of Critical and Scientific. Depending on what we are looking for, specific cases may be more illuminated by emphasizing one axis over another. Nor need we stop with merely a two-dimensional analysis; other possible criteria might be introduced to make sense of the variegated history of Marxism, for example, the tension between nationalist and internationalist currents. Although Gouldner has correctly led us to probe for the repressed contradictions in Marxism, we ought not to expect that they can be clustered around the poles of one or even two axes. In short, if we consider Gouldner, to use his own terms, a "paradigm patriarch," it is incumbent on those of us who want to use his work creatively, to become, at least in part, "paradigm rebels."[61] It is hard to imagine that Gouldner, who himself rebelled against an accepted paradigm or two in his day, would have really minded.

Rather than finishing on this somewhat obstreperous note, let me conclude by pointing to what seems far less an anomaly in Gouldner's work than a fundamental insight, one that brings us back to our earlier theme of "the American Ideology." As we have seen, Gouldner defended the continuing importance of sociology as a corrective to the totalitarian tendencies in Marxism because of its concern for "the problems connected with developing a *self*-maintaining civil society, social organizations, and social systems." With the recent turmoil in Eastern Europe, Gouldner's contention seems to be in the process of being historically confirmed. In a recent interview the former Hungarian prime minister turned dissident Marxist, Andras Hegedüs, gave as the reason for his shift away from orthodoxy "an intensive study of Western sociology," which taught him that what had happened in 1956 "was not a counterrevolution; that the rebels were not necessarily to be regarded as enemies of socialism; that there were among the rebels many workers and communists who had good reason to be dissatisfied."[62] Their goal, he came to understand, was the creation of autonomous social organizations that escaped domination by the state. Today, Hegedüs contended, a similar desire is being expressed throughout Eastern Europe:

> The Eastern European power structure, on the one hand, and the Eastern European opposition, on the other, stand before a great historical compromise. Those in power must desist from wanting to immediately integrate every movement, as before. They must, first, legally permit autonomous organizations. At the same time the opposition must limit itself. It must from the start renounce the traditional goals of politics—the achievement of power—indeed, even the moral questioning of current power . . . I venture to say that they have no other choice. For if they do not make the historical compromise, they are left only with two sad possibilities: either a neo-Stalinism, which no one wants, or an even more frequent sequence of social upheavals until the system collapses completely.[63]

The test case for these assertions today is, of course, Poland, whose resistance to Soviet hegemony has been characterized, as Andrew Arato points out,[64] by participants and observers alike as a struggle of civil society against the state. In fact, if one wanted to make a broad comparison between the events in Czechoslovakia in 1968 and those in Poland today using Gouldner's categories, it might be argued that whereas the "Socialism with a Human Face" of the Prague Spring represented the reaction of Critical Marxism to Scientific Marxism, the Solidarity movement in Poland is an uprising of civil society against Marxism of both kinds. That is, whereas the former was more of a quarrel within the radical intelligentsia, with to be sure considerable public sympathy and support for one faction, the latter seems a more genuinely mass-based social phenomenon that arose largely from below. Instead of trying to realize the Critical Marxist dream of a completely dealienated, dereified totality in which the split between citizen and bourgeois man is fully overcome, the Polish rebels seem anxious only to regain the relative autonomy of civil society that had been denied by bureaucratic communism's distorted version of that dream. Whether or not they will succeed, of course, is now even more doubtful than it was before the crackdown of December 13, 1981.

In any event, Gouldner's argument for the importance of appropriating sociology's concern for social autonomy as a corrective to the totalitarian potential in Marxism appears to be enjoying growing influence. What is being legitimated, however, is not merely Gouldner's defense of sociology, but also his particular indebtedness to what Therborn called "the American Ideology." Or at least, to put it in less loaded terms, it demonstrates his debt to the special place America has had in the development of sociological theory. I am thinking in particular of a figure, who alongside Mannheim, Durkheim, and Weber, must be seen as having a formative, if unacknowledged, influence on Gouldner's thought: Alexis de Tocqueville. For it was, of course, in the work of de Tocqueville on America that the vital importance of a healthy civil society as a bulwark against the tyrannical potential in mass democracy was most classically expressed. It was not by chance that Marx in "On the Jewish Question," that founding document of Critical Marxism, singled out de Tocqueville's argument for the survival of private, nonestablished religion in America as evidence of its allegedly incomplete emancipation in truly "human" terms. For what de Tocqueville was defending was the autonomy of social organizations and moral communities against the homogenizing power of the state. Authentic politics, he argued, took place as much if not more so on the level of civil society as that of the state.

Gouldner, in arguing for the same relative autonomy, was thus very much in de Tocqueville's spirit, even though he almost studiously neglected to cite him in his work.[65] Outlaw Marxism is for this reason, as well as the others mentioned above, very much an American phenomenon. It is difficult to believe that Gouldner, who exhorted us so often to see the theorist behind the theory, would have been chagrined by our making clear the nurturing context of his own thought. Nor need we feel discomforted by the awareness that a Marxism, if also cognizant of recent European theoretical developments, owes something to domestic influences. At a time when there are many "ideologies" to chose from, it is by no means clear that, say, the French or Chinese are so superior to our own in actualizing the emancipatory potential in Marxism and checking its opposite. In the extraordinary body of work left us by Gouldner, as well as in the personal example he provided for many who knew him, we have ample evidence of the continued vitality of the Marxist tradition when filtered through an American prism. Although he was a powerful force for what Paul Piccone called "the systematic deprovincialization of American sociology,"[66] he showed as well what a shrewd man from the provinces can do to demystify the inflated claims of those who wander too far from home.

8

Against Fragmentation Against Itself: Contradictions and Anomalies in the Development of Gouldner's Theory

"One of the central tasks of social theory in our time is to attempt to rethink the position of theory's own group involvements and to re-examine the conditions, social and organizational, requisite for the development of an effective community of theorists committed to the understanding of the social totality."[1] So ends Alvin Gouldner's posthumously published second installment of his remarkable exploration of the origins and implications of the Marxist tradition. By advocating so explicitly the goal of a theoretical grasp of the social whole, Gouldner demonstrated how deeply indebted he was to the Marxist quest for a viable concept of totality, which, as I've tried to show elsewhere,[2] was a special obsession of its "Western" branch. And yet paradoxically, what makes *Against Fragmentation* such a stimulating and valuable book is the tension between its author's avowed goal and the abundant evidence he supplies of the manifold obstacles to its realization. For with the fierce intellectual integrity that was the hallmark of all Gouldner's work, he spared no effort in detailing the internal contradictions within Marxism itself, which thwarted the totalizing intentions he clearly shared.

In part, Gouldner's keen sensitivity to a wide variety of unreconciled binary oppositions immanent in Marxism may have come from his own unreflected proclivity for dualistic models. His personal paleosymbolic code, the deep structure of his work, favored what he liked to call "binary fissions" between, for example, Marxism and sociology or

This essay is a discussion of Alvin W. Gouldner's *Against Fragmentation: The Origins of Marxism and the Sociology of Intellectuals* (New York: Oxford University Press, 1985).

Critical and Scientific Marxism.[3] There were few dialectical triadic syntheses, balanced quaternities or disseminating pluralities in his analyses, which almost always tended to revolve around nuclear contradictions instead. *Against Fragmentation*, despite its call for a holistic overcoming of partial and incomplete perspectives, proves no exception to this rule.

Its first section, "Marxism and the Intellectuals," continues Gouldner's earlier analyses, largely inspired by the sociology of knowledge, of the suppressed secret of Marxism's embarrassing social origins in the radicalized bourgeois intelligentsia. Because of the difficulty of accounting for his own theoretical production in the terms of his theory, Karl Marx neglected the growing importance of intellectuals as a nascent class of their own. Instead, he sought to decontextualize the roots of radical theory, offering instead vague organismic metaphors about philosophy as the "head" of the revolution with the working class as its "heart." The result, as Gouldner correctly notes, was an "ineluctable contradiction in Marxism: for it, *theory* is absolutely necessary for social transformation, yet *theorists* may not be trusted."[4] Because Marxism refused to confront its social origins in the radicalized intelligentsia, it was forced to search for an agent impelled by concrete historical interests to fulfill its revolutionary goals. But in so doing, it produced another dichotomy, which it never fully overcame: "Marxism's shopping for an agent premises a distinction between *theory*-guided intellectuals and *interest*-prompted agents."[5] Here the myth of disinterested intellectual activity prevented Marxist theoreticians from reflecting on their own social status and the potentially self-serving implications of their radicalism.

Drawing on his earlier work, Gouldner contends that the intellectuals were beholden to the norms of a "culture of critical discourse." Their radicalization, however, followed more from the blockage of upward social mobility than from the discourse itself. As blocked ascendants, radical intellectuals from the Jacobins onward often looked to state service as a possible way to salvage their positions, while at the same time serving the general cause of social rationalization. Ironically, even the culture of critical discourse harbored its own form of potential elitism. For although self-consciously egalitarian in terms of its own adherents, it was hierarchically related to those outside its boundaries. The absolute commitment to rationality, at least as a regulative ideal, could easily conflict with the specific material interests of the non-intellectual agents, whose linguistic code, to borrow the terms of Basil Bernstein used by Gouldner, was "restricted" rather than "elaborated."[6] Indeed, the very notion of a material interest suggested an undiscussable given outside the realm of rational discourse. As a result, so Gouldner darkly concludes, "the rationality in which the permanent revolution of our time is grounded is a self-contradictory, self-confounding structure. Its voice is the voice of universal equality, but its hands are the hands of a new elitism. Insofar as a Marxist socialism embodies this rationality it also partakes of these contradictions."[7] Thus, although Gouldner certainly sought to distance himself from the familiar debunking use of this analysis, which simply reduces radical intellectuals to cynical manipulators of the masses in whose name they falsely claim to speak, his subtle account showed the difficulties of deriving a holistic theoretical analysis from a social context in which two groups implicitly vied for the role of universal class.

The second section of *Against Fragmentation* deepens and fleshes out the implications of this analysis in a number of ways. "The Ecology of Marxism" begins with an original interpretation of Marx's relation to the popular materialism of his day, showing that in his hands it underwent a binary fission. For Marx, a healthy materialism linked to productive industrial expansion and the domination of nature, a materialism derived from honest, need-satisfying, unalienated labor, was contrasted with a malevolent alternative associated with commerce, exchange, credit, money, and unproductive toil. Reinforcing Marx's animus towards the latter, so Gouldner contends, was his self-hating identification of it with Jewish huckstering.[8] By splitting materialism in this way, Marx could envisage a socialism that would build on the progressive side of capitalist industrialization, while jettisoning its pathological counterpart. This solution had its costs, however, not only in its sinister denigration of "Jewish" unproductive capitalism (a theme repeated in the Nazi distinction between *schaffendes* and *raffendes Kapital*), but also in its underestimation of the progressive effects of commercial formal rationality itself. Despite his allegiance to the Enlightenment project of rationalization, Marx thus failed to grasp all of its implications.

But perhaps more consequential than these theoretical inadequacies, Gouldner suggests, were their expression in the internal tensions within the movement Marx helped found. In a masterful reconstruction of Marx's relations with a series of competitors, Wilhelm Weitling, Andreas Gottschalk, Joseph Dietzgen,[9] and most notably Mikhail Bakunin, Gouldner reveals a paradigmatic and never resolved contradiction between intellectuals and workers (or more precisely, radical artisans) in the socialist tradition. Reacting against such current defenders of Marx in these disputes as Hal Draper and Paul Thomas, Gouldner insists that his opponents often sensed a potential for abuse in Marx's sympathy for a strong, if putatively transitional, state, which would provide a justification for the elite function of intellectuals.

Gouldner's eagerness to show the justice on both sides occasionally leads him towards a compensatory defensiveness about Marx's opponents. Thus, for example, he invidiously contrasts Marx's "instrumental" view of politics with the expressive and "prefigurative" version practiced by Bakunin,[10] which is an odd way to characterize the Russian's penchant for violent destruction as a way to cleanse society of any bourgeois residues. One shudders to think of what is being prefigured in Bakunin's call for "the purifying fire of holy retribution."[11] Indeed, one might say that Marx's grudging allowance for parliamentary politics in the struggle for socialism provided at least some space for politics as a legitimate end in itself, whereas Bakunin with his typically anarchist impatience wanted an apocalyptic end to politics per se. Gouldner himself gives ammunition to this interpretation when he notes that the Marxist strategy of playing the parliamentary game had more of an attraction for intellectuals than Bakunin's plea for direct, expressive action. For it was precisely the relation between this type of political interaction and the culture of critical discourse that can itself be seen as prefigurative of a future socialist public sphere. Gouldner's further claim that Critical Marxism was in some way more a recovery of Bakunin's position than Marx's is thus questionable, as is his contention that the Frankfurt School in particular was more Bakuninist than Marxist.[12] For figures like Antonio Gramsci and Jürgen Habermas have been especially sensitive to the need to build a new politics out of the old, rather than merely negate it. Thus when Gouldner sees Habermas's quest for an "ideal speech situation" as a "lineal descendent less of Marx than of Bakunin's struggle against the New Class's educational privileges,"[13] he is only telling half of the story. The anti-elitism of Habermas may set him apart from Marx in the latter's more authoritarian moments, but it can scarcely be derived from Bakunin's decisionist fetish of direct action and his voluntarist repudiation of all rational deliberation.

Still, these reservations aside, Gouldner's general point about the symptomatic conflict between Marx and a series of similar opponents is very well taken. And it is made even sharper by the insight that like Critical and Scientific Marxism, the warring twins of his earlier book, it is a conflict within the bosom of Marxism itself. "Bakuninism and Marxism," he shrewdly comments, "cannot be understood as two adversaries, each external to the other. Rather, they were doctrines which had certain communalities and overlapped at important points. Each had a living part of his enemy *in* himself."[14]

If the second section of Gouldner's book argues that Marx's apparent antipode was internalized within Marxism, the final section, which is also called "Against Fragmentation," deepens still further the paradoxical conclusion that Marxism is no less "against holism." For here Gouldner carries his argument into the very totalizing method of Marxism itself, showing both inadvertently and deliberately its contradictions. The former implication can be drawn from Gouldner's very stimulating analysis of the paleosymbolic code of Marxism, which he sees as rooted in an iconic metaphor of slavery and a conceptual metaphor of subjects treated as objects. At the deepest immanent level of Marxist discourse, he argues, these metaphors allow a series of substitutions to fill the slot of the enslaved and subjugated subject, the proletariat being only one of many possibilities. But as a genetic center of the entire Marxist enterprise, this metaphoric code gives Marxist holism its normative drive.

There is a great deal to be said for this understanding of Marxism's deep structure, but what makes Gouldner's analysis an inadvertent source of tension with his larger point about Marxism's yearning to overcome fragmentation is its implicit conflict with another tropological reading of the theory. For, as Hayden White has pointed out,[15] Marx's concept of totality can be understood less in metaphoric than in metonymic and synecdochal terms. In other words, Marx's narrative strategy, the way he emplots history, is to see pre-communist society in terms of mechanistically, causally related linkages, which privilege syntagmatic contiguities rather than paradigmatic substitutions. The final overcoming of alienation in communism will occur through a synecdochal integration of contraries, in which a comic resolution of contradictions will be achieved. Metaphor because of its representational dynamic, its stress on the substitution of one signifier for another, cannot be the ground of a totalizing integration of oppositions. Thus, White sees it as more appropriate for a Romantic historiography of unfulfilled quests than a Marxian one of holistic unification. Metaphor, he suggests, provides "no rule by which the individual elements appearing in the field can be brought together in such a way as to encourage any confidence that *the whole process* has a comprehensible meaning."[16]

There are two interesting inferences to be drawn from this argument. First, if we juxtapose Gouldner's emphasis on the metaphoric dimension of Marxism with White's stress on its metonymic and synecdochal, we can see that the theory itself was inherently divided from the beginning. For all its explicit yearning for a holistic overcoming of fragmentation, it was itself tropologically fragmented at its core. Second, we can understand Gouldner's own inability to arrive at a satisfactory holism of his own, despite his avowed hope for one, in terms of his obvious bias for metaphoric displacements, specifically that of the binary fissions that appear throughout his work. Although this inclination gave him the sensitivity to uncover all of the unreconcilable oppositions we have seen him expose in Marxism, it perhaps limited his ability to find a way out of the bind such a bias created, at least for someone interested in overcoming fragmentation.

One need not, however, strain to discern an inadvertent argument against holism in Gouldner's last section, for he also provides a very powerful explicit one in his treatment of what he calls "the dialectic of recovery and holism." By recovery, Gouldner means the anamnestic impulse in Marxist epistemology, its insistence on restoring forgotten and repressed truths.[17] Here the realization, to borrow Max Horkheimer and Theodor Adorno's famous phrase, that "all reification is a forgetting" means that emancipation requires the collective remembering and working through of the debilitating residues of past history. What puts this imperative in potential conflict with Marxism's holistic intentions is its penchant for a fetishistic focus on *only* the repressed dimension of the historical process. "It is typical," Gouldner notes, "that, in the very process of recovering the neglected part, the previously consolidated larger whole itself, and its once firmly established other parts, could become precarious."[18] Put differently, the quest for some essential, but forgotten aspect of the whole can blind us to the relative autonomy of those seemingly nonessential dimensions that are irreducible to a hidden genetic center. These more obvious elements in the whole get their revenge in what might be called a "return of the unrepressed."

The validity of this observation is, in fact, demonstrated by Gouldner's own privileging of the hidden metaphoric dimension of Marx's paleosymbolic code and concomitant indifference to its metonymic and synecdochal competitors. Here the "unrepressed" exacts its vengeance in a displaced form in Gouldner's own observation that Marxist holism is itself split between a Scientific Marxist concept of a mechanical system and a Critical Marxist concept of an organic totality.[19] That is, the metonymic causality he brackets in his emphasis on Marxism's metaphoric paleosymbolic code returns in the stress on system rather than totality prominent in one basic tendency in Marxist theory. Although at one point in his argument Gouldner forgets his own injunction to grant equal status to Scientific and Critical Marxism as present from the beginning,[20] the general implication of his analysis is that both systemic and totalistic readings of Marxism have their legitimacy.

In short, wherever we look in Gouldner's richly textured, brilliantly nuanced account of Marxism's struggle "against fragmentation," we discover dichotomies, antinomies, fissures, and contradictions. As suggested earlier, these may reflect the binary paleosymbolic code of

Gouldner himself. But it would be hard to deny that they are reflections as well of the actual dilemmas of a tradition of thought and practice that has never achieved the viable concept of totality it so fervently sought.

At moments in his argument, Gouldner seems aware of the vanity of this quest, indeed of its potential costs. Marxism's hope for reconciliation in history, its indifference to the suffering that no amount of historical change might alleviate, made it relatively callous towards the human pain that transcended irrational social conditions. "The human condition," Gouldner soberly notes, "was rejected on behalf of the historical condition. In short, Marxism, like any ideology, shunned the tragic."[21] One expression of this insensitivity to tragedy was surely the Marxist refusal to confront the contradictions in its own origins and history that made the goal of a theory or a society completely beyond fragmentation a vain one.

Can one say in conclusion that Gouldner with his final call for "an effective community of theorists committed to the understanding of the social totality" was equally unaware of a blind spot in his own work? Is there an unresolved tension between his own intuitive sympathy for dualities and his call for wholeness? Is there a no less intractable gap between his debunking, sociology-of-knowledge sensitivity to the concrete interests underlying allegedly disinterested theory and his yearning for a universal class, however imperfect? Might it not be possible that Marxism, after we see it through Gouldner's powerful optic, can no longer be understood as a constructive contributor to any quest for holistic knowledge or totalizing practice? And as a result, should we celebrate with a kind of resigned gaiety, the virtues of fragmentation, non-identity, heterogeneity, etc., that are preached by a wide variety of *soi-disant* post-Marxist philosophies?

No review can hope to do justice to these questions or help extricate Gouldner from the predicament into which his own penetrating analysis led him. But if a start is to be made, it would have to begin by abandoning a questionable premise in Marxism, which Gouldner saw as still active in the present: the quest for a single historical agent through which the world can be made a meaningful whole. Although at times Gouldner may have seemed to be searching for one himself in his fascination with the intellectuals as "new class," by and large, he recognized its dangers. Thus in an earlier essay entitled "The Politics of Mind,"[22] he explicitly warned against trying to collapse the distance between radical theorists and party activists, praising the Frankfurt School's intellectual independence as a model to emulate. But how radical intellectuals, especially when isolated from any social group, historical agent or otherwise, were to achieve a genuinely totalistic perspective is not very clear. The Frankfurt School's own later history, in which both the concepts of totality and of agent were criticized as potentially dangerous, shows how hard the task can be. Perhaps only a forthright abandonment of the very idea of a totalizing historical force as the epistemological ground of holistic knowledge, the premise of most Hegelian Marxism from Georg Lukács on, will allow some escape from the dilemma. Whatever totalizations are permitted to us will then no longer have to be grounded in a dubious consciousness philosophy writ large, based on the implicit metaphor of a totalizing gaze from afar or the generative power of a collective metasubject "making" the history it then understands. Instead, we will have to rest content with the slower, more laborious, and indeed highly precarious project of creating some sort of consensus from a shifting constellation of groups, none of which can claim absolute pride of place. Fragmentation cannot therefore be overcome through some sort of Hegelian mediation of contradictions, which always smacked of an extorted reconciliation to those left subordinate in the outcome. It is to Gouldner's great credit that we now see how riven Marxism really was by the very splits its own rhetoric claimed it wanted to overcome. Like all works of true distinction, *Against Fragmentation* thus transcends what seem to have been the intentions of its author. As the parting gift of a remarkable man, it makes us even more keenly aware than before of how much we miss the giver.

9

Habermas and Modernism

In an important, but neglected, essay published in 1976, entitled "Aesthetic Experience and Self-Reflection as Emancipatory Processes: Two Complementary Aspects of Critical Theory,"[1] Shierry Weber located a fundamental, albeit often subterranean, tension in the Frankfurt School's work. Although emphasizing their potential complementarity, she singled out two impulses in Critical Theory that have been subtly at odds through much of its history: aesthetic experience as a prefigurative cipher of redemption and rational self-reflection as a critical tool in the struggle to achieve that utopian state. Recalling Critical Theory's debt to German Idealists like Friedrich Schiller, she contended that it is the artistic representation of wholeness that explains the Frankfurt School's fascination for aesthetics which embodies "a non-alienated relationship between man and nature, subject and object, and reason and the senses."[2] In contrast, Weber contended, "the process of self-reflection is focused more on man conceived in his universal aspect as a rational member of a socio-historical species."[3] Rather than leading towards the reconciliation anticipated by aesthetic wholeness, rational self-reflection encourages man's increasing liberation from what Karl Marx called his *Naturwüchsigkeit* or embeddedness in nature.[4]

The Critical Theorists who paid most attention to aesthetic experience are Walter Benjamin, Leo Lowenthal, Herbert Marcuse, and Theodor W. Adorno. The last works of the latter two were in fact called, respectively, *The Aesthetic Dimension* and *Aesthetic Theory*.[5] Although their work did not always adopt Weber's Schillerian characterization of the aesthetic as a model of reconciled wholeness—Adorno's defense of natural beauty as an embodiment of a non-identical relationship between subject and object is a counterexample— art often did serve as a refuge for their never completely abandoned utopian aspirations. The same, however, has rarely been said of a more recent figure in the history of the Frankfurt School, Jürgen Habermas, who has stressed instead the process of rational self-reflection and explicitly abjured all hopes for a reconciliation of man and nature. As Weber notes, in his work "interest in the subjective or interactional components of domination has led to a more systematic return to the original problems of the nature of reason and its role in history, without, as yet, a similar reconsideration of the nature of the aesthetic and its relation to reason."[6]

Although Weber's cautious "as yet" has not become entirely outmoded in the years since she wrote her essay, Habermas has nonetheless come increasingly to dwell on aesthetic issues. If by no means at the actual center of his latest work, which has been devoted primarily to the development of a theory of communicative action and the reconstruction of historical materialism, art has found a modest place in his elaborate theoretical system. In particular, Habermas's recent attempt to formulate a theory of the modern has led him not only to reflect on modernization, understood in sociological terms, but on aesthetic modernism as well. He has thus, somewhat haltingly, returned to one of the fundamental themes of the classical Frankfurt School. But he has done so without abandoning his preference for rational self-reflection. Precisely what that return has meant for Habermas's reformulated version of Critical Theory has not, however, been widely discussed.[7] What follows is an attempt to rectify that omission, which has resulted in a failure to understand the full complexity of Habermas's exceptionally complicated undertaking.

Habermas's interest in aesthetic issues can in fact be detected even in his earliest works, such as his influential essay of 1963 "Between Science and Philosophy: Marxism as Critique."[8] But it was not until the early 1970s that he first seriously attempted to integrate his consideration of these issues with his more general theoretical position. In his 1972 essay on Walter Benjamin, and in the book published the following year entitled *Legitimation Crisis*, Habermas reflected on the importance of art in the process of emancipation.[9] To take the much briefer discussion in the latter first, Habermas upheld the traditional Frankfurt School position that art is an enclave of negation against the totalizing power of one-dimensional society:

Only bourgeois art, which has become autonomous in the face of demands for employment extrinsic to art, has taken up positions on behalf of the victims of bourgeois rationalization. Bourgeois art has become the refuge for a satisfaction, even if only virtual, of those needs that have become, as it were, illegal in the material life-process of bourgeois society. I refer here to the desire for a mimetic relation with nature; the need for living together in solidarity outside the group egoism of the immediate family; the longing for the happiness of a communicative experience exempt from imperatives of purposive rationality and giving scope to imagination as well as spontaneity . . . Thus, along with moral universalism, art and aesthetics (from Schiller to Marcuse) are explosive ingredients built into bourgeois ideology.[10]

Focusing more precisely on how aesthetic negation occurs in the modern world, Habermas then turned to the implications of what he called, borrowing Benjamin's term, "post-auratic art." Whereas traditional art was surrounded by a ritually induced aura that distanced it from everyday life, thus encouraging its cultic enjoyment as a beautiful illusion, modern art abandoned both its aura and the accompanying illusion of its autonomy from society.[11] The break between auratic and post-auratic art came where Benjamin had located it: "Surrealism marks the historical moment in which modern art destroyed the shell of the no-longer-beautiful illusion in order to pass desublimated over into life."[12]

Habermas, however, was enough of Adorno's student to challenge the essentially optimistic implications Benjamin drew from the de-auraticization of art. Not only did he call into question Benjamin's overemphasis on the technology of mass production as an explanation of the change, he also pointed out the costs of a premature integration of art and life. The surrender of artistic claims to autonomy, he warned, "can just as easily signify the degeneration of art into propagandistic mass art or into commercialized mass culture as, on the other hand, transform itself into a subversive counterculture."[13] Although he was not willing either to endorse Adorno's unequivocal defense of autonomous art without acknowledging its own limitations, most notably its *a priori* denial of the possibility of an exoteric art, he nonetheless concluded that "as long as avant-garde art is not completely deprived of its semantic content and does not share the fate of the more and more powerless religious tradition, it strengthens the divergence between the values offered by the socio-cultural system and those demanded by the political and economic systems"[14]

This conclusion, which drew on Daniel Bell's then widely discussed argument about the "cultural contradictions of capitalism,"[15] but reversed Bell's conservative application of it, was also based on the much more detailed analysis of aesthetic issues Habermas had made the year before in his remarkable essay on Walter Benjamin.

"Consciousness-Raising or Redemptive Criticism: the Contemporaneity of Walter Benjamin" began with a comparison of the aesthetic theories of Marcuse and Benjamin and stressed four central differences. First, whereas Marcuse employed the traditional Marxist critique of ideology to expose the contradiction between art's ideal essence, which transcends the current reality, and its consoling function as a means of helping persons endure that same reality, Benjamin sought to conserve and rescue the truth content of works of art themselves. His was, therefore, in the terms of Habermas's title, more a "redemptive" than "consciousness-raising" criticism, a theory of aesthetic experience rather than reflection.[16] Second, while Marcuse, in the tradition of idealist aesthetics, was biased towards classical works of art, whose essence appeared through symbols, Benjamin defended the non-affirmative, non-totalizable works of art dependent more on allegory, which registered suffering rather than attempted to transfigure it. Third, whereas Marcuse only fleetingly contemplated the meaning of the avant-garde's destruction of auratic art, Benjamin emphasized the implications of that very destruction, which Surrealism in particular had carried out.[17] Fourth and finally, Marcuse differed from Benjamin in denying the responsibility of technological changes alone for the de-auraticization of modern art, its turn towards exoteric rather than esoteric forms.

Without immediately taking sides in this implicit debate, Habermas then turned to a similar comparison of Benjamin's aesthetics with those of Adorno, focusing on their celebrated dispute in the 1930s over the implications of the loss of the aura. Here, perhaps more than in *Legitimation Crisis*, he stressed the drawbacks of Adorno's faith in the critical power of autonomous, inaccessible, still auratic art which led, so Habermas argued, to a "strategy of hibernation, whose obvious weakness lies in its defensive character."[18] Adorno's dark vision of a totally controlled Culture Industry which allows no room for any negation outside of the most esoteric and incomprehensible works of art was, so Habermas argued, an unwarranted exaggeration. "A noticeable development of arts with a collective mode of reception," he optimistically insisted, " . . . points beyond mere culture industry and does not *a fortiori* refute Benjamin's hope for a universalized secular illumination."[19]

Adorno was also at fault in reducing Benjamin's position to an unnuanced celebration of modern art's loss of the aura, whose ambivalent implications Benjamin, in fact, had fully understood. Whereas Benjamin had not mourned the loss of the specifically cultic and irrational aspects of the aura, he was afraid that the experiential source of the aura's power, its derivation from a primitive moment of perfect plenitude, might also be entirely forgotten. As Habermas put it, "Since the historical experience of a past *Jetztzeit* needs to be recharged, and because this experience is locked within the aura of a work of art, the undialectical disintegration of the aura would mean the loss of this experience."[20] Moreover, so Habermas argued, Benjamin had not been content with merely redeeming the experiential origin of the aura; he wanted to generalize it in the lived experience of everyone in the present. Benjamin's goal, Habermas insisted, is "a state of affairs in which the esoteric experience of happiness has become public and universal; for only in a context of communication into which nature has been included in a mutual way—as if once again stood up straight— can subjects return one another's gaze."[21]

Habermas's introduction of the theme of universal communication, which some commentators were to contend he illegitimately imposed onto Benjamin's actual argument,[22] shows the extent to which he identified with Benjamin's position. He was, however, unwilling to endorse all of its dimensions. On the question of technological determinism, for example, he sided with Marcuse and Adorno, whereas on the issue of preserving artistic autonomy in the contemporary world he remained ambivalent. Nor did he express an unequivocal preference for allegory over symbolism, although in the 1963 essay mentioned above he had claimed that Benjamin's concept of the allegorical "has proved its singular appropriateness especially for modern art, though it had first been formed in terms of the baroque."[23] But perhaps Habermas's most interesting uncertainty concerned the fundamental choice between consciousness-raising and redemptive criticism.

In important ways, he clearly felt attracted to the latter alternative. In order to explain what Benjamin had wanted to redeem, Habermas turned to his highly idiosyncratic theory of language which was based on a mimetic concept of meaning. In arguing that meaning was something to be preserved rather than created, Benjamin, so Habermas suggested, was probably "thinking of the semantic potential from which human beings draw and with which they invest the world with meaning, permitting it to be experienced. This semantic potential is deposited in myth to begin with and must be released from it—but it cannot be expanded, just continually transformed."[24] The original source of the semantic potential for Benjamin was in fact mixed, simultaneously mimetic and expressive. Once again in Habermas's words, language for Benjamin "is merely a form of the animal instinct manifest in expressive gestures. Benjamin combines these in turn with the mimetic capacity (*Vermögen*) to perceive and reproduce similarities."[25] Thus what is actually expressed in language is not merely the subjective interiority of the speaker, but also an imitation of surrounding nature. Originally onomatopoetic, imitation is evidenced as well in the non-sensuous correspondences preserved in written script. What makes this type of combined expression and mimesis so attractive to Benjamin is its priority to the break between subject and object; in other words, that Schillerian motif of reconciliation which Shierry Weber identified in Critical Theory is evident here in Benjamin's linguistic speculations.

Now, in general, Habermas was sceptical of precisely such claims to reconcile man and nature through a new, non-dominating science. His objections to Marcuse's faith in this possibility are well known. Yet, in this essay, he demonstrates a certain cautious approbation of the goal insofar as it is represented by art. "As odd as this mimetic theory of language sounds," he contended, "Benjamin is right in assuming that the oldest semantic stratum is that of expression. . . . One could speculate that a semantic store of original subhuman forms of communication has found a place in human language and represents a potential that cannot be augmented. With the meanings that comprise this potential, human beings interpret the world in terms of their own needs and create thereby a net of correspondences."[26] The mediated preservation of these primitive expressive-mimetic linguistic experiences is at the heart of the *promesse de bonheur* in art. According to Habermas, Benjamin understood that "we need those rescued semantic potentials if we are to interpret the world in terms of our own needs, and only if the source of these potentials does not run dry can the claim to happiness be fulfilled."[27] Insofar as Habermas himself shared Benjamin's anxiety over the loss of these potentials, he endorsed the redemptive impulse of the latter's criticism.

But Habermas drew back from accepting the nostalgic, and perhaps even conservative, implications of Benjamin's linguistic theory which "can but comprehend itself as identification and *repetition* of emphatic experiences and utopian contents—and not as reflection in a formative process."[28] Benjamin, to be sure, had also recognized the regressive possibilities in his linguistics and had tried to counter it by adopting a materialist theory of history. But his attempt had failed, so Habermas concluded, because "the materialist theory of social development cannot be simply fitted into the anarchistic conception of *Jetztzeiten* which intermittently come crashing through fate as if from above. An anti-evolutionary concept of history cannot be tacked onto historical materialism as if it were a monk's cowl . . . "[29]

Habermas's own concept of history was anything but anti-evolutionary.[30] Without returning to an orthodox Marxist insistence on the inevitability of progress, he nonetheless combined the arguments of a wide range of thinkers, most notably, Max Weber, Niklas Luhmann, Talcott Parsons, Jean Piaget, and Lawrence Kohlberg, to fashion a highly tentative rational reconstruction of the past as progressive from which the possibility of positive change in the future could be extrapolated. The species, Habermas hoped, might achieve what he called a "participatory remodelling of administrative structures"[31] which would approach the regulative, hitherto counter-factual ideal of the perfect speech situation latent in communicative action.

All of the implications and problems of Habermas's reconstruction of historical materialism need not concern us now. What is of interest is the role art might play in the process of emancipation as he reconceptualized it. For it was precisely to Benjamin's redemptive criticism that he turned for an account of the positive content that might be rationally discussed in the formal symmetry of the perfect speech situation. His essay on Benjamin concludes with the troubling question "Could an emancipated humanity one day confront itself in the expanded scope of discursive will-formation and nevertheless still be deprived of the terms in which it is able to interpret life as good life?"[32] The answer Habermas offers shows how seriously he took Benjamin's linguistic theory, despite all his reservations about its regressive implications: "Without the store of those semantic energies with which Benjamin's redemptive criticism was concerned, there would necessarily be a stagnation of the structure of practical discourse that had finally prevailed."[33] In short, communicative rationality is not enough to insure true emancipation; the experiential memories still contained, however faintly, in art are necessary to give humankind a motivational stimulus to the search for happiness.

In Habermas's more recent work on modernity, most notably his 1980 Adorno Prize address on *"Die Moderne: Ein unvollendetes Projekt,"* translated under the title "Modernity versus Postmodernity," and his mammoth two-volume *Theorie des kommunikativen Handelns,*[34] the implications of his reliance on art as a repository of endangered meanings have become clearer. Arguing once again against Daniel Bell's neo-conservative attack on cultural modernism as the major source of our ills, he defended the ultimate value of modernization in which science, morality, and art are separated into autonomous spheres, each with its own internal logic. Based on institutionalization of professional expertise, "there appear the structures of cognitive-instrumental, moral-practical, and of aesthetic-expressive rationality, each of these under the control of specialists who seem more adept at being logical in these particular ways than other people are. As a result, the distance has grown between the culture of the experts and that of the larger public".[35]

But if cultural modernization has implied differentiation and specialization, which for art was most clearly expressed in the *l'art pour l'art* movement of the 19th-century, it has also produced a counter-move designed to reunite the increasingly autonomous spheres with the life-world out of which they emerged. The project of modernity, Habermas argued, "intended to release the cognitive potentials of each of these domains to set them free from their esoteric forms. The Enlightenment philosophers wanted to utilize this accumulation of specialized culture for the enrichment of everyday life, that is to say, for the rational organization of everyday social life."[36] In our own era, this same desire has been manifested in those modernist movements, most notably Surrealism, which attempted to de-auraticize art in the hope of revolutionizing life. This attempt, however, failed, so Habermas contended, for two essential reasons. The first, which Adorno had noted in his dispute with Benjamin, was that the destruction of autonomous art merely dispersed its contents without leading to a really emancipatory change in mass consciousness. The second, which Habermas called more important, followed from the fact that

> In everyday communication, cognitive meanings, moral expectations, subjective expressions and evaluations must relate to one another. Communication processes need a cultural tradition covering all spheres—cognitive, moral-practical and expressive. A rationalized everyday life, therefore, could hardly be saved from cultural impoverishment through breaking open a single cultural sphere—art —and so providing access to just one of the specialized knowledge complexes. The surrealist revolt would have replaced only one abstraction.[37]

Like the aborted *Aufhebung* of philosophy in the Marxist attempt to realize it through the proletarian revolution, Surrealist and other anti-auratic movements have not really succeeded in reuniting their sphere of esoteric truth with everyday life. To do so, Habermas claimed, all three spheres of specialized knowledge would have to be made accessible at once. "A reified everyday praxis," he contended, "can be cured only by creating unconstrained interaction of the cognitive with the moral-practical and the aesthetic-expressive elements."[38]

Such an outcome is, needless to say, highly improbable, but Habermas claims that there is at least one example of something approaching it. In his book *The Aesthetics of Resistance*, Peter Weiss describes an incident in Berlin in 1937 when a group of politicized workers sought to reappropriate the cultural heritage of Europe, then being systematically distorted by the Nazis, for their own life experience.[39] This attempt to recapture the energies of the objective *Geist* for personal life, Habermas claims, shows that the Surrealists' dream can perhaps still be accounted viable, even if their own efforts to realize it foundered.

Whether or not this isolated example is really convincing, it shows Habermas's continued determination to redeem those semantic potentials that Benjamin had located in auratic art. But significantly, Habermas hopes to do so without aiming at the complete reversal of the process of differentiation which he identifies with the modern. What must be reversed, however, is the unbalanced relationship between the subsystems of rationality that characterize the types of modernization—capitalist and bureaucratic socialist—that have so far taken place. In particular, the domination of the subsystem of cognitive-instrumental (or what he calls in his new book, functional rationality) over both moral-practical and aesthetic-expressive rationality must be undone. What hitherto has been a relationship of colonization must be replaced by one of constructive mediation. Habermas admits that the prospects for this change to occur are very slim. But he warns against abandoning the unfulfilled project of modernity which, among other things, would mean a loss of hope in the creative reappropriation of aesthetic rationality into an increasingly rationalized everyday life. Thus, although Habermas must still be accounted a far less aesthetically inclined thinker than his mentors in the Frankfurt School, it will no longer do to claim that he gives no weight at all to the role of art in the process of emancipation.

That the way in which he does so is by no means without its problems has not escaped many of his commentators. Some, for example, have charged that he misconstrues Benjamin's theory of language by underestimating the extent to which it sees mimesis as a "*technical* act of human production."[40] By privileging human communication over representational construction, so these critics argue, Habermas has falsely emphasized the expressive moment of semantic potentiality in Benjamin's theory. This reading of Benjamin has, however, itself been called into question by Anson Rabinbach,[41] who claims that although Benjamin may have not understood language in communicative terms comparable to those, say, of Martin Buber's "I-Thou" relationship, he nonetheless was even more hostile to a purely technical or instrumental concept of language. As another commentator, Richard Wolin, has recently put it, Benjamin's essays on language "coincide in their rejection of an instrumentalist view of language and their emphasis on language as a privileged medium through which a 'flashing image' of reconciliation between man and nature can be glimpsed."[42] However much Benjamin may have admired and learned from Stéphane Mallarmé's anti-communicative theory of language, he never embraced a purely technical alternative, as his critical response to the Soviet linguists Nikolay Y. Marr and Lev Vigotsky demonstrates.[43] Still, it is clear that he did distinguish between the mimetic and communicative (or what he called "semiotic") dimensions of language. The latter may have been the "bearer"[44] of the former, but they lacked its utopian energies.

Yet Habermas himself, it should be noted, does not ignore the difference between the communicative and expressive-mimetic dimensions of language, as his refusal to collapse communicative and aesthetic rationality into one category makes clear. The belief that he wants to do so, however, motivates the work of several of his other critics, most notably the French post-structuralist philosopher Jean-François Lyotard. In a recent essay on post-modernism, Lyotard asks what sort of unity between spheres Habermas seeks.[45] Is it, he wonders, an organic unity of the type posited by G. W. F. Hegel or a synthetic unity of heterogeneities like that suggested in Immanuel Kant's *Critique of Judgment?* Even if the latter, Lyotard contends, Habermas fails to address the severe criticisms recent post-modern thinkers have made of the Enlightenment ideas of a unified goal of history and a totalizing subject. In neglecting to confront these objections, Habermas thus shows himself to be less the partisan of cultural modernism than he claims. In fact, his implicit aesthetic ideal, Lyotard argues, is that of the beautiful as opposed to the sublime. Modernism, however, depends on the latter, even if it evinces some nostalgia for the allegedly lost wholeness and harmony captured in the traditional ideal of beauty.[46] Post-modernism, with which Lyotard more closely identifies, is equally dependent on an aesthetic of the sublime, although without the nostalgia for its beautiful opposite still apparent in modernism.

A similar accusation is made against Habermas by Andreas Huyssen, who claims that he

> ignores the fact that the very idea of a wholistic (sic) modernity and of a totalizing view of history has become anathema in the 1970's, and precisely not on the conservative right. The critical deconstruction of enlightenment rationalism and logocentrism by theoreticians of culture, the decentering of traditional notions of identity, the fight of women and gays for a legitimate social and sexual identity outside the parameters of male, heterosexual vision, the search for alternatives in our relationship with nature, including the nature of our own bodies—all these phenomena, which are key to the culture of the 1970's, make Habermas's proposition to complete the project of modernity questionable, if not undesirable.[47]

Huyssen, however, goes beyond Lyotard by arguing that Habermas's holistic impulse is shared by modernist art itself, which is no less universalistic and totalizing in its assumption about a positive future anticipated by an avant-garde in the present. There is thus a "secret bond between avant-garde and official culture in advanced industrial societies,"[48] which Habermas with his Adornoesque faith in the critical power of modernism fails to register.

An even more extensive critique of Habermas's position has been made by the German literary critic Peter Bürger, who nonetheless professes solidarity with many of his social and political goals.[49] According to Bürger, who worries, like Lyotard and Huyssen, about Habermas's smoothing over the ruptures of culture, there are three major problems in his theory of modernism. First, Habermas's assertion of a parallel development of the three spheres of science, morality, and art towards autonomy and specialization misconstrues the structural and social differences between each sphere. In particular, it underestimates the primacy of cognitive-instrumental rationalization in the modernization process. And perhaps even more significantly, it fails to acknowledge the fatal absence of an impulse in science to reintegrate itself with everyday life. "While autonomous art carries with it the idea of its self-transcendence," Bürger writes, "this cannot be said to be true of science in the same way."[50] Thus Habermas's hope for a simultaneous reintegration of the three spheres into a rationalized life-world seems highly unrealistic.

Secondly, there is a much greater contradiction between the two aspects of the modernization process—the growing differentiation of the separate spheres and the contrary desire for their reintegration with the life-world—than Habermas admits. "In fully developed bourgeois society 'autonomy' and 'use' of art have increasingly come to oppose each other. They will not be so easily reconciled as Habermas's construction of modernity suggests."[51]

And finally, the exaggerated tendency of art to proclaim its total autonomy creates a danger that Habermas fails to take seriously enough: the atrophy of that semantic potential in art derived from its original expressive-mimetic relation to nature. Habermas is thus wrong, Bürger contends, in so quickly dismissing the Surrealists' attempt to revitalize art. "Even the failure of the demand for sublation should not be regarded as a mistake without results. On the contrary. If it is possible today to think about free productivity for everyone, then it is certainly due to the fact that the avant-gardists questioned the legitimacy of the term 'great art work'.[52] Bürger, who elsewhere has made clear his opposition to Adorno's defense of autonomous modernist art for being no longer viable in the age of the post-avant garde,[53] thus chastizes Habermas both for not abandoning that defense rigorously enough and for thinking that, should it be abandoned and art reintegrated with life, a genuinely emancipatory result would ensue!

Although Bürger's critique has these contradictory implications, it does point to certain unresolved difficulties in Habermas's treatment of modernism. In conjunction with the others mentioned above, it suggests two major ambiguities that require clarification before Habermas's attempt to include cultural modernism, despite the qualms of neo-conservatives like Daniel Bell, in his general defense of modernity can be accounted a success. First, he must clarify the extent to which his vision of a mediated rather than colonizing relation between the subsystems he posits as inevitable differentiations in the modernization process is qualitatively superior to the old and largely discredited idealist dream of a perfectly harmonious and rational totality. That he has not expressed himself with complete clarity on this issue is demonstrated by the fact that whereas Lyotard, Huyssen, and Bürger, as well as other recent deconstructionist critics, fault him for still dreaming this dream, others like Thomas McCarthy and Henning Ottmann attack him precisely for having abandoned it.[54] Against the former, Habermas has explicitly written,

> Nothing makes me more nervous than the imputation—repeated in a number of different versions and in the most peculiar contexts—that because the theory of communicative action focuses attention on the social facticity of recognized validity-claims, it proposes, or at least suggests, a rationalistic utopian society. I do not regard the fully transparent society as an ideal, nor do I wish to suggest *any* other ideal—Marx was not the only one frightened by vestiges of utopian socialism.[55]

Against the latter, who are particularly hostile to his refusal to countenance the overthrow of humanity's instrumental relationship to nature and its replacement by an entirely aesthetic one, he has replied that both are necessary aspects of an emancipated society. Not only is it impossible to extend a communicative ethic based on full reciprocity to inorganic nature or even plant life, it is difficult to know how to ground such a naturalistic ethic without regressing to discredited religious or metaphysical world views. Science, therefore, must be instrumental. Still, "the discussion from Kant to Adorno concerning natural and artistic beauty could provide grounds for the thesis that the *expressive attitude* to external nature opens up a domain of experience that can be exploited for *artistic production*."[56] The best that can be hoped for between these separate spheres is the non-colonizing interpenetration that may be reestablished on the level of everyday experience.

But precisely what that mediated relationship might look like, especially when the cognitive and aesthetic attitudes towards nature may be more contradictory than complementary, is not really clear. Nor is it easy to grasp how the return to the life-world as the arena of cooperation can be reconciled with the continued differentiation of the separate cultural spheres. Here Habermas's ambivalence about the implications of the debate between Adorno and Benjamin over the de-auraticization of art reveals a larger tension in his work which needs to be more explicitly addressed. As Bürger contends, it may be much harder to reconcile the autonomy of art with its usefulness in the life-world than Habermas imagines.

The second major issue which needs clarification concerns the status of the artistic sphere itself. With that partiality for reason demonstrated throughout his work, Habermas contends that alongside cognitive-instrumental and moral-practical rationality, there is also a kind of "aesthetic-practical rationality."[57] What he seems to mean by this term is that the aesthetic sphere has come "under the control of specialists who seem more adept at being logical"[58] in artistic terms than are laymen. Here certain remarks of Adorno in his *Aesthetic Theory* about the way in which increased technical virtuosity in art combines the mimesis of nature with non-instrumental rationality are tacitly assumed.[59] But precisely how this type of increased mastery of technique can be seen as rational in the same evolutionary sense that Habermas attributes to the other types of rationality is not clear. For there are certainly many other standards of judgment in aesthetic matters besides technical virtuosity which makes the idea of artistic progress highly problematic.

Nor are we nearer to an understanding of aesthetic rationality if we remember Habermas's Benjaminian identification in his 1963 essay "Between Science and Philosophy: Marxism as Critique" of modernist art with allegory rather than classical symbolism. Although this argument gives the lie to Lyotard's contention that Habermas's aesthetics is closer to the beautiful than the sublime, it makes it difficult to see the rationality in modernist art, except insofar as it provides a critique of the false wholeness of affirmative culture. It may do so in order to redeem the semantic potentials that Benjamin saw preserved in art as a residue of its original mimetic-expressive relationship with nature, but it does not seem clear why the non-sensuous correspondences that allegedly underlie art can be said to be *rational* in any normal sense of that term.[60] Indeed, Habermas very explicitly warns against attributing to mimesis "the role of representative of an original Reason, whose place has been usurped by instrumental rationality."[61] More-over, if Bürger is right about the atrophy of the original semantic potential of art as a result of too much autonomous technical virtuosity, there may even be a contradictory relationship between increased artistic rationalization and its redemptive function.

One possible way in which Habermas might turn for help in resolving these problems is to draw on the work of a theorist whose concepts of rational development have been useful for him in other contexts: Jean Piaget. Following the art historian Suzi Gablik in her controversial analysis of *Progress in Art*,[62] he might then argue that increasingly non-representational modern art expresses a cognitive advance from Piaget's concrete-operational to formal-operational stages. But the difficulties of this solution are not hard to discern. Aside from the limited applicability of this schema to the visual arts and its blissful unawareness of the social underpinnings of too much abstraction in reification, it fails to provide a place for that reintegration of artistic rationality into everyday life which Habermas wants to defend. Nor is it in any way compatible with his Benjaminian stress on mimesis as a source of art's ultimate value. In fact, it would lead to the very collapse of aesthetic into cognitive and moral rationality that Habermas's critics accuse him of fostering and which he has been at such pains to refute.

In short, although I would not want to ally myself with those deconstructionists who reach for their gun every time they hear the word reason, I do think Habermas owes us a more explicit explanation of the nature of the aesthetic-practical rationality he wants to defend in modernism. It is difficult enough to grasp what a mediated relationship among cognitive-instrumental, moral-practical, and aesthetic-expres-sive rationalities would look like, even if they all might be simultane-ously reintegrated with the life-world. It is even harder if the rational status of the third remains somewhat of a mystery. Habermas has devoted an enormous amount of intellectual energy in the effort to define and defend a communicative concept of rational action. But he has recognized, although many of his critics have been slow to acknowledge it, that its full realization alone cannot provide us with the substantive visions of the good life which will make discussion worthwhile. If the aesthetic is to come to the rescue, without, however, leading to an Adornoesque strategy of hibernation, Habermas will need to expand his still rudimentary treatment of it. Not only is modernity an uncompleted project, so, too, is Habermas's enormously ambitious attempt to salvage its still emancipatory potential.

10

Habermas and Postmodernism

In the burgeoning debate over the apparent arrival of the postmodern era (or over the implications of a discourse that claims such an era has arrived), no contributor has been as forthright and unflinching a defender of the still uncompleted project of modernity as Jürgen Habermas. In several recent works, *Der philosophische Diskurs der Moderne, Die neue Unübersichtlichkeit,* and his response to the essays collected by Richard Bernstein in *Habermas and Modernity,*[1] he has expanded his critique far beyond the first, tentative essays he published in the early 1980s.[2] These initial efforts, in part because of their imperfect command of the French intellectual scene and in part because of their controversial attribution of a conservative political implication to postmodernism, proved a lightning rod for criticism. In many quarters, Habermas was pilloried as a naively one-dimensional celebrant of an outdated liberal, Enlightenment rationalism. His attempt to formulate a theory of social evolution was damned as a new version of a discredited objectivist philosophy of history.

Although the relation of Habermas's critique to the specific context out of which it emerged, that of the cynically anti-political *Tendezwende* in the West Germany of the late 1970s, was on occasion acknowledged,[3] by and large, he was chided with having superficially reversed the profound analysis of the Enlightenment's failure offered by the older generation of the Frankfurt School. Indeed, because he has been understood as a staunch defender of universalist, totalizing reason, his work has been accused of being only the most recent and subtle version of an intellectual tradition which inadvertently fostered the authoritarian political uniformity it claimed to resist. Habermas, the passionate defender of democratically achieved consensus and generalized interests, was thus turned into the terrorist of coercive Reason *malgré lui*.

Whether or not his more recent works will dispel this caricature remains to be seen. From all reports of the mixed reception he received in Paris when he gave the lectures that became *Der philosophische Diskurs der Moderne*, the odds are not very high that a more nuanced comprehension of his work will prevail, at least among certain critics. At a time when virtually any defense of rationalism is turned into a brief for the automatic suppression of otherness, heterogeneity, and non-identity, it is hard to predict a widely sympathetic hearing for his complicated argument. Still, if such an outcome is to be made at all possible, the task of unpacking his critique of postmodernism and nuanced defense of modernity must be forcefully pursued. One way to start this process is to focus on a particularly central theme in his work, which has hitherto been relatively ignored. Because it concerns an issue closely related to his similar critique of post-structuralism, it will also illuminate Habermas's no less virulent hostility to the other leading "post" phenomenon of our no longer modern world.

The theme in question is what might be called the opposition between differentiation and *différance*. The latter term, a neologism coined by Jacques Derrida in a seminal essay now twenty-one years old, doubtless needs little introduction to contemporary readers of cultural criticism. I would only like to emphasize that Derrida specifically emphasizes its distance from differentiation. "Among other confusions," he notes, "such a word would suggest some organic unity, some primordial and homogeneous unity, that would eventually come to be divided up and take on difference as an event. Above all, formed on the verb 'to differentiate,' this word would annul the economic signification of detour, temporalizing delay, 'deferring.'"[4] Differentiation, in other words, implies for Derrida either nostalgia for a lost unity or conversely a utopian hope for a future one. Additionally, the concept is suspect for deconstruction because it implies the crystallization of hard and fast distinctions between spheres, and thus fails to register the supplementary interpenetrability of all subsystems, the effaced trace of alterity in their apparent homogeneity, and the subversive absence undermining their alleged fullness or presence.

Now, although deconstruction ought not to be uncritically equated with postmodernism, a term Derrida himself has never embraced, one can easily observe that the postmodernist temper finds *différance* more attractive than differentiation as an historical or, better put, post-historical conceptual tool. The meta-narrative of a process of original unity progressively articulating itself into a series of increasingly autonomous and internally homogeneous subsystems is far less compelling to it than an anti-narrative of heterogeneous, but interpenetrating movements that flow in no discernible historical or evolutionary direction. Even though the prefix "post" implies temporal irreversibility, it has become a favorite pastime to find the postmodern already evident in such earlier figures as Gustave Flaubert.[5] Postmodernists like Jean-François Lyotard explicitly eschew any yearning for the restoration of a pre-differentiated unity or the construction of a dedifferentiated totality in a reconciled future. Instead, they valorize a fluid network of proliferating and incommensurable *différances*, which escape reduction to a finite number of common denominators. In the neo-Wittgensteinian language Lyotard adopted in *The Postmodern Condition* (but later abandoned as too anthropocentric in *Le Différend*), he contends that "there is no possibility that language games can be unified or totalized in any meta-discourse."[6] But if unity or totality is denied, so too is the apparent necessity of those binary oppositions that characterize traditional thought. Thus, the recent postmodernist "non-exhibition" staged at the Centre Pompidou in Paris by Lyotard was called "Les Immatériaux" to stress the overturning of the rigid separation between mind and matter, subject and object, consciousness and body, even life and death.[7] Furthermore, as Jacques Bouveresse, one of Lyotard's most persistent critics, notes in his recent diatribe *Rationalité et Cynisme*, "the deliberate effacement of conventional frontiers that exist for the moment among sciences, philosophy, literature and art is the shibboleth (*mot d'ordre*) *par excellence*, it seems to me, of postmodernity."[8]

If we also look more closely at the aesthetic dimension of the postmodern condition, we will see the same anti-differentiating impulse at work. Thus, the art critic Suzi Gablik notes in *Has Modernism Failed?* that a great deal of performance art in particular makes us anxious because "it violates our sense of boundaries; no distinction is made between public and private events, between real and aesthetic emotions, between art and self."[9] As such, postmodernism can be seen in part as the non-utopian anti-climax to what Peter Bürger has defined as the avant-garde, as opposed to the modernist project: the abolition of the separate institution of art and its reabsorption into the life-world out of which it originally came.[10] Typical of this postmodernist penchant for violating boundaries is the breakdown of the differences between high and low art, culture and kitsch, and the sacred space of the museum and the profane world without. In architecture in particular, which has been widely recognized as the cutting edge of the postmodernist offensive, what Charles Jencks called "radical eclecticism"[11] has meant the disruption of the time-honored distinctions between different styles in favor of an historical pastiche, as well as the breakdown of the hierarchical superiority of "serious" architecture over a more popular and vulgar vernacular, such as that celebrated by Robert Venturi in his defense of Las Vegas.[12]

What is, however, important to recognize in all of these transgressions of various frontiers is the abandonment of any hope for a new totalization in the sense of a dialectical *Aufhebung* or sublation. Instead, an untotalized network of supplementary *différances* is posited as the superior alternative to the seemingly rigid and unyielding dichotomies of modernist differentiation. Georges Bataille's model of a carnivalesque disruption of all hierarchies in the sacred and ecstatic community of expenditure can be found lurking behind much post-structuralist social theorizing. The postmodernist sensibility has also borrowed a great deal from that dimension of feminist thought which rejects the abstract universalism underlying any homogenizing humanist discourse, while also remaining suspicious of the essentializing opposition between the sexes so much a part of patriarchal culture.[13]

Now, because Habermas has been outspoken in his distrust of both post-structuralist and postmodernist theories, and has heretofore not really absorbed the feminist critique of the Western tradition,[14] he has variously been accused of hoping for a utopian totalization based on the universal power of rationality and rigidly holding on, like a typically German anal-compulsive, to the existent differentiations of a modernization process still worth salvaging. The first charge is exemplified by Lyotard's complaint that "what Habermas requires from the arts and the experiences they provide is, in short, to bridge the gap between cognitive, ethical and political discourses, thus opening the way to a unity of experience."[15] Habermas, he believes, still remains hostage to the fantasy of "humanity as a collective (universal) subject"[16] seeking a perfect consensus in a meta-language game transcending all others.

The second and in some ways contrary criticism is typified by the Derridean argument of Dominick LaCapra, who concedes Habermas's strong distaste for Hegelian or other meta-subjects, but still questions his alternative:

> The problem, however, is whether, in rejecting reductionism and dialectical synthesis, Habermas goes to the extreme of analytic dissociation which is itself constitutive of a logic of domination. Habermas does not directly see how his own analytic distinctions, which are useful within limits, may be rendered problematic, especially when they are taken as categorical definitions of realms of thought or action.[17]

As an antidote, LaCapra urges Habermas to pay more attention to the supplementary and carnivalesque play of language, which would undermine the apparently rigid differentiations posited in various ways during the development of his work. More recent deconstructionist critics of Habermas like Michael Ryan and Jonathan Culler have echoed this advice, in each case defending *différance* as superior to categorical distinctions.[18]

A more patient reading of Habermas's demanding corpus than is evident in these critiques would, I want to suggest, allow us to appreciate the virtues of defending a certain notion of differentiation against postmodernist *différance*. First, it is clear that although the very early Habermas may have espoused the position attributed to him by Lyotard, that of believing in a meta-subjective species being capable of achieving a universal consensus, at least as early as 1972 and possibly even during the positivist dispute of the 1960s, he had explicitly abandoned this position.[19] Repudiating the idea of a Hegelian-Marxist universal subject as a residue of a discredited consciousness philosophy, he began to call instead for the nurturing of a plurality of intersubjectively grounded speech communities. In fact, his main complaint against post-structuralism is that it merely inverts consciousness-philosophy by denying the subject, and thus ironically, is as holistic as the logocentric traditions it opposes. Rather than calling for a unity of experience, as Lyotard contends, Habermas has scrupulously defended the value of distinctive forms of interaction, not merely among human beings, but also between human beings and nature. In fact, his scepticism towards the project of reconciling humanity and the natural world has brought him under fire from such advocates of a more Marcusean or Blochian strain in Western Marxism, such as Thomas McCarthy, Joel Whitebook, and Hennng Ottmann.[20] Instead of holding out hope for a utopian reenchantment of our disenchanted world, Habermas has resolutely acknowledged humanity's disembeddedness, that is, differentiation from the natural world.

But second, while valorizing differentiation, Habermas has fully recognized that the process has been plagued by severe difficulties. Even as he has called modernity an uncompleted project worth carrying forward, he has been very sensitive to the deep discontents it has spawned. Unlike the more sanguine defenders of modernization who peopled the American and West German academies in the postwar era, he has always been enough of a student of Max Horkheimer and Theodor Adorno's *Dialectic of Enlightenment* to recognize that the mere refinement of analytic categories and the increased complexity of modern society are by no means emancipatory in themselves.

Habermas's attitude towards differentiation is, thus, a highly complicated one. To do justice to it would require tracing its origins in at least two traditions, sociological and philosophical. To make sense of the former would mean beginning with Herbert Spencer and Emile Durkheim in the 19th century and passing on to 20th-century theorists like Max Weber, Talcott Parsons, Niklas Luhmann and Wolfgang Schluchter, all of whom are critically appropriated in Habermas's massive *Theory of Communicative Action* and elsewhere.[21] We would then have to reconsider the heated sociological controversies over evolutionism and functionalism and make distinctions among segmental, stratified, and functionalist forms of differentiation. And finally, we would have to consider the responses of such contemporary sociologists as Anthony Giddens to Habermas's reading of the tradition.[22]

To probe the second, philosophical tradition, we would have to go back at least as far as Immanuel Kant and examine his three critiques with their separation among forms of judgment. We would then have to trace efforts to undo Kant's differentiations, beginning perhaps with Hegel and continuing up through the Western Marxist struggle to articulate a defensible concept of totality.[23] And we would have to conclude with a consideration of Habermas's recent exchanges with Hans-Georg Gadamer and other defenders of a radical hermeneutics, who try to provide a new foundationless foundation for a holistic approach to understanding.

Rather than attempt so ambitious and foolhardy a reconstruction of the roots of Habermas's attitude towards differentiation, let me simply point to the major implications he has drawn from his contact with these disparate sources. Habermas's rational reconstruction of the evolution of Western societies posits a relatively undifferentiated society of hominids who became what can be called human through both the division of labor and the development of kinship structures.[24] At the very beginning of the evolutionary process, as he conceptualizes it, there is thus already a form of differentiation between subsystems of the whole. Similarly, the distinction between labor and language means that any universal explanation of human development, say, a vulgar Marxist productivism or a vulgar deconstructionist pantextualism, must be rejected as reductionist. For the process of evolution takes place on several levels, which roughly can be grouped under two rubrics. The first, which Habermas calls system integration, derives from an instrumental relationship between humanity and its natural environment. Initially generated by the dialectic of labor, system integration spawns steering mechanisms, like money and bureaucratic power, which achieve a certain autonomy of their own. The second level, which Habermas calls social integration, refers to norms and values, which are derived from a communicative rather than instrumental relationship among actors, who have the capacity to be active agents rather than mere bearers of structural forces. It is only in the modern period beginning in the 18th century, so Habermas contends, that the distance between system and social integration becomes especially evident with the differentiation of subsystems of economics and administration, the decentering of world views (what Weber calls the "disenchantment of the world") and the uncoupling of law from morality.

Unlike more complacent functionalist theorists of evolutionary differentiation, Habermas recognizes the potential for radical distress in this process. In particular, he is sensitive to the disproportionately advanced development of system as opposed to social integration in modern capitalist and bureaucratic socialist societies. Both types of integration can be understood as emerging against the background of a life-world in which rationalization takes place when communicative argumentation supplants more authoritarian and coercive forms of social coordination. System rationalization, however, entails means-ends rationalism, whereas social or communicative rationalization involves other forms of reciprocal intersubjective integration. In the modern world, the former has revealed itself as more powerful than the latter, leading to what Habermas calls the "colonization" of the life-world by system or instrumental rationality. Hostility to this trend has expressed itself in many ways, including the derogation of all forms of reason as dominating and coercive. It is, however, Habermas's contention that unless we carefully distinguish among types of rationalization, we risk regressing beyond the genuine achievements of modernization. Thus, he writes, the deconstructionist critique of logocentrism becomes legitimate when it understands its target, "not as an excess, but as a deficit of reason"[25] because of the partiality of the subject-centered, instrumental rationality it misidentifies with reason *tout court*. It is illegitimate, however, when it rejects any rational adjudicating of competing truth claims because of the inherent undecidability of all language, a belief whose practical consequences is an irrationalist decisionism.

Following Weber and before him Kant, Habermas stipulates a differentiation among three basic types of reason in the sphere of values: cognitive (or scientific), moral, and aesthetic. The Enlightenment had hoped that the emancipatory potential of each of these spheres could ultimately be harnessed for practical purposes. "The 20th century," Habermas admits, "has shattered this optimism. The differentiation of science, morality and art has come to mean the autonomy of the segments treated by the specialist and at the same

time their splitting off from the hermeneutics of everyday communication. This splitting off is the problem that has given rise to those efforts
to "negate" the culture of expertise."[26] Although understanding the
motivation behind these attempts to dedifferentiate and thus end the
alienation of the separate spheres from each other and from the
everyday life-world, Habermas is nonetheless very reluctant to
abandon the Enlightenment project entirely. For with it came the
refinement of rationalization itself, which resists the reduction of
modern life to any one common denominator, rational or otherwise.

Habermas's argument in this regard is worth following in some
detail, because it has so often been misconstrued by those who see him
as the advocate of a terroristically universal form of reason. First of all,
although Habermas sees each sphere as having undergone a variant of
what can be called rationalization, he nonetheless explicitly rejects the
idea that reason means the same thing in each case. In an earlier essay
on his attitude towards modernism, I challenged him in particular to
clarify what he meant by rationality in the aesthetic sphere.[27] Was he
claiming in the manner of, say, Suzi Gablik in her book on *Progress in
Art* that Jean Piaget's developmental cognitive categories could be
applied to aesthetics, as he argued they could to cognitive and moral
development? His reply was that art criticism, which arose with the
differentiation of autonomous art from its religious-ceremonial context,

> has developed forms of argumentation that specifically differentiate it
> from the forms of theoretical and moral-practical discourse. As
> distinct from merely subjective preference, the fact that we link
> judgments of taste to a criticizable claim presupposes non-arbitrary
> standards for judgment of art. As the philosophical discussion of
> "artistic truth" reveals, works of art raise claims with regard to their
> unity (harmony: *Stimmigkeit*), their authenticity, and the success of
> their expressions by which they can be measured and in terms of
> which they may fail.[28]

Thus, in the discourse about art, there is an argumentative rationality
that resists reduction to moral or scientific reason.

Not only does aesthetic discourse reveal such a rationalization,
Habermas continues, so too does art immanently considered. In art
itself, there is a type of learning process, which is cumulative. "What
accumulates are not epistemic contents," Habermas contends, "but
rather the effects of the inner logical differentiation of a special sort of
experience: precisely those aesthetic experiences of which only a
decentered, unbound subjectivity is capable."[29] The increasingly
decentered and unbounded subjectivity of artistic experience has an
ultimately emancipatory potential, for it "indicates an increased

sensitivity to what remains unassimilated in the interpretive achievements of pragmatic, epistemic, and moral mastery of the demands and
challenges of everyday situations; it effects an openness to the
expurgated elements of the unconscious, the fantastic, and the mad,
the material and the bodily."[30] Thus, "art becomes a laboratory, the
critic an expert, the development of art the medium of a learning
process—here, naturally, not in the sense of an accumulation of
epistemic *contents*, of an aesthetic 'progress'—which is possible only in
individual dimensions—but nonetheless in the sense of concentrically
expanding, advancing exploration of a realm of possibilities opened up
with the autonomization of art."[31] In short, instead of providing a
straightjacket for transgressive, heterogeneous experiences, as those
who formulate a simple opposition between art and reason assume,
aesthetic rationalization—in the dual sense of critical and productive
learning processes—allows, indeed encourages, a proliferation of
artistic stimuli to a widened consciousness. Only the modernist
autonomization of art, its differentiation as an institution of its own,
makes such a rationalization possible.

The extreme autonomization of both esoteric art and hermetic
aesthetic criticism does, to be sure, create pressures for their
reintegration with the life-world out of which they originally emerged.
Here Habermas admits to a certain ambivalence. On the one hand, he
rejects what he sees, following Adorno, as the premature, forced, and
impotent *Aufhebung* of art and life in such movements as Surrealism.
Yet on the other hand, he recognizes that too rigid and inflexible a
detachment of art from life courts the danger of forfeiting art's ultimate
capacity to reinvigorate the life-world by giving it a higher level access
to those expurgated experiences it normally marginalizes or sup-
presses. Too radical a break between art and life also threatens to cause
the wellsprings of aesthetic expression themselves to run dry. He
hesitates to affirm an immediate reintegration, however, because he
contends that the utopian dedifferentiation of art *by itself* is insufficient
to undo the pathologies of modernization. A new constellation of the
separate value spheres with their expert rationalized discourses and
the communicative life-world of everyday experience is needed in
order to maximize the emancipatory potential in the project of
modernity. This neither necessitates the collapse of all of these now
distinct realms into one universal language game, as Lyotard accuses
him of advocating, nor the rigid maintenance of the boundaries of the
differentiated spheres, as his deconstructionist critics aver he upholds.
Instead, a more nuanced mediation of relatively, but not absolutely
commensurable realms is a preferable alternative.[32]

In a recent essay on "Modern and Postmodern Architecture,"[33]

Habermas spells out the implications of this argument in the aesthetic field that is now at the cutting edge of the debate. Modernist architecture, he points out, was at once functional and formalist, following both the socially progressive imperatives of, say, early Bauhaus radicalism and the anti-ornamental purism of constructivist abstraction. In both ways, it sought to break with a sterile traditionalism and use the methods and materials of the modern world. As such, it was based on a mediated interaction between non-aesthetic needs and the development of immanent aesthetic reflexivity. The postmodernists are right, Habermas admits, in recognizing that the utopian social intentions of the early modernists went awry when the international style became the emblem of corporate capitalism and the excuse for alienating and impersonal mass housing. But here the problem was not so much the Enlightenment ambition at the root of the modernist quest, as its distorted application in terms more of instrumental, system rationality than communicative, social rationality.

The postmodernists go too far, Habermas suggests, in reaction to this failure by seeking to separate formalist and functional imperatives entirely. Either they retreat into an eclectic celebration of historical styles, which conservatively affirm all of them merely because they once existed. Or "like surrealist stage designers," they "utilize modern design methods in order to coax picturesque effects from aggressively mixed styles."[34] Any attempt, moreover, to generate a vitalist architecture, which would immediately restore all severed ties with the life-world—here perhaps Habermas is thinking of the Heideggerian-inspired call for a Critical Regionalism by Kenneth Frampton and others[35]—risks turning into an anti-modernist nostalgia for a pre-differentiated form of life. An immanent critique of the limitations of modernist architecture, acknowledging its achievements as well as its failures, is thus preferable to a wholesale turning of the page, which offers only pseudo-solutions to the pathologies of modern life.

Premature dedifferentiation is, in fact, one of the most troubling of those false answers, which Habermas sees as legitimated by the postmodernist discourse of *différance*. In his latest book, *Der philosophische Diskurs der Moderne*, he criticizes Michel Foucault, Derrida, and also Adorno for their undifferentiated critique of modernity: "Enlightenment and manipulation, conscious and unconscious, forces of production and forces of destruction, expressive self-realization and repressive desublimation, freedom-guaranteeing and freedom-eliminating effects, truth and ideology—all of these moments are confused with each other."[36] The dedifferentiation of the value spheres of modernity are, moreover, purchased at the cost of the tacit elevation of one of them, aesthetics, understood in an essentially irrationalist sense.

For Habermas, the current fascination with Friedrich Nietzsche betrays this inclination, for the new Nietzscheanism "represents the different-iation of science and morality as the developmental process of a reason that at the same time usurps and stifles the poetic, world-disclosing power of art,"[37] which it seeks to resurrect. But in making art somehow prior to differentiation, in assuming that rhetoric is somehow more fundamental than philosophy,[38] it fails to see that the very sphere of art itself is the result of a process of differentiation. In other words, it is mistaken to offer an aesthetic colonization of the life-world as an antidote to its instrumental rational counterpart produced by the hypertrophy of science and system integration in modern capitalism.

Similarly, Foucault's effort to collapse cognition and power is based on a problematic dedifferentiation of the will to knowledge and the will to power, which reduces all the human sciences to little more than subtle instruments of discipline and normalizing control. Likewise, Derrida's critique of J. L. Austin fails to register the linguistic differentiations of the communicative life-world in which fictional discourse has been usefully distinguished from other language games.[39] In short, much postmodernist analysis has been vitiated by a confusingly ahistorical failure to recognize that certain patterns of differentiation have emerged in ways that defy the attempt to say that they are always already undermined. And moreover, it is precisely the separate rationalizations of the distinct spheres that must be defended as a way to avoid a holism of indiscriminate *différance* that merely turns on its head the logocentric holism of reductive sameness. Albrecht Wellmer puts Habermas's alternative cogently when he writes,

> we have to distinguish between those irreversible differentiation processes, which signify the end of traditional society and the emergence of specifically modern, universalist conceptions of ration-ality, freedom, and democracy on the one hand, and the specific form in which these differentiation processes have been articulated and institutionalized in capitalist societies. It is obviously to the *latter* only that the ideas of a sublation of formal law, politics, or art can meaningfully apply. What they can mean is that could be called a new "permeability" of the relatively autonomous subsystems or cultural spheres for each other.[40]

Such an answer may, to be sure, raise a few questions of its own. How can we tell, for example, when a healthy balance has been struck between permeability and boundary maintenance? If, on the one hand, the boundaries become too fluid, aren't we forced into a postmodernist *différance* in which supplementarity reigns supreme? If, on the other, they have become too rigid, might it no longer be possible to assume even the partial commensurability that is at the root of Habermas's guarded optimism about the modernist project? How can we, moreover, be certain that it is only the specific differentiations of the Western modernization process that possess enough rationality to be worth defending? As Thomas McCarthy points out in questioning Habermas's debt to Luhmann's systems theory, it is important to insure that "the possibility of democratization as dedifferentiation of economy and state not be metatheoretically ruled out of court by systems-theoretic borrowing. Here again, the question arises of whether it should be superseded by some non-regressive form of dedifferentiation."[41] The same question arises for the other forms of articulation defended by Habermas in his eagerness to avoid abandoning the modern project before its emancipatory potential is fully tapped. It is perhaps not by chance that *différance* has often come to be the rallying cry for many who feel excluded by the dominant forms of rationality in our culture.

And yet, after having acknowledged all of these questions, it still seems justifiable to conclude by stressing the value of Habermas's alternative to postmodernist *différance*. A recent critic of his position, Peter Uwe Hohendahl, complains that

> It is not quite evident why Habermas is not willing to use the critical force of deconstruction against the logic of differentiated systems. It seems that Habermas overstates his case when he describes deconstruction as a purely literary approach without concern for problem-solving in the realm of the life-world. Thus my suggestion would be: if we want to free the life-world from the constraints of the overarching system and its institutions, there is room for the project of deconstructive criticism, precisely because it questions the logic of systems.[42]

The answer to this complaint is that for Habermas, the differentiation of systemic institutions cannot be construed *solely* as a constraint on an oppressed life-world, but rather as the source of certain rationalizations that are worthy of continued preservation. It would therefore be dangerous to turn deconstruction from an essentially literary approach into a more universal solvent of all structures and systems, in the hope of recovering the sacred community of Bataille's ecstatic general economy. For the result would be a night of endless *différance* in which all cows were piebald, which is as deceptive as the old idealist trick of turning them all black. Instead, we should be more sensitive to the enlightening as well as obscuring implications of a much-maligned modernity whose promise is still greater than is assumed by those who counsel a leap into the postmodernist dark.

11

Blumenberg and Modernism:
A Reflection on
The Legitimacy of the Modern Age

When does an epoch become conscious of itself as a distinct and coherent historical period, qualitatively different from its predecessors? What leads, in fact, to the conceptualization of historical time in epochal terms rather than as a homogeneous chronological continuum or as a cyclical eternal return? Under what circumstances does an epoch feel itself threatened and in need of legitimation? Indeed, what can the criteria of epochal legitimacy actually be?

These and similar questions are now being heatedly contested by students of contemporary Western culture and society, aware that what Jürgen Habermas once called a "legitimation crisis" has spread from the political arena to threaten the self-confidence of the age itself. A long-festering discontent with the ideas and practices of modernity and modernism has recently erupted into a full-fledged allegation that a new historical formation is now upon us. What sociologists began calling a while ago post-industrial society has merged in complicated ways with what cultural critics call post-modernist art and post-structuralist philosophy to become what one leading interpreter of the phenomenon has dubbed "the postmodern condition."[1] Like it or not—and there have been many critics suspicious of an era that can define itself only in terms of what it claims to have replaced—it is fast becoming widely accepted that *"il faut être absolument post-moderne!"*[2]

It is in the context of the still often muddled and inchoate debate over the significance of this alleged rupture, with all its implied denigration of modernity and modernism, that the English translation of Hans Blumenberg's *The Legitimacy of the Modern Age* comes as an especially welcome event.[3] For although never addressing itself directly to the post-modernist challenge to modernity, it makes very clear the implications of the latter's abandonment, as well as the enormousness of the task faced by any new epoch that will have to answer the questions left unresolved by its predecessor. Written in 1966 and emended in a second edition, published in three installments in 1973, 1974, and 1976, *The Legitimacy of the Modern Age* is, in fact, directed at a very different challenge to the modern from that posed by the defenders of its alleged successor. It is a challenge that came from German philosophers like Karl Löwith, Martin Heidegger, and Carl Schmitt, who were less concerned with what follows modernity than with what it claimed to replace. Readers more familiar with Anglo-American literature will recognize the issues raised by their critique in the debates stimulated by J. B. Bury on progress, Carl Becker on the Enlightenment, and M. H. Abrams on Romanticism. Rather than delegitimating the modern by claiming that it was already being surpassed, these authors attempted to call it into question by reducing it to a disguised version of what went before.[4]

In more specific terms, they sought to discredit the modern by seeing it as little more than a secularized version of Christian, medieval culture. As Blumenberg convincingly shows, this secularization thesis has taken an astonishingly wide variety of forms: for example, bourgeois progress as a secularized version of providential Christian eschatology; radical social utopias like Marxism as secularizations of millenial dreams of paradise; modern political leaders as secularized theocratic monarchs; the modern work ethic as a secularized version of Christian asceticism; modern psychological self-examination as secularized confessionalism; or modern political egalitarianism as the secularization of the Christian idea of man's equality in the eyes of God. Even modern science has been derived from the Christian faith in an intelligible and rational world designed by a trustworthy deity.

What made these interpretations of the hidden meaning of the modern a challenge to its legitimacy—aside from their often being coupled with an explicit nostalgia for a lost world, such as Löwith's for the age of Stoic reverence for a cyclical cosmos—was their denial of modernity's claim to the original ownership of its cultural content. Borrowing the old trick of early Christian polemicists, who accused the ancient Greeks of having secretly stolen their best ideas from the Bible, the secularization theorists located the unacknowledged paternity of the modern in originally religious ideas. Illegitimacy comes therefore not from lacking a proper parent, but rather from denying his generative power. This charge is itself, so Blumenberg astutely notes, a negative variant of an argument that can be traced as far back as Plato's notion that whatever is true is merely a copy of an original Truth, which can be identified with a divine author. Its positive residues linger today in the kind of proof by etymological priority evident in the work of thinkers like Heidegger or Hannah Arendt, who reach back before the Christian era to an original language whose authentic meaning has somehow been corrupted.

The Legitimacy of the Modern Age sets out in almost 600 extremely subtle, dense and, alas, often maddeningly difficult pages to contest this paternity suit and defend the legitimacy of the modern on other grounds. Although, as we shall see, they are not without difficulties of their own, it should be noted immediately that Blumenberg does not set out to refute the historicist argument of continuity by committing the opposite mistake of assuming an absolute originality for the modern. Legitimacy does not mean beginning *ex nihilo* or through an immaculate conception. Indeed, the modern age's characteristic founding gesture of starting with radical doubt à la René Descartes and ignoring the hold of the past over the present is one he resolutely rejects. The grand narrative he offers is not one of radical and inexplicable discontinuities between epochs in the manner of, say, Michel Foucault's early works. Blumenberg makes his case instead by introducing a subtle distinction between the continuity of transfigured substances, which he opposes, and the continuity of problems and functions, which he defends. In place, therefore, of the secularization thesis he proposes instead what can be called a reoccupation argument. In his words, "What mainly occurred in the process that is interpreted as secularization, at least (so far) in all but a few recognizable and specific instances, should be described not as the *transposition* of authentically theological contents into secularized alienation from their origin but rather as the *reoccupation* of answer positions that had become vacant and whose corresponding questions could not be eliminated," (p. 65).

To spell out what the perennial questions have been and to show how they have been answered in different historical epochs, Blumenberg divides his massive work into four major sections. The first deals explicitly with the secularization thesis, whose misreading both of the religious legacy and its modern replacement he subjects to ruthless criticism. The second section introduces an alternative reading of the history of the West in which questions originally posed by the Gnostic challenge to orthodox Christianity are shown to reappear in a new guise and with new answers at the threshold of the modern epoch. Blumenberg's next section explores what he terms the "trial" of theoretical curiosity, demonstrating how what medieval Christianity originally condemned as a vice became a central virtue for the modern mind. The fourth and final section of the book compares in great detail the intellectual journeys of Nicholas of Cusa and Giordano Bruno, who serve for Blumenberg as exemplary figures on opposing sides of the medieval/modern divide.

Blumenberg's highly ingenious refutation of the secularization thesis begins by conceding the power of what might be called its weaker version, which argues that certain forms of, say, the modern idea of progress may well draw on medieval antecedents. Thus, for example, the expansion of the idea of possible progress into a totalistic philosophy of history with faith in an inevitable future is, to a great extent, open to the secularization charge. But in its stronger form, which argues that the concept of progress per se in all of its manifestations is always secularized eschatology, the thesis is in error. To demonstrate its flaws, Blumenberg adduces a wide variety of contrary evidence. First, he argues that in an important sense, the world was already "secularized" shortly after the onset of the Christian era, when the immediate eschatological hopes of the earliest church fathers were disappointed. Because the apocalypse did not arrive, it was necessary to see the world as bereft of eschatalogical significance, more "worldly" than the locus of the imminent kingdom of God. As a result, profane history could begin in the space vacated by the failed apocalypse. For Blumenberg, this means that "the early historicization of the essential contents of salvation consumes the substance that as a later secularization could have served to explain the modern age" (p. 40). Or in other words, there could never have been a modern secularization *of* eschatology, as Löwith and others contend, because there had already been a secularization *by* eschatology, which took place at the threshold of the medieval epoch.

Second, Blumenberg contends that the failure of these early eschatological expectations meant a reinterpretation of the eschaton as having already happened, in the sense that all the events needed for personal salvation had taken place with the incarnation. Individuals could therefore have an inner certainty through faith of their ultimate fate, which was already somehow judged. "Consequently," Blumenberg concludes, "the basic eschatological attitude of the Christian epoch could no longer be one of hope for the final events but was rather one of fear of judgment and the destruction of the world. . . . The concept of history that could be constructed from this basic attitude is at most one of an interval of grace, not of an expectation directed toward a future in which it seeks fulfillment" (p. 44). It is this anxiety about the future that helps account for the importance of memory in such Christian thinkers as Augustine, who had no optimistic eschatology to secularize.

Third, insofar as Christian eschatology had both a cosmic and individual strain, the latter drove men to be obsessed more and more with their personal fate rather than with that of the community of believers. In contrast, the modern concept of progress was predicated on an essentially collective project in which individual salvation, indeed individual happiness, was less important than the continuation of an open-ended task that transcended the lifetime of any individual and could have no parallel with personal salvation in an afterlife. The collective nature of this project was clearly evident in the fundamental, modern idea of scientific method, which began with Francis Bacon and Descartes. According to Blumenberg, "the idea of method is not a kind of planning, not a transformation of the divine salvation plan, but rather the establishment of a disposition: the disposition of the subject, in his place, to take part in a process that generates knowledge in a transsubjective manner" (p. 33).

Moreover, as a side effect of the modern belief in a transsubjective method open to everyone, the older notion of intellectual property deriving from authorial authority—the very notion, as we have seen, underlying the secularization theorists' attempt to delegitimate the modern—was itself called into question for scientific knowledge. Although remaining in force in humanist pursuits, at least until the recent critique of the author made by writers like Foucault and Roland Barthes,[6] the sovereignty of original creativity was jettisoned by a scientific method that was interested only in results and not intellectual pedigree. Thus the battle between the ancients and the moderns was more than just a struggle for new ideas; it was also a fundamental challenge to the traditional way of conceptualizing the truth. Here too no simple secularization could have taken place.

Fourth, because the collective project was quintessentially a human and not a divine one, immanent in history and not the product of transcendent intervention, the idea that the modern could be an illegitimate pseudomorph of the medieval is radically untenable. For what defines the modern is precisely its attempt to ground itself on the basis of human self-assertion rather than theological dispensation. Self-assertion, which is one of Blumenberg's key terms, means "an existential program, according to which man posits his existence in a historical situation and indicates to himself how he is going to deal with the reality surrounding him and what use he will make of the possibilities that are open to him" (p. 138). A corollary of this program was the attempt to define the modern age in epochal terms as different from its predecessor; even though absolute self-grounding was in a certain sense a delusion, it nonetheless functioned to distinguish the modern from other epochs, which felt no need to legitimate themselves in this fashion.

In all these ways and others that Blumenberg also explores, the modern age cannot be reduced to a transfigured Christianity covertly owing "an objective cultural debt" (p. 117) to the past. But in terms of the questions posed to both the medieval and modern periods and the functional reoccupation of the sites left for answers, one can, so Blumenberg concedes, speak of important continuities. The second part of *The Legitimacy of the Modern Age* is therefore devoted to exposing the common pattern of question and response underlying both epochs. In particular, it seeks to defend the thesis that "the modern age is the second overcoming of Gnosticism" (p. 126), whose challenge the medieval period ultimately failed to meet.

What exactly was the Gnostic challenge as Blumenberg understands it? Confronted by the burning question of the origin of evil in the world, a question which classical philosophy had not satisfactorily resolved, Marcion, the greatest Gnostic thinker of the second century, sought an answer by radically devaluing the world and locating the good entirely outside of it. The dualism that ensued presented an especially dangerous threat to mainstream Christian orthodoxy that was in the process of formation at the same time. For it contested the unity of a God who had both created the world, a world admittedly rife with evil, and who could redeem it. According to Blumenberg, "the formation of the Middle Ages can only be understood as an attempt at the definitive exclusion of the Gnostic syndrome. To retrieve the world as the creation from the negative role assigned it by the doctrine of its demiurgic origin, and to salvage the dignity of the ancient cosmos for its role in the Christian system, was the central effort all the way from Augustine to the height of Scholasticism" (p. 130).

The most fateful early response to Gnosticism was that of Augustine, who contended that the source of evil was not a malign demiurge, a rival of the Christian God of salvation, but rather a fallen mankind. In assuming, however, that there was a distinction between those who could be saved from the fall, an elect blessed by grace, and those who could not, Augustine actually displaced Marcion's dualism onto mankind itself. But he also opened a new space for the revalorization of God's creation, which was filled when classical thinking, most notably Aristotle's cosmology, was adopted by the Scholastics. The cost of this solution was, however, enormous. As Blumenberg describes it, the price of this preservation of the cosmos was not only the guilt that man was supposed to assign himself for the condition in which he found the world but also the resignation that his responsibility for that condition imposed upon him: renunciation of any attempt to change for his benefit, through action, a reality for the adversity of which he had himself to blame. The senselessness of self-assertion was the heritage of the Gnosticism which was not overcome but only "translated" (p. 136).

Self-assertion could appear as the new alternative to Gnostic dualism only when the medieval synthesis itself began to unravel. As Blumenberg sees it—characteristically offering an explanation solely on the level of ideas—the change occurred when the providential, intelligible, and essentially rational cosmos of the Scholastics, with their recycled Aristotelianism, was called into question by William of Ockham's nominalism. Although a similar radical doubt about the intelligibility of the cosmos had haunted the Hellenistic world with the onset of atomism, it was essentially neutralized by the desire of leading atomists like Epicurus to maintain at least a minimum of order underlying the apparent chaos of the experienced world. The nominalists were denied this consoling option paradoxically by their faith in a Christian God, whose will was understood to be unlimited, even by reason. The implication of this faith in unchecked divine voluntarism became apparent only in the late thirteenth century, when Aristotle's proof of the uniqueness of this world was condemned by the Church as incompatible with the doctrine of God's omnipotent will. For with an awareness of the infinity of possible worlds which could be created by such a God came a dizzying sensation of the utter contingency and groundlessness of this particular one. In other words, the cosmos as we know it and as Aristotle had described it could no longer be valorized as inherently intelligible and rational.

Once again the specter of Gnostic dualism was revived, as the metaphysical guarantees provided by Scholasticism were undercut and God became a Deus Absconditus. Set adrift, man did not, however, seek an explanation in his own corrupt state, as he had during the early Middle Ages. For with the devaluation of Aristotle's finite universe had come the realization that the Incarnation, God's sacrifice for mankind, could no longer be seen as the central moment in the history of the universe. The result, as Blumenberg describes it, was equally fatal to man's self-aggrandizing assumption that his fallen state could account for the irrationality, evil, and chaos of the created world. In Blumenberg's words, "nothing less than the loss of this location of man in the theological system of reference had come about during the decline of the Middle Ages: the speculative self-renunciation of 'anthropological "egoism"'" (p. 177).

But ironically, as man lost his special religious role in a universe he could no longer assume was the manifestation of divine order, he began to assert a more active role in mastering and controlling the world in which he somehow had to live. "Deprived by God's hiddenness of metaphysical guarantees for the world, man constructs for himself a counterworld of elementary rationality and manipulability" (p. 173). Searching for the means to build such a counter-world amenable to his designs, modern man combined the ontological postulate of material reality with that of mathematical regularity and set out to fill the gap left by the collapse of the Scholastic cosmology. Unlike classical theory, which counseled a merely passive observation of a world already constructed; unlike Gnostic dualism, which taught man to disdain the world altogether as utterly chaotic and corrupt; unlike Hellenisic atomism, which advised man to live in such a world without trying to change it; and unlike medieval Scholasticism, which revived classical cosmology and charged it with divine teleology, modern science was based essentially on human self-assertion in a world which lacked any a priori intelligibility.

As a result, the modern worldview untimately abandoned the quest for objective truth, turning instead to efficiency as the criterion of highest value. Rather than having the hubris to measure himself against a God whose knowledge was perfect, modern man simply gave up the belief that such knowledge could exist at all. As Blumenberg puts it, "As an instrument of self-assertion, theory has no need of the luxury of relating its hypotheses to—and taking part in—the truth possessed by divinity itself. The involvement with technique integrates theory and the theoretical attitude into the functional complex of the immanent teleology of human self-assertion, and weakens its—until then—irreducible claim to truth" (p. 208). The new importance of quantitative as opposed to qualitative knowledge was evidence of the shift away from truth, insofar as mathematics was recognized as only asymptotically related to a putative truth, for which even the nominalists had still nostalgically yearned.

The new epochal self-consciousness of the modern era emerged when this nostalgia was finally put aside, although to be sure there were many revivals of it in the years to come. Descartes, for example, can be seen as a still transitional figure by Blumenberg because of his desire to retain a correspondence theory of truth based on a trustworthy God. He can also be seen inversely as making too much of the break with the past implied by his method of radical doubt, which masked from itself its debt to the legacy of questions and answers bequeathed to the modern by its predecessors. But despite the substantialist and functionalist debts he owed to the past, Descartes was still on the threshold of a modernity which could not be reduced to a secularized version of its Christian antecedent. For Blumenberg, the full weight of the break came perhaps only with Immanuel Kant's critical philosophy, which "concentrated all directed, purposeful processes in man's rational action, and this meant that the world could participate in this sort of directedness only by becoming a substrate subject to man's purposes" (p. 214). When later thinkers—Blumenberg singles out Thomas Malthus and Charles Darwin—tried to subjugate man once again to some version of a natural order, modern self-assertion, expressed above all in technological breakthroughs, resisted the counsel to return. Indeed, according to Blumenberg, "the greatness of the much reviled nineteenth century lay in the fact that, at least in the greater part of what it actualized historically, it opposed this advice" (p. 225).

Modern man did not, however, turn his back on the world in the service of a narcissistic self-absorption. Indeed, it was the unleashing of curiosity, so Blumenberg contends in the third major section of his book, that marks the modern sensibility. Turning a remarkable amount of erudition on the question of why that unleashing took so long, Blumenberg presents a brilliant account of what he calls the "trial" of theoretical curiosity. Theory in its classical guise was, as we have already had occasion to note, contemplative rather than experimental, which meant that the ancients refrained from doing more than passively "reading" a cosmos whose objective existence they did not doubt. What made it even more inimical to the full unleashing of curiosity was the assumption that such contemplation could produce human happiness, an assumption itself tied to the belief, still held by many medieval thinkers, that knowledge of the Truth was the road to contentment. In this sense, both classical and medieval theory could be called "pragmatic," for its ultimate goal was not knowledge per se, but the happiness its possession would bring. But this kind of pragmatism, which perhaps can be traced back as far as the Socratic quest for the good life, proved hostile to any kind of knowledge that does not translate into personal fulfillment. Thus, Blumenberg concludes, it created an impediment, more passive than active, to the complete valorization of human curiosity no matter what its purpose.

With the Stoics, Blumenberg argues, came a further obstacle to unlimited curiosity. Far more skeptical than their predecessors about the possibility of achieving a human version of divine truth, they preached against the inevitable disappointment that seeking it would engender. Instead of an open-minded and open-eyed contemplation of the world, they counseled a therapeutic form of ataraxia, in which disillusionment is avoided by a preemptive refusal to seek the truth at all. For the Stoics, Blumenberg writes, "intellectual curiosity is now the disastrous drive that misleads us into violating the boundary settlement between the human and the divine sphere" (p. 264). Although Christian thinkers like Augustine had to work their way through the skeptical implications of this doctrine, they nonetheless did not come to accept theoretical curiosity as a viable alternative. For now the road to happiness was understood to be through faith, not philosophy and certainly not science. Augustine was particularly uneasy about worldly curiosity because of its potential to distract man from his proper sacred concerns. Moreover, insofar as legitimate knowledge comes only from its rightful author—here the Platonic residue was still potent—the Truth can be grasped not by examining the world through the fallible senses, but rather through the unmediated acceptance of God's word. What Augustine damned as "ocular desire" (p. 312), because it led man into temptation, was thus as far removed from the classical emphasis on contemplative vision as the modern stress on its experimental counterpart.

Although the Scholastics were poised ambiguously between Aristotle's affirmation of a contemplative knowledge of the cosmos and Augustine's warning against all curiosity as a vice, it was not really until the modern age that the verdict of the "trial" was finally rendered in favor of unconstrained curiosity. One major reason for the change was the uncoupling of happiness and salvation from knowledge, which followed the growing popularity of the doctrine of predestination prepared by the nominalists and brought to a head by John Calvin. For if man's redemption had nothing to do with his practical life on earth, then it was unnecessary to be so anxious about the distracting effects of curiosity about allegedly superfluous matters. In addition, the growing hiddenness of God in the early modern era meant the world could no longer be passively read as a divine text. A Deus Absconditus meant a "speechless" world lacking the marks of the divine word, a world as a result open to man's own constructs and manipulations.

The vindication of curiosity was therefore closely linked to the emergence of self-assertion as an alternative answer to the still unresolved Gnostic question of the meaning of an imperfect and corrupt world. Only when the qualitative knowledge assumed to be the analogue of divine wisdom was abandoned as a goal and replaced by an inevitably imperfect knowledge expressed in quantitative terms could modern science begin. Only then could man break through the forbidding Pillars of Hercules standing as the image of transgression as far back as the *Odyssey* and embark, as the famous title page of Bacon's *Instauratio Magna* implies, on uncharted seas.

Moreover, only when personal happiness was decisively severed from the collective pursuit of a truth that could be sought but never completely won, only when the hope for immortality was displaced from the individual soul to the species as a whole, only then could curiosity be utterly without limits. As such, it could then be extended from nature to man himself by philosophers like Thomas Hobbes and projected by others like Ludwig Feuerbach into a desire to know what is not yet knowable. Faust's famous pact with the devil, an early modern invention that expressed a still ambiguous attitude towards the "vice" of curiosity, could ultimately become a triumphant symbol of modern man's insatiable desire to know, which Sigmund Freud would later naturalize into a sublimation of an infantile sexual curiosity to see.

If Faust was a fictional figure at the cusp of the medieval and modern, there are two genuine historical thinkers Blumenberg takes to be exemplary of attitudes on each side of the divide. The fourth section of *The Legitimacy of the Modern Age* is devoted to a comparison of Nicholas of Cusa and Giordano Bruno as representative of their respective epochs. Beginning with a subtle discussion of the necessity of conceptualizing history in epochal terms in order to avoid an anachronistic historicism, Blumenberg uses each figure to illuminate the oppositions that he claims distinguish the modern from its predecessor. Scholars better versed than I in the works of the Cusan and the Nolan, as Blumenberg calls them, will doubtless find enormous stimulation in his reading of their place in the grand drama of epochal change outlined in this remarkable book. Indeed, it is safe to say that the wealth of analytical insights into an astonishingly wide range of topics and thinkers in Blumenberg's work should make it required reading for anyone seriously concerned with the course of Western civilization.

Beneath the richly textured surface of his argument, there are, however, certain main themes that can be brought into the light of critical scrutiny even by someone lacking the breadth and depth of his erudition. It is particularly rewarding to examine these in the context of the recent debate over post-modernity, to which we have already alluded.

First and most obvious is Blumenberg's challenge to the widely shared secularization thesis. It seems clear that he had dealt a death blow to the thesis in its strong form. For although his various arguments may have differing degrees of plausibility, taken as a whole, they make it impossible to return to the assumption that modernity *tout court* is little more than an illegitimate transfiguration of religious substance into profane form. Doubts, however, may be raised about the extent to which the argument still stands in its weaker form. For example, Blumenberg's emphasis on the fears rather than hopes of the early Christian eschatologists is convincing, but it perhaps underplays the persistence of another, more optimistic Christian tradition which may well have anticipated the later doctrine of progress in certain respects. Although admittedly heterodox, the millenarianism associated with figures like Joachim of Fiore, a figure strangely ignored by Blumenberg, may still be accounted a substantialist rather than merely functionalist link with secular utopias of the modern age. The same might be said of Jewish messianic traditions, such as the Sabbatianism of whose power Gershom Scholem had made us all so aware.

It is, in fact, only by acknowledging the continuities between these future rather than past-oriented eschatologies in the religious legacy that we can make sense of such modern figures as the great utopian Marxist, Ernst Bloch, who is also virtually missing from Blumenberg's account. For unlike Löwith and other secularization theorists who turn their arguments against the modern era's claim to legitimacy, Bloch praises rather than condemns the modern precisely for its transfiguration of religious substance into profane form. Blumenberg is, of course, correct in emphasizing the role of memory rather than hope in Augustine and other Christian thinkers, but in the hands of a Bloch—and here one might add other twentieth-century figures like Walter Benjamin and Herbert Marcuse—memory and hope could be yoked together for forward-looking purposes. All these thinkers were, to be sure, deeply suspicious of bourgeois notions of gradual and evolutionary progress, but they were nonetheless willing to secularize the explosively utopian potential of the religious past. Perhaps because Blumenberg is so sensitive to the debunking function of the secularization thesis, he underestimates its possibly legitimating role in the hands of those who want to preserve the emancipatory moment in the pre- and even counter-Enlightenment past for radical purposes in the present.

As for Blumenberg's highly imaginative and brilliantly argued alternative, the reoccupation thesis, here too a possible objection might be raised. For if I've understood him correctly (not always an easy task), there may be a contradiction between the weight he assigns to the nominalist demolition of the Scholastic faith in a rational and intelligible world and the importance he claims elsewhere for the modern belief in the regularity of the natural order. The latter is evident, for example, in the importance of astronomy in the great exploration of the early modern period, the very same astronomy whose bold claim to foretell the celestial future was denounced, as he notes, by Augustine for checking God's will. Faith in the regularity of nature was also apparent in the valorization of theoretical and experimental curiosity by early modern defenders of the scientific method like Bacon. As Blumenberg himself admits "For Bacon, the great world hide-and-seek of the hidden God of late-medieval nominalism, which Descartes intensified into the suspicion of the universal deception of a *Dieu trompeur* [deceiving God] and sought to break through by grounding all certainty on absolute subjectivity, has exactly the innocence of a game laid out with the goal of eventual discovery and solution and free of any suggestion of jealousy of man's insight into the secret of the creation" (p. 387). It would indeed be difficult to know what men could be curious about, if there were no sense of a reality to be discovered and not merely posited by self-assertion.

Blumenberg might, of course, reply that Bacon's residual desire for a correspondence theory of truth marks him as only a transitional figure, as we have seen him claim for Descartes. But it would be difficult to demonstrate the endpoint of the transition, insofar as the battle between realist and conventionalist accounts of science still continues to rage well into the twentieth century. The seriousness of Albert Einstein's often quoted remark about God not playing with dice shows the continuing power of the correspondence theory among many scientists even in our own day. Although this observation by no means undercuts Blumenberg's contention about the liberating effects of the nominalist road to the hidden God, it shows that too unnuanced a reliance on self-assertion to describe the modern age is not without its problems.

If one were, however, to point to what may be the most vulnerable element in the reoccupation thesis, it might well be the concept of self-assertion itself. Here the post-modernist critique of the modern may perhaps be useful, for one of its major targets is the relatively unreflective notion of selfhood or subjectivity in the discourse of modernity. What actually is the self whose assertion, according to Blumenberg, marks the modern turn? Interestingly, he himself implicitly undercuts one typically modern concept of the self in his denigration of the importance of individual happiness and salvation in the scientific method. As he explicitly notes, without pausing to ponder the potential dangers to personal rights in the formula, "in the progress of knowledge, individuals are only functionaries, who operate within the totality of the process as transmitters, without ever partaking of this totality" (p. 444).

In identifying as much as he apparently does with this functionalist view of individuality, which relativizes the value of personal happiness, Blumenberg shows himself to be even more in the tradition of German Idealism than he does by his utter indifference to materialist explanations of historical change. For the self that is doing the asserting is essentially a transcendental one developing itself over time, engaging in what might be called a species *Bildung*. Blumenberg admits as much when he points to Kant's critical philosophy as the culmination of self-assertion, opening, as it does, the uncompleted future as the arena for human mastery and self-expression.

But what if the transcendental subject itself can be understood as a transfiguration of the divine self? This, of course, is the argument of certain secularization theorists like Heidegger and Carl Schmitt, the latter turning it also against the Romantic subject in his famous study of political romanticism.[7] It has been brought to an even finer point in the antihumanism of such recent thinkers as Foucault, Louis Althusser, Gilles Deleuze, and Jacques Derrida, who have contributed to the postmodernist sensibility. Blumenberg is, needless to say, aware of the critique of the transcendental subject in Heidegger and others, but nowhere in *The Legitimacy of the Modern Age* does he offer a plausible account of its origins. Who is the "man" who "posits his existence in a historical situation," to cite once again his definition of self-assertion? In fact, the question also arises, might there be a substantialist and not merely functionalist link between modern humanism and the Gnostic version of a deity who confronts a world that is utterly contingent and irrational? This, of course, is the argument of the conservative political theorist Eric Voegelin, whose claim that the modern age "would be better entitled the Gnostic age" Blumenberg quotes approvingly without probing its full implications (p. 126).

One of these implications is made clear in the work of another famous student of Gnosticism, Hans Jonas, who has explored the affinities among this ancient doctrine, modern science, and modern philosophies of nihilism like existentialism.[8] Unlike classical theory with its passive, but nonetheless worshipful attitude towards nature, all of these movements express a contempt for the natural world, which is denuded of all intrinsic worth. Perhaps because Blumenberg is so intent on finding a legitimacy for the modern epoch in terms of self-assertion, he never really addresses the domination of nature which it entails. Perhaps, as he intimates, Max Horkheimer and Theodor Adorno may have been in error in projecting the origins of that domination all the way back to a dialectic of enlightenment beginning with the dawn of Western civilization; perhaps Heidegger may have exaggerated in dating the fall to the collapse of pre-Socratic philosophy; but surely they were on to something in deploring the rise of an aggressive self treating the world as nothing more than a means to human ends. Blumenberg himself indicates he shares some of this feeling when he points to the cost of functionalizing theory into a tool for arbitrarily selected purposes. But he then backs away from the full implications of the argument that technology has become virtually autonomous in the modern era, rejecting the imputation that "purposes posited by a *technical* will must play the primary and motivating role for the technical process" (p. 200). It is not so much the "must" as the "can" that the critics of technological self-assertion worry about.

Blumenberg, to be sure, is not trying to legitimate every aspect of modernity, but rather merely attempting to establish its relative autonomy—in substantialist, not functionalist terms—from the era that preceded it. But interestingly, by remaining on the ground of the legitimation problem itself, Blumenberg may be revealing the extent to which he remains very much within the modernist camp. For if, as he persuasively shows, the very idea of a discrete epoch needing such grounding is modern rather than classical or medieval, one of the earmarks of a possible epochal shift into the post-modern is a crisis of the very concept of legitimacy itself. Indeed, to return to Jean-François Lyotard's *Postmodern Condition*, one of its targets is the thesis of a legitimation crisis, most elaborately developed by Habermas. Although his claim that the idea of legitimacy can be traced back as far as Plato's legislator, who joins in himself the right to decide what is both good and true, may not hold up against Blumenberg's account of the modernness of the problematic, his more general point is worth pondering. For what Lyotard calls into question is the grand narrative or mythic self-representation of modern self-assertion as a possible ground for legitimacy. The master idea of humanity as a collective, universal metasubject, which is so important for Blumenberg's defense of the modern, is precisely what post-modernists like Lyotard decry as itself incapable of legitimation. They do so, not merely because, as Adorno and others have warned, there is a link between such subjects and coercive terror, but also because the very role of grand narratives as a device of legitimation is problematic. Although even the post-structuralists find it difficult to avoid telling stories—what, after all, is Foucault's account of the rise of the carceral society or the discourse of sexuality, if not a kind of narrative?—they do so without claiming that legitimation can be derived from the tales they tell, or indeed from any others as well.

It may, of course, seem premature to abandon all need for legitimation, just as it may appear dangerous to celebrate the putative death of the subject without pausing to consider its replacement. The metasubject of the Idealist tradition, whose self-assertion Blumenberg identifies with the modern age, may no longer be viable, but some other more nuanced notion of intersubjectivity of the kind developed in the work of, say, Habermas might be a worthy successor. Still, what does seem clear is that the modern attempt to answer the vexing questions posed by Gnosticism through the means Blumenberg so fascinatingly explores has now foundered. Although its outline can now only be dimly perceived, the new occupant of the site it is rapidly vacating will have to provide yet a new response to the Gnostic challenge whose importance for Western culture Blumenberg has shown to be so decisive. It is no small tribute to *The Legitimacy of the Modern Age* that for the first time, we can appreciate how high the stakes are and how demanding the task really will be.

12
Concluding Unhistorical Postscript

Remarking on the professional pressures to compose a series of occasional papers rather than concentrate on one focused project, Wlad Godzich has recently argued that at least in the case of the late Paul de Man, the results were surprisingly positive. "Whereas some scholars live in a tragic mode, the disjunction between what they consider their proper intellectual pursuits and the demands made upon them by their profession, Paul de Man had come to think of this disjunction as the relation between the contingency of the historical and the necessity of coherent thought, with the former imposing a salutary heterogeneity upon the latter's inevitable drift toward single-minded totalization."[1]

Although it would be foolishly immodest to measure the essays assembled in the present collection against those comprising de Man's *Blindness and Insight*, *Allegories of Reading*, or *The Resistance to Theory*, Godzich's observation seems especially apt here as well. For the pieces in *Fin-de-siècle Socialism* were all composed in the shadow of a larger, unified study whose theme was in fact the crisis of totalization itself, most notably in the tradition of Western Marxism.[2] Thus, although that work was conceived as a holistic narrative tracing the collapse of most versions of holism, these disjointed essays provide a more allegorically appropriate expression of such a history. Their very heterogeneity, in other words, bespeaks the difficulty of composing a totalized account of the crisis of totalization. As such, they can be construed as inadvertently proving the "failure" of that attempt.

In the case of a deconstructionist like de Man, such a "failure" provided welcome confirmation of a larger argument about the impossibility of any form of totality. As Godzich notes of de Man's own scattered essays, "he drew a certain pleasure from the ironies that attended their publication."[3] But as will have become clear to the reader of the present collection, no such unalloyed glee in the undoing of my own synthesizing inclinations can be assumed. For in many instances, the essays themselves express uneasiness with the obsessively detotalizing implications of deconstruction or other programmatically anti-holistic schools of thought. As such, they come closer than those of de Man to the mood of such earlier defenders of the essay form as Georg Lukács and Theodor Adorno, who recognized the costs as well as the necessity—at least at the moment—of such a stylistic imperative.[4]

There is, therefore, a certain tension in this collection between its non-totalized, heterogeneous structure and its author's reluctance to abandon entirely the impulse toward at least some larger, synoptic coherence. Indeed, the very attempt to compose this concluding postscript suggests such an impulse, which is, however, implicitly undercut by its title's reference to Kierkegaard's anti-totalizing attack on Hegel. Substantively, the same tension is played out in terms of an alternative that, without any premeditation, runs throughout many of the discrete pieces. Although not always couched in precisely the same terms, it might be called the struggle between redemptive and communicative notions of wholeness. Several of the essays address attempts to defend a strongly normative notion of totalization, which, even in secular contexts, carries with it connotations of redemption. Others examine, usually with some sympathy, less grandiose notions of coherence and consensus, grounded in communicative rationality. None embraces a fully anti-holistic ethic of radical heterogeneity and transgressive dissemination as the only antidote to the failures of redemptive thinking.

This pattern is evident in the earliest of the essays, "Vico and Western Marxism," written for a colloquium on Giambattista Vico and Venice in 1978.[5] Its theme is the initial adoption and then progressive disillusionment with the *verum-factum* principle as a grounding assumption of a radical epistemology. Such a premise was at the heart of Western Marxism at its most redemptive, when the neo-Hegelian hope for an identical subject-object in the proletariat was still considered viable as an answer to reification and alienation. But abandoning it, the essay suggests in conclusion, need not lead to resignation in the face of the discontents it was introduced to remedy.

In the two essays devoted to the sociologist Alvin W. Gouldner, the first a tribute written for a special memorial issue of *Theory and Society* in 1982, the second, a consideration of his posthumously published *Against Fragmentation* four years later,[6] the same theme appears in somewhat displaced form. Rather than a contest between redemptive and communicative rationalist moments within Marxism, it is expressed in terms of a tension between Gouldner's "outlaw Marxism" and his adherence to many of the tenets of "bourgeois" sociology. Gouldner's inability to force a reconciliation between these two traditions was manifest even against his overt intentions, as the latter essay tried to demonstrate. For all his hopes in the intellectuals as a "flawed universal class," replacing the proletariat as the totalizer of history, he always stopped short of assigning it a fully redemptive function.

Similarly, the essay comparing Max Horkheimer and Siegfried Kracauer's respective attitudes toward mass culture, prepared for a conference in Konstanz, Germany in 1984,[7] traced the decline of the long-standing German fascination with the aesthetic as a placeholder for a future cultural redemption. By identifying their different approaches to the relationship between art and mass culture with the modernist and avant-garde projects, as formulated by Peter Bürger, and then arguing that neither succeeded in keeping alive the goal of aesthetic redemption, the essay concluded that the Western Marxist faith in what Herbert Marcuse would have called "the aesthetic dimension"[8] could no longer be confidently held.

A final essay that dealt with the crisis of redemptive politics, this time more explicitly than before, is the most recent, written for a conference in Gröningen, Holland in 1987 organized to discuss the future of socialism.[9] In "Fin-de-siècle Socialism," the widespread collapse, even on the left, of the belief that a new mode of production would necessarily produce a radically differerent and fully emancipated form of life is compared to a similar crisis of bourgeois expectations at the end of the nineteenth century. Whereas the latter, however, often led to a search for new forms of cultural or political redemption—including, of course, socialist versions—its more recent counterpart, our own fin-de-siècle socialism, is far less inclined to indulge such yearnings. The sad experience of the twentieth century, in which redemptive politics has so often led to dystopian results, has had its sobering effect.

At the same time as these and other essays in this collection register a cooling of what Ernst Bloch liked to call the "warm current" of Marxism, they also express a strong reluctance to toss the baby out with the now tepid bathwater. This is, they resist the more quietistic and despairing implications of a resolutely anti-totalizing discourse, which repudiates all attempts at narrative coherence or synoptic theorizing as inherently repressive. As such, they point toward a possible alternative beyond the deconstructionist polarization between "a salutary heterogeneity" and "a single-minded totalization" (a binary opposition that deconstruction itself would be the first to decry, even if it refuses to posit a way outside it).

Thus, for example, "Hierarchy and the Humanities," an essay defending the radical implications of the normally conservative idea of hierarchy (prepared for a Canadian national conference on the humanities in 1983[10]), takes as its target the indiscriminate leveling of all differences in value in the name of either Christian populism or deconstructionist Marxism. Similarly, the long review essay on Hans Blumenberg's *Legitimacy of the Modern Age* endorses his critique of the debunking secularization thesis, which undermines the modern narrative of emancipation.[11] Although Blumenberg is himself no friend of that narrative as it understands itself, he gives us a useful way to conceptualize the continuities of the story in terms of questions and answers rather than transfigured substances.

Of all the essays in this collection, those dealing explicitly with the work of Jürgen Habermas are the most directly concerned with a constructive replacement for redemptive politics. For they focus, as did the culminating chapter in *Marxism and Totality*, on his remarkable attempt to recast the search for a viable concept of totality in a post-redemptive age. Perhaps the most fundamental element in that effort is his struggle to define and defend an intersubjective, communicative notion of rationality, which will avoid the pitfalls of the neo-Hegelian alternative based on the *verum-factum* principle so important for earlier Western Marxists. Because of his stubborn partiality for reason, Habermas has often been accused of being a latterday *philosophe*, building yet another heavenly city of coercive, restrictive, homogenizing rationality. There are, in fact, moments in his work when such an interpretation might well seem plausible, moments in which his anxiety about the threat of irrationalism and decisionism overwhelms his ability to credit alternative positions with anything but sinister implications. Here perhaps his sensitivity to the abuses of the counter-enlightenment in the Germany of his youth makes such a predilection at least understandable.

Read more generously, however, Habermas's project can be seen as transcending such a narrow goal. Despite his unfashionable desire to wrest some coherence from the meta-narrative of Western civilization, he explicitly distinguishes between such a rational reconstruction of the past and any objective historical account of it. And however much he wants to retain a synoptic view of the current whole, one of his most recent collections is significantly entitled *Die neue Unübersichtlichkeit*,[12] roughly translatable as the "new unsurveyability." As for his spirited defense of a communicative notion of rationality, it is important to note that he eschews the goal of unifying all versions of reason, a reluctance which makes him even less utopian than the Kant to whom he is often compared.[13] Instead, he recognizes the legitimacy of non-communicative rationalities, such as instrumental or technical, which have developed their own immanent logic. Because of his sober refusal to postulate a reconciled, harmonious reason embodied in a homogeneous, totalized form of life, Habermas can, I would argue, justly be placed in the company of the more explicitly anti-totalizing *fin-de-siècle* socialists discussed in the essay opening this collection.

At times, to be sure, Habermas has elicited the reproach that his categorical articulation of a non-redemptive totality nonetheless works to shut out all disruptive "noise" from his system. My own expression of this concern appeared in "Habermas and Modernism," which probed the implications of his underdeveloped notion of aesthetics and aesthetic rationalization. If the redemptive mission of art as a placeholder of utopia posited by the older Frankfurt School is abandoned, I wondered, what role does it play in the reflective learning process of the species, as Habermas understood it? In his thoughtful and constructive response to that essay,[14] Habermas went a long way toward dispelling my concern, by clarifying the implications of his differentiated notion of rationalization. Although it might be argued that he still failed to acknowledge those aspects of aesthetic experience that defy any concept of reason, he suggestively pointed to ways in which both the tradition of reflecting on art and the production of art itself are not utterly foreign to certain forms of rationalization. As the later essay on "Habermas and Postmodernism" tries to argue, the result is more encouraging than the tacit transformation of art into the ground of all other aspects of human culture by Heideggerian and post-structuralist celebrants of *rhétorique avant tout choses*. For in so doing, he avoids the temptation of what might be called the ecstatic totalization that lurks beneath the surface in the work of writers from Georges Bataille to Gilles Deleuze and Félix Guattari. Such a non-rationalist redemption is no less problematic than one forged in the manacles of a hyper-rationalism.

Just what constitutes a more modest and less aggressive notion of reason is, of course, by no means self-evident. These concluding observations are not the place to attempt a thorough analysis of so weighty a topic, but perhaps a few remarks are in order. Despite the implied uniformity entailed by their sharing the same term, it is important to relinquish the hope for a single common denominator underlying all variants of reason. For in such a quest lies the threat of privileging one variant over the others as the normative standard. It is less dangerous to construe what we might call a congeries of rationalities—formal, substantive, instrumental, procedural, communicative, etc.—in Wittgenstein's familiar term, as sharing certain "family resemblances." If we keep the differentiation of rationalities in mind, remaining open to the possible tensions between or among them, we can avoid the fallacy of essentializing one as reason *tout court* and then using arguments against it as an excuse to dismiss all the others as well.[15]

The second observation concerns the fraught relationship between reason and rhetoric, which in certain of its forms seems at the heart of the deconstructionist critique of rationality, especially in its communicative form. If all philosophy is dependent on an irreducible rhetorical or metaphorical mediation because of its inevitable expression in language, so the now familiar argument goes, then the telos of rational transparency and clarity is only a chimerical hope. Even the less explicitly rationalist forms of hermeneutics, which strive for common meaning, are open to the same charge because of their indifference to the complicating mediation of language's unavoidable materiality.

A useful consideration of this vexed question can be found in a recently translated essay by the figure whose nuanced defense of the modern age I have already mentioned, Hans Blumenberg. In "An Anthropological Approach to the Contemporary Significance of Rhetoric,"[16] Blumenberg postulates the necessity of an indirect, symbolic, rhetorically mediated relation to reality because of what the religious tradition called our "creaturely" inadequacies. "The axiom of all rhetoric," he notes, playing on Gottfried Leibniz's famous phrase, "is the principle of insufficient reason . . . It is a correlate of the anthropology of a creature who is deficient in essential respects."[17] But because we are compelled to relate to the world through the mediation of an inevitably metaphorical and even catachrestic language does not mean the inevitability of an irrationalist decisionism or paralyzing undecidability:

> the principle of insufficient reason is not to be confused with a demand that we forego reasons, just as "opinion" does not denote an attitude for which one has no reasons but rather one for which the reasons are diffuse and not regulated by method. One has to be cautious about making accusations of irrationality in situations where endless, indefinitely extensive procedures have to be excluded; in the realm of reasoning about practical activities in life, it can be more rational to accept something on insufficient grounds than to insist on a procedure modeled on that of science, and it *is* more rational to do this than to disguise decisions that have already been made in arguments that are scientific in form.[18]

In fact, Blumenberg notes, the delaying function of rhetoric, its retardation of immediate decisions because of the need to clarify linguistic imprecisions, is at one with the deliberative process of reasoning itself. It contributes therefore to the communicative rationality that a Habermas would counterpose to the irrationalist decisionism of a, say, Carl Schmitt[19] or the technical rationalism that demands quick and unequivocal results. Thus Blumenberg concludes that rhetoric can itself be construed as a form of human rationality—"a rational way to come to terms with the provisionality of reason."[20] In so arguing, Blumenberg supports from a linguistic point of view what Gouldner always defended from a sociological one: no absolute reflexivity is possible, yet a culture of critical discourse is viable nonetheless.

Although some aspects of Blumenberg's argument are troubling, such as his overemphasis on the Vichian "man makes history"[21] metaphor as characteristic of modernity, his general defense of the compatibility of rhetoric with a modest notion of reason seems to me extremely promising. And if we recall Goethe's famous plea, "Do not forbid me use of metaphor; I could not else express my thoughts at all," which Franz Mehring invoked in his analysis of Karl Marx's style,[22] then such an argument can be seen as also compatible with a fin-de-siècle socialism that no longer tries to ape an allegedly non-rhetorical scientificity.

To draw on the work of Blumenberg in this endeavor is to raise one final question, which the collection as a whole also tacitly poses: what role can intellectual history play in current theoretical debates? Blumenberg's essay is included in a collection provocatively entitled *After Philosophy: End or Transformation?*, which suggests the growing uncertainty of the boundary between orthodox, problem-oriented philosophizing and the historical reconstruction of the philosophical tradition. Aside from a piece by Michel Foucault, Blumenberg's contribution to the anthology seems the only example of work by someone who is closer to the history of ideas than mainstream philosophy. But it is grouped with other essays by several thinkers—Hans-Georg Gadamer, Paul Ricoeur, Alasdair McIntyre, and Charles Taylor—who are deeply sensitive to the historical dimension in all theorizing.

Another recent collection, *Philosophy in History*, edited by Richard Rorty, J. B. Schneewind, and Quentin Skinner,[23] also testifies to the breakdown of the time-honored distinction between addressing perennial philosophical problems and writing the history of thought. In this re-narrativization of philosophy, intellectual history necessarily plays a more constructive and active role than earlier, when it was often reduced to providing quickly forgotten background contexts for present-minded theorizing. If one also contemplates the recent and widely remarked emergence of a "new historicism" in literary studies, following the waning of the excitement over deconstruction, the growing centrality of intellectual history in our current cultural discourse is difficult to gainsay.

One result of this transformation has been a greater boldness on the part of those of us trained in traditional history departments as intellectual historians to engage more deeply in the current debates whose roots we have explored. In my own case, it would be easy to cite specific stimuli to this development. Having written my dissertation and first book on the Frankfurt School, a group of thinkers then on the verge of gaining an enormous international audience, I was inevitably assumed to be an adherent and defender of their ideas, or at least someone with a considered opinion about all of them. Although the range of their work was extremely wide and it would have been foolishly presumptuous of me to pretend to have an informed position on all of the issues they treated, being pressed to do so often enough had its effect. Two encounters in particular stand out in this regard, one with the Brandeis sociologist Kurt Wolff and the other with the Oxford philosopher Alan Montefiore, both of whom exhorted me to reach my own conclusions about the issues I had been treating with historical distance. Although there will doubtless be readers of this collection who wish I had never heeded their advice, it has been enormously challenging to try to do so.

What seems to me far more important than any anecdotal account of this kind, however, is the emblematic way in which my own trajectory has been so often shared by other intellectual historians of my generation. From discussing the ideas and careers of historical figures and movements, we have been inexorably drawn into the contemporary debates over their current relevance. Interestingly, it was often through intellectual history that the more controversial and transgressive ideas of heterodox thinkers made their way into the more respectable halls of the American academy. The reception of Western Marxism, for example, provides an excellent proof of this pattern. Where would our understanding of that tradition be today without the work of such intellectual historians as Andrew Arato, Paul Breines, Susan Buck-Morss, Lee Congden, Mary Gluck, David Gross, Russell Jacoby, Dominick LaCapra, Eugene Lunn, Mark Poster, Paul Robinson, and Richard Wolin, to name only some of the most prominent? Inevitably, their accounts have been deeply marked by an engagement, to be sure not always supportive, with the ideas themselves. The same can easily be said of other intellectual historians like Michael Ermarth, Hans Kellner, Allan Megill, and Hayden White, who have been students of the trends in structuralist, post-structuralist and hermeneutic thought that are so influential today. And when such scholars as

Jerrold Seigel or James Kloppenberg write about historical topics like Parisian Bohemianism or the social democratic and pragmatist movements of the late nineteenth century, they display a palpable eagerness of apply the lessons of their work to contemporary concerns. The result, to borrow LaCapra's phrase, is a "hybridized" discourse that combines attentiveness to the voices of the past with a keen concern for current cultural problems. It is a discourse, moreover, increasingly self-conscious about the challenges presented by contemporary cultural criticism to the traditional assumptions of historical scholarship.

For these and other reasons, intellectual history, which a scant decade ago seemed to be reeling before the onslaught of social history and an anthropologically informed "history of meaning,"[24] has enjoyed a remarkable resurgence of interest. *Fin-de-siècle* intellectual history, it can be conjectured in conclusion, promises to be as lively, experimental and open-ended as the socialism to whose elaboration it may well provide some useful sustenance.

Notes

1. Fin-de-siècle Socialism

1. Thomas Masaryk, "Die Krise innerhalb des Marxismus," *Die Zeit*, 17 and 19 (1898 and 1899), pp. 65–66 and 72–74, 86–87.

2. Georg Lukács, "Healthy or Sick Art?", in *Writer and Critic and Other Essays*, ed. and trans. Arthur D. Kahn (New York, 1974). For a general analysis of the concept of decadence in Marxist criticism, see Matei Calinescu, *Faces of Modernity: Avant-Garde, Decadence, Kitsch* (Bloomington, 1977), p. 195f.

3. David Gross, "Left Melancholy," *Telos*, 65 (Fall, 1985), pp. 112–121. The term was originally coined by Walter Benjamin in 1931 to attack left-liberal writers like Kurt Tucholsky, Erich Kästner, and Walter Mehring. See his "Linke Melancholie," *Die Gesellschaft*, VIII (1931), pp. 181–184.

4. Friedrich Nietzsche, *The Birth of Tragedy and The Case of Wagner*, trans. Walter Kaufmann (New York, 1967), p. 170.

5. Martin Jay, *Marxism and Totality: The Adventures of a Concept from Lukács to Habermas* (Berkeley, 1984).

6. See especially, Georg Lukács, *History and Class Consciousness: Studies in Marxist Dialectics*, trans. Rodney Livingstone (Cambridge, Mass., 1971), p. 24.

7. Theodor W. Adorno, "The Idea of Natural History," *Telos*, 60 (Summer, 1984), pp. 111–124.

8. For a good account of this alternative, see Fred R. Dallmayr, *Twilight of Subjectivity: Contributions to a Post-individualist Theory of Politics* (Amherst, Mass., 1981).

9. Thomas Ebermann and Rainer Trampert, *Die Zukunft der Grünen: Ein realistisches Konzept für eine radikale Partei* (Hamburg, 1984).

10. This argument is made compellingly by Adorno in "Sociology and Psychology," *New Left Review*, 46 (November-December, 1967) and 47 (January-February, 1968). For a more orthodox attempt to reassert the primacy of the social, see Richard Lichtman, *The Production of Desire: The Integration of Psychoanalysis into Marxist Theory* (New York, 1982).

11. Barry Hindess and Paul Hirst, *Pre-Capitalist Modes of Production* (London, 1975) and *Mode of Production and Social Formation* (London, 1977). For a useful overview of the Althusserian moment, see Ted Benton, *The Rise and Fall of Structural Marxism: Althusser and His Influence* (London, 1984).

12. Claus Offe, *Disorganized Capitalism: Contemporary Transformations of Work and Politics,* ed. John Keane (Cambridge, Mass., 1985).

13. Ernesto Laclau and Chantal Mouffe, *Hegemony and Socialist Strategy: Toward a Radical Democratic Politics,* trans. Winston Moore and Paul Cammack (London, 1985), p. 111.

14. André Gorz, *Farewell to the Working Class: An Essay on Post-Industrial Socialism,* trans. Michael Sonenscher (London, 1982). Laclau and Mouffe claim that Gorz should go farther than he does in repudiating the entire Marxist problematic. They argue that he merely fills in the place of the discredited proletariat with a "non-class of non-workers," whereas they want to abolish the very search for any group to play such a dominant role. See *Hegemony and Socialist Strategy,* p. 169.

15. For an analysis of the initial embrace and ultimate repudiation of Vico's principle, see Martin Jay, "Vico and Western Marxism," in Giorgio Tagliacozzo, ed., *Vico: Past and Present* (Atlantic Highlands, N.J., 1981), vol. II, p. 195–212. Reprinted here as Chapter Five.

16. Alvin W. Gouldner, *The Future of Intellectuals and the Rise of the New Class* (New York, 1979); *The Two Marxisms: Contradictions and Anomalies in the Development of Theory* (New York, 1980); *Against Fragmentation: The Origins of Marxism and the Sociology of Intellectuals* (New York, 1985). For an analysis of Gouldner's contribution to Marxism, see Chapter Seven, "For Gouldner: Reflections on an Outlaw Marxist." This essay originally appeared in *Theory and Society,* 11, 6 (November, 1982), p. 759–778.

17. Michel Foucault, *Power/Knowledge: Selected Interviews and Other Writings, 1972–1977,* ed. Colin Gordon, trans. Colin Gordon et al. (New York, 1980).

18. See for example, Clive Scott, "Symbolism, Decadence and Impressionism," in Malcolm Bradbury and James McFarlane, eds., *Modernism: 1890–1930* (London, 1976), pp. 206–227.

19. John Goode, "The Decadent Writer as Producer," in Ian Fletcher, ed., *Decadence and the 1890s* (New York, 1979), p. 129.

20. See for example, Stanley Aronowitz, *The Crisis in Historical Materialism: Class, Politics and Culture in Marxist Theory* (South Hadley, Mass., 1981), p. 124f.

21. See for example, Foucault's critique of the politics of sovereignty in *Power/Knowledge,* p. 121, or Derrida's consideration of Rousseau in *Of Grammatology,* trans. Gayatri Chakravorty Spivak (Baltimore, 1976). For Derrida's thoughts on representation, see his "Sending: On Representation," *Social Research,* 49, 2 (Summer, 1982), pp. 294–326.

22. Jacques Rancière, "La représentation de l'ouvrier ou la classe impossible," in *Le retrait du politique,* eds. Philippe Lacoue-Labarthe and Jean-Luc Nancy (Paris, 1983), p. 90.

23. Claude Lefort, *L'invention démocratique* (Paris, 1981).

24. Jean L. Cohen, *Class and Civil Society: The Limits of Marxian Critical Theory* (Amherst, Mass., 1982).

25. The classical case is perhaps Vienna. See Carl E. Schorske, *Fin-de-Siècle Vienna: Politics and Culture* (New York, 1980).

26. Norberto Bobbio, "The Future of Democracy," *Telos*, 61 (Fall, 1984), p. 15.

27. Agnes Heller and Ferenc Fehér, *Eastern Left: Western Left: Totalitarianism, Freedom and Democracy* (Cambridge, 1986); Mihaly Vajda, *The State and Socialism: Political Essays* (London, 1981); Cornelius Castoriadis, *Crossroads in the Labyrinth*, trans. Kate Soper and Martin Ryle (Cambridge, Mass., 1984) and *Domaines de l'homme: les carrefours du labyrinthe* II (Paris, 1986); Claude Lefort, *L'invention démocratique*; Jean Cohen, *Class and Civil Society*; Seyla Benhabib, *Critique, Norm and Utopia* (New York, 1986). Although all of these writers have different views of what democracy is, they all share a strong concern for the totalitarian implications of its reduction to an epiphenomenon of economic or social forces.

28. Peter Dews has been the most important representative of this trend at the *New Left Review*. See for example, his introduction to *Autonomy and Solidarity: Interviews with Jürgen Habermas*, ed. Peter Dews (London, 1986).

29. See for example, A. J. Polan, *Lenin and End of Politics* (Berkeley, 1984).

30. It can, of course, be argued that a radical, Rousseauist notion of democracy, shorn of any liberal implications, is the forerunner of socialist or communist notions of a sovereign general will. See for example, Galvano della Volpe, *Rousseau and Marx and Other Writings*, trans. John Fraser (London, 1978); Carl Schmitt, *The Crisis of Parliamentary Democracy*, trans. Ellen Kennedy (Cambridge, Mass., 1985); and J. L. Talmon, *The Origins of Totalitarian Democracy* (New York, 1961). These books have very different readings of the value of Rousseau and his socialist descendents. What seems to characterize *fin-de-siècle* socialism is a recognition that the radical separation of democracy from liberalism is deeply problematic. See for example, Jürgen Habermas, "Sovereignty and the *Führerdemokratie*," *Times Literary Supplement* (London, September 26, 1986) and Norberto Bobbio, "The Future of Democracy."

31. Jürgen Habermas, "Die Moderne: Ein unvollendetes Projekt," *Die Zeit*, 39 (September 26, 1980); English trans. as "Modernity versus Postmodernity," *New German Critique*, 22 (Winter, 1981) pp. 3–14.

32. Jürgen Habermas, *Autonomy and Solidarity*, p. 91.

33. Agnes Heller and Ferenc Fehér, *Eastern Left, Western Left*, p. 42.

34. The term is originally Carl Schmitt's. Benjamin used it in his "Theses on the Philosophy of History," *Illuminations: Essays and Reflections*, ed. Hannah Arendt, trans. Harry Zohn (New York, 1968), p. 259.

35. For an account of the collapse of the redemptive project of the avant-garde, see Peter Bürger, *Theory of the Avant-Garde*, trans. Michael Shaw, foreword Jochen Schulte-Sasse (Minneapolis, 1984).

36. A. E. Carter argues that hopes for the return of the noble savage lurk behind the decadents' disillusionment with Western civilization. See his *The Idea of Decadence in French Literature, 1830–1900* (Toronto, 1958), p. 151. The religious revival that attracted certain decadents is another example of their craving for redemption. See the discussion in Jean Pierrot, *The Decadent Imagination, 1880–1900*, trans. Derek Coltman (Chicago, 1981), p. 79f. Others who succumbed to cultural despair sought ways out in mythic politics. See the discussion in Fritz Stern, *The Politics of Cultural Despair: A Study in the Rise of Germanic Ideology* (Berkeley, 1961).

37. For an analysis of this pattern, see M. H. Abrams, *Natural Supernaturalism: Tradition and Revolution in Romantic Literature* (New York, 1971).

38. Theodor W. Adorno, "Spengler After the Decline," in *Prisms: Cultural Criticism and Society*, trans. Samuel and Shierry Weber (London, 1967), p. 72.

39. Joel Whitebook, "The Politics of Redemption," and Ferenc Fehér, "Redemptive and Democratic Paradigms in Radical Politics," *Telos*, 63, (Spring, 1985), pp. 147–167.

40. Paul Breines, "Redeeming Redemption," and Richard Wolin, "Against Adjustment," *Telos*, 65 (Fall, 1985), pp. 152–163. See Whitebook's response in *Telos*, 69 (Fall, 1986).

41. Ernesto Laclau and Chantal Mouffe, *Hegemony and Socialist Strategy*, p. 190.

42. *Ibid.*

43. Jürgen Habermas, *Autonomy and Solidarity*, p. 212.

44. As Jean Cohen has noted, the new social movements "are often defensive and reactive but do not protect preexisting communities from outside incursions. Rather, they defend spaces for the creation of new identities and solidarities." "Strategy or Identity: New Theoretical Paradigms and Contemporary Social Movements," *Social Research*, 52, 4 (Winter, 1985), p. 689.

2. Reflectiòns on the Habermas-Gadamer Debate

1. For a general history of philosophies of language, see Ernst Cassirer, *The Philosophy of Symbolic Forms*, tr. Ralph Manheim, vol. I (New Haven, 1953), 117–176. Cassier's survey is, to be sure, selective and ignores figures like Nietzsche who anticipated the twentieth-century linguistic turn. See also Ian Hacking, *Why Does Language Matter to Philosophy* (Cambridge, 1975), and Richard Rorty, *Philosophy and the Mirror of Nature* (Princeton, 1979).

2. Wittgenstein's fidelity to this view of language in the actual writing of the *Tractatus* has, however, itself been called into question. See Dominick LaCapra, "Reading Exemplars: *Wittgenstein's Vienna* and Wittgenstein's *Tractatus*," *Diacritics* 9 (Summer 1979), 65–82.

3. Wittgenstein's later philosophy was preeminently expressed in his posthumously published *Philosophical Investigations* (New York, 1955); Austin's major work is *How to Do Things with Words* (Cambridge, 1962); Ryle's is *Concept of Mind* (London, 1949). For a general comparison of ordinary language philosophy and hermeneutics, see Gerard Radnitzky, *Contemporary Schools of Metaphysics*, 3d ed. (Chicago, 1973).

4. The qualifier "generally" is necessary because there were and are French philosophers whose view of language is closer to German hermeneutics than to structuralism, i.e., Paul Ricoeur, Maurice Merleau-Ponty, and Georges Gusdorf.

5. For a discussion of Sartre's relative neglect of language, see Dominick LaCapra, *A Preface to Sartre* (Ithaca, 1978), p. 26, and Joseph R. Fell, *Heidegger and Sartre: An Essay on Being and Place* (New York, 1979), 268f. It should be noted that in the decade before his death in 1961 Merleau-Ponty discovered Saussure and began to reflect on his importance in *Le visible et l'invisible*, published posthumously in 1964. For a discussion, see Albert Rabil, Jr., *Merleau-Ponty: Existentialist of the Social World* (New York, 1967), 197–204.

6. See David C. Hoy, "Taking History Seriously: Foucault, Gadamer, Habermas," *Union Seminary Quarterly Review* 34 (Winter 1979), and Hubert L. Dreyfus and Paul Rabinow, *Michel Foucault: Beyond Structuralism and Hermeneutics* (Chicago, 1982).

7. Derrida began the quarrel with an attack on Foucault's *Folie et déraison* (Paris, 1961) in *L'ecriture et la différence* (Paris, 1967). For an excellent account of their differences, see Edward W. Said, "The Problem of Textuality: Two Exemplary Positions, *Critical Inquiry* 4 (1978).

8. J. C. Dannhauer, *Hermeneutica sacra sive methodus exponendarum sacarum litterarum* (1654). See the discussion in Richard Palmer, *Hermeneutics: Interpretation Theory in Schleiermacher, Dilthey, Heidegger, and Gadamer* (Evanston, 1969), 34.

9. On Hamann's views of language, see James C. O'Flaherty, *Unity and Language: A Study in the Philosophy of Johann Georg Hamann* (Chapel Hill, 1952); and Harold Stahmer, *Speak That I May See Thee* (New York, 1968).

10. Although idealism was antihermeneutic, its proponents did not lack an interest in language. Hegel, in particular, was concerned with its importance. See Daniel J. Cook, *Language in the Philosophy of Hegel* (The Hague, 1973). It should also be noted that Wilhelm von Humboldt's very influential theory of language was in part indebted to Kant. See the discussion in Cassirer, 155f.

11. Emilo Betti, *Teoria generale della interpretazione*, 2 vols. (Milan; 1955); E. D. Hirsch, Jr., *Validity in Interpretation* (New Haven, 1967); Quentin Skinner, "Motives, Intentions and the Interpretation of Texts," *New Literary History* 4 (Winter 1972), and "Hermeneutics and the Role of History," *New Literary History* 8 (Autumn 1975). For critiques of Betti and Hirsch from a Gadamerian standpoint, see Palmer, *Hermeneutics*; and David C. Hoy, *The Critical Circle: Literature and History in Contemporary Hermeneutics* (Berkeley, 1978).

12. For a discussion of their work, see Stahmer, *Speak That I May See Thee.*

13. Paul Ricoeur, *Freud and Philosophy: An Essay on Interpretation*, tr. Denis Savage (New Haven, 1970), 26f.

14. For a discussion of Heidegger's philosophy of language, see Palmer, *Hermeneutics*, chapters 9 and 10, and the essays in Joseph J. Kockelmans, *On Heidegger and Language* (Evanston, 1972).

15. Derrida's critique of Heidegger comes in his discussion of Heidegger's reading of Nietzsche in "La question du style," in *Nietzsche aujourd'hui* (Paris, 1973). See the discussion in Gayatri C. Spivak's translator's preface to Jacques Derrida, *Of Grammatology* (Baltimore, 1976). It should be noted that Derrida's reading of Nietzsche is more radical than Ricoeur's in that he denies a desire for ultimate truth beneath Nietzsche's hermeneutics of suspicion. For Derrida, Nietzsche posits an infinite play of metaphoricality.

16. Habermas, *Zur Logik der Sozialwissenschaften* (Frankfurt, 1970); tr. in *Understanding and Social Inquiry*, ed. Fred Dallmayr and Thomas McCarthy (South Bend. Ind., 1977). Habermas's critique was aimed at Gadamer's *Wahrheit und Methode* (Tübingen, 1965); tr. as *Truth and Method*, by Garrett Barden and John Cumming (New York, 1975); several further exchanges are collected, with other contributions, in *Hermeneutik und Ideologiekritik* (Frankfurt, 1971). An English translation of one of Gadamer's replies can be found in his *Philosophical Hermeneutics*, tr. and ed. David E. Linge (Berkeley, 1976); another, with a rebuttal by Habermas, appeared in *Continuum* 8 (1970). The third edition of *Wahrheit und Methode* (1975) contains yet another reply.

   The debate has stimulated widespread discussion; see Albrecht Wellmer, *Critical Theory of Society*, tr. John Cumming (New York, 1971); Karl-Otto Apel, *Transformation der Philosophie* (Frankfurt, 1973); Paul Ricoeur, "Ethics and Culture: Gadamer and Habermas in Dialogue," *Philosophy Today* 17 (Summer 1973); Dieter Misgeld, "Critical Theory: The Debate between Habermas and Gadamer," in *On Critical Theory*, ed. John O'Neill (New York, 1976); Anthony Giddens, *Studies in Social and Political Theory* (London, 1977), Thomas McCarthy, *The Critical Theory of Jürgen Habermas* (Cambridge, Mass., 1978); Hoy, *The Critical Circle*; and Jack

Mendelson, "The Habermas-Gadamer Debate," *New German Critique*, 18 (Fall 1979). See also the special issue of *Cultural Hermeneutics* 2 (February 1975) devoted to the hermeneutics—Critical Theory controversy, which contains an extensive bibliography of relevant works.

17. Peter Winch, *The Idea of a Social Science and its Relation to Philosophy* (London, 1958); A. R. Louch, *Explanation and Human Action* (Berkeley, 1969); Hanna F. Pitkin, *Wittgenstein and Justice* (Berkeley, 1972); for a critique of the work of Winch and Louch in particular, see Richard J. Bernstein, *The Restructuring of Social and Political Theory* (Philadelphia, 1978).

18. Gadamer, *Truth and Method*, 354–355.

19. Habermas, *Communication and the Evolution of Society*, tr. Thomas McCarthy (Boston, 1979), 6. Habermas's confidence in the formal analysis of language's pragmatic dimension seems to stem from the early work of Searle, who has more recently retreated from this position.

20. For a discussion of Habermas's departures from classical Critical Theory, see Axel Honneth, "Communication and Reconciliation: Habermas' Critique of Adorno," *Telos* 39 (Spring 1979).

21. For Habermas's criticisms of Heidegger, see *Philosophisch-politische Profile* (Frankfurt, 1971). Gadamer, it should be noted, also differed with Heidegger on certain issues. For an illuminating discussion of some of them, see Hubert L. Dreyfus, "Holism and Hermeneutics," *Review of Metaphysics* 34 (September 1980).

22. Heidegger, *Platons Lehre von der Wahrheit: Mit einem Brief über den "Humanismus"* (Bern, 1947), 53.

23. This term is Ricoeur's: see his "Ethics and Culture," 156.

24. Gadamer, *Truth and Method*, 264.

25. Gadamer, "The Problem of Historical Consciousness," in *Interpretative Social Science: A Reader*, ed. Paul Rabinow and William M. Sullivan (Berkeley, 1979), 147.

26. Gadamer, *Truth and Method*, 269.

27. See, for example, the mistaken equation of Gadamer and Dilthey by Sande Cohen, "Structuralism and the Writing of Intellectual History," *History and Theory* 17 (1978), 176–177.

28. Hoy, *The Critical Circle*, 77–84.

29. Said, *Beginnings: Intention and Method* (Baltimore, 1975) 324.

30. Gadamer, *Truth and Method*, 266.

31. Gadamer, "The Problem of Historical Consciousness," 156.

32. For an interpretation suggesting Gadamer's allegiance only to the hermeneutics of recollected meaning, see David Halliburton. "The Hermeneutics of Belief and the Hermeneutics of Suspicion," *Diacritics* 6 (Winter 1976), 9.

33. Gadamer has, in fact, written extensively on Hegel. See his *Hegel's Dialectic: Five Hermeneutic Studies*, tr. P. Christopher Smith (New Haven, 1976). For a brief discussion of his affinities to Hegel, see Palmer, *Hermeneutics*, 215–216.

34. Rüdiger Bubner, "Theory and Practice in the Light of the Hermeneutic-Criticist Controversy," *Cultural Hermeneutics* 2 (February 1975). Bubner contends that Adorno's negative dialectics should properly be called reflection rather than theory, because the latter implies system.

35   Habermas, *Zur Logik der Sozialwissenschaften*, 287. In stressing the extralinguistic existence of power, Habermas is making a criticism of Gadamer similar to that of Derrida made implicitly by Foucault.

36.   In *The Critical Circle*, Hoy goes so far as to argue that "Habermas's own later shift toward a linguistic theory of communication as the basis for a *universal* hermeneutics vindicates Gadamer's reply" (124). What should, however, be added is that Habermas does not rely on his universal pragmatics alone to ground his emancipatory interest, but integrates it with several other theoretical schemes which are nonhermeneutically defended.

37.   Habermas, "What Is Universal Pragmatics?" in *Communication and the Evolution of Society*. For good accounts of Habermas's intentions, see McCarthy. *The Critical Theory of Jürgen Habermas*, 272f., and Albrecht Wellmer, "Communications and Emancipation: Reflections on the Linguistic Turn in Critical Theory," in *On Critical Theory*, ed. O'Neill.

38.   Searle, *Speech Acts*, (Cambridge, 1969).

39.   In earlier versions of Habermas's position, the transcendental nature of the anthropological interests he posited (an instrumental interest in the mastery of nature, a hermeneutic interest in linguistic consensus, and an emancipatory interest in liberation from illegitimate authority) was such that a number of critics argued that he had returned to Kant. In the introduction to a later edition of *Theory and Practice*, tr. John Viertel (Boston, 1973), he modified this position somewhat: "As long as these interests of knowledge are identified and analyzed by way of a reflection on the logic of inquiry that structures the natural and the human sciences, they can claim a transcendental status; however, as soon as they are understood in terms of an anthropology of knowledge, as results of natural history, they have an 'empirical' status." And in "What Is Universal Pragmatics?" he specifically distanced himself from Apel's "transcendental hermeneutics" for two reasons: "The idea underlying transcendental philosophy is—to oversimplify—that we constitute experiences in objectivating reality from invariant points of view. . . . However, I do not find any correspondent to this idea under which the analysis of general presuppositions of communication might be carried out. Experiences are, if we follow the basic Kantian idea, constituted; utterances are at most generated . . . Moreover, adopting the expression *transcendental* could conceal the break with apriorism that has been made in the meantime" (p. 24). Despite these disclaimers, some Gadamerian critics continue to talk of Habermas's "transcendental narcissism." (See Hoy, "Taking History Seriously," 94.) Although this epithet, which is actually from Foucault's *Archaeology of Knowledge*, seems to me unwarranted, it is nonetheless true that Habermas's attempt to find a quasi- or nontranscendental vantage point is not without its problems. As McCarthy puts it, "the spectre of ultimate foundations still haunts the theory of cognitive interests; Habermas is not unaware of the problem but seems to feel that it can be remedied (if at all) only to the extent that the future progress of science leads to a unified theory of nature and society" (*The Critical Theory of Jürgen Habermas*, 403).

40.   Habermas, "What Is Universal Pragmatics?." 63.

41.   Habermas's distinction between these two dialectics was developed in one of his earliest works, *Technik und Wissenschaft als 'Ideologie'* (Frankfurt, 1968), as a corrective to the collapse of symbolically mediated interaction into the dialectic of labor in Marx.

42. Habermas's first complete book, *Strukturwandel der Öffentlichkeit* (Neuwied, 1962), dealt with the concept of the public sphere and its historical implementation. His later work on language clearly follows from this early interest in public discourse. See the discussion in Jean Cohen, "Why More Political Theory?" *Telos* 40 (Summer 1979).

43. Quoted in, and used as the inspiration for the title of, Fredric Jameson, *The Prison-House of Language: A Critical Account of Structuralism and Russian Formalism* (Princeton, 1972).

44. Gadamer, *Philosophical Hermeneutics*, 35.

45. Ibid., 34.

46. Hoy, *The Critical Circle*, 130. It should also be noted that Gadamer strongly rejects the accusation that his position is relativistic in its refusal to seek absolutes outside of the hermeneutic circle. Following Heidegger, he sees hermeneutic reflection as allowing truth to be disclosed, contending that "the anticipation of perfect coherence presupposes not only that the text is an adequate expression of a thought, but also that it really transmits to us the *truth*" ("The Problem of Historical Consciousness," 154). But how perfect coherence and the disclosure of truth are to be verified Gadamer does not convincingly say.

47. For a comparison of Gadamer and Mannheim, see A. P. Simonds, *Karl Mannheim's Sociology of Knowledge* (Oxford, 1978), 92–96. Hoy, however, warns against too harmonistic an interpretation of Gadamer's position: "The term 'fusion' (*Verschmelzung*) is indeed misunderstood if it is believed, as some accounts of Gadamer seem to indicate, that the fusion is a *reconciliation* of the horizons, a flattening out of the perspectival differences. Although Gadamer does claim that a *single* horizon results . . . it must be remembered that a horizon is in flux and that the hermeneutic consciousness maintains a *tension* between the historical consciousness (of the past) and the strictly present horizon (*Gegenwartshorizont*)."

48: For a discussion of their criticisms, see Martin Jay, "The Frankfurt School's Critique of Karl Mannheim and the Sociology of Knowledge," *Telos* 20 (Summer 1974).

49. Samuel Weber, *RückKehr zu Freud, Jacques Lacans Ent-stellung der Psychoanalyse* (Frankfurt, 1978). For a discussion of this and other Lacanian critiques of Habermas, see Rainer Nägele, "The Provocation of Jacques Lacan: Attempt at a Theoretical Topography apropos a Book about Lacan," *New German Critique* 16 (Winter 1979).

50. LaCapra, "Habermas and the Grounding of Critical Theory," *History and Theory* 16 (1977).

51. Ibid., 263.

52. McCarthy, *The Critical Theory of Jürgen Habermas*, 353.

53. Mendelson, "The Habermas-Gadamer Debate," 73.

54. Hayden White, *Metahistory: The Historical Imagination in Nineteenth-Century Europe* (Baltimore, 1973), and *Tropics of Discourse: Essays in Cultural Criticism* (Baltimore, 1978). See also the suggestive use of Saussure's notion of syntagmatic relations in George Armstrong Kelly. *Hegel's Retreat from Eleusis* (Princeton, 1978).

55. Hans Robert Jauss, *Literaturgeschichte als Provokation* (Frankfurt, 1970); for a discussion of Jauss's debt to Gadamer, see Hoy, *The Critical Circle*, 150f.

56. Harold Bloom, *The Anxiety of Influence: A Theory of Poetry* (New York, 1973), 152. For a comparison of Bloom and Gadamer, see Hoy. *The Critical Circle*, 159f.

57. Gadamer argues for a kind of surrender when he claims that "understanding involves a moment of 'loss of self' that is relevant to theological hermeneutics and should be investigated in terms of the structure of the game" (*Philosophical Hermeneutics*, 51).

58. Lévi-Strauss once acknowledged that structure could be grasped only from the outside, whereas process and change can never be understood in this way ("La notion de structure en ethnologie" in *Sens et usages du terme structure* [The Hague, 1962], 44–45). It is thus highly questionable to assume the role of a detached anthropologist in examining the history of one's own tradition. See the discussion in Said, *Beginnings*, 335.

59. The same objection might be made against some of the post-structuralists—such as Derrida, who, in Hayden White's words, "is the minotaur imprisoned in structuralism's hypostatized labyrinth of language" (*Tropics of Discourse*, 280).

60. Ricoeur, "Ethics and Culture," 162.

61. Ricoeur, "The Model of the Text: Meaningful Action Considered as a Text," in *Interpretative Social Science*, ed. Rabinow and Sullivan.

62. Hoy, "Taking History Seriously," 94.

63. Gadamer, "The Problem of Historical Consciousness," 153.

64. Gadamer, *Wahrheit und Methode*, 3d ed., 534.

65. Said, *Beginnings*, 343. LaCapra argues that "Derrida's approach does not sterilize utopian hope" (*A Preface to Sartre*, 224), but it is difficult to see how his nihilism avoids just this sterilization.

66. White, *Tropics of Discourse*, 269.

67. For an acute discussion of Habermas's attitude toward nature, see Joel Whitebook, "The Problem of Nature in Habermas," *Telos* 40 (Summer 1979).

3. The Radical Implications of a Conservative Idea

1. Adorno, *Negative Dialectics*, trans. E. B. Ashton (New York, 1973), p. 367. Translation slightly altered.

2. Crane, *The Idea of the Humanities*, vol. I (Chicago, 1967), p. 7.

3. Quoted in Adorno, p. 366. Similar sentiments were voiced by their mutual friend Walter Benjamin, who claimed in a frequently cited remark that "there is no document of civilization which is not at the same time a document of barbarism," *Illuminations: Essays and Reflections*, ed. with introduction, Hannah Arendt, trans. Harry Zohn (New York, 1968), p. 258.

4. Horkheimer, "Egoismus und Freiheitsbewegung," *Zeitschrift für Sozialforschung*, V, 2 (1936), p. 219; see also Herbert Marcuse, "The Affirmative Character of Culture," in *Negations: Essays in Critical Theory*, trans. Jeremy J. Shapiro (Boston, 1968).

5. For a discussion of these distinctions in Babbitt, Paul Elmer More, and other "New Humanists," see J. David Hoeveler, Jr., *The New Humanism: A Critique of Modern America, 1900–1940* (Charlottesville, 1977), p. 128f.

6. Steiner, *Language and Silence: Essays on Language, Literature, and the Inhuman* (New York, 1967), p. ix.

7. Horkheimer and Adorno, *Dialectic of Enlightenment*, trans. John Cumming (New York, 1972).

8. Adorno, *Minima Moralia: Reflections from Damaged Life*, trans. E. F. N. Jephcott (London, 1974), p. 86.

9. The transition from the pre-modern to modern world view in these terms is classically expressed in Alexandre Koyré, *From the Closed World to the Infinite Universe* (Baltimore, 1957). The challenge to the hierarchical ordering of the universe presented by the new emphasis on infinity in the work of Nicholas of Cusa and others is spelled out in C. A. Patrides, "Hierarchy and Order," *Dictionary of the History of Ideas*, vol. II (New York, 1973).

10. Bouwsma, "Intellectual History in the 1980's: From History of Ideas to History of Meaning," *Journal of Interdisciplinary History*, XII, 2 (Autumn, 1981); Michael Ryan, *Marxism and Deconstruction: A Critical Articulation* (Baltimore, 1982).

11. Bouwsma, p. 279. This obituary may, however, be premature. In his summary remarks in a recent volume dedicated to *Modern European Intellectual History*, eds. Dominick LaCapra and Steven L. Kaplan (Ithaca, 1982), Hayden White notes his surprise at "the general air of buoyancy and self-confidence in [the earlier essays]—a pervasive sense that a renaissance of a field that had been, to say the least, recessive with respect to that social historiography which has predominated in our discipline in the last two decades, was in the offing" (p. 280).

12. Bouwsma. pp. 280–281.

13. *Ibid.*, p. 283. The argument that intellectual history should be the history of meaning is now widespread. See, for example, the articles by Roger Chartier and Keith Michael Baker in LaCapra and Kaplan.

14. Geertz, *The Interpretation of Cultures* (New York, 1973), p. 6. The term is actually Gilbert Ryle's but it is Geertz who has popularized it. For a critique of his impact on historiography, see Ronald G. Walters, "Signs of the Times: Clifford Geertz and Historians," *Social Research*, XLVII, 3 (Autumn, 1980).

15. Bouwsma. p. 289.

16. Bouwsma, "Christian Adulthood," *Daedalus*, CV, 2 (1976).

17. *Ibid.*, p. 78.

18. *Ibid.*, p. 81.

19. Bouwsma, "Intellectual History in the 1980's," pp. 282–283.

20. Antonio Gramsci, *Selections from the Prison Notebooks*, ed. and trans. Quintin Hoare and Geoffrey Nowell Smith (New York, 1978), p. 9.

21. Marvin Harris, *Cultural Materialism: The Struggle for a Science of Culture* (New York, 1979), p. 281f.

22. Ronald G. Walters, p. 553.

23. Alvin W. Gouldner, *The Future of Intellectuals and the Rise of the New Class* (New York, 1979); George Konrád and Ivan Szelényi, *The Intellectuals on the Road to Class Power: A Sociological Study of the Intelligentsia in Socialism*, trans. Andrew Arato and Richard E. Allen (New York, 1979).

24. Basil Bernstein, *Class Codes and Control*, vol. 1, *Theoretical Studies Towards a Sociology of Language* (London, 1971), vol. II, *Applied Studies Towards a Sociology of Language* (London, 1973), vol. III, *Towards a Theory of Educational Transmission* (London, 1975). See also, William Labov, *Sociolinguistic Patterns* (Philadelphia, 1972).

25. Quoted in Bouwsma, "Christian Adulthood," p. 86.

26. Benjamin spoke of the Surrealist project as winning the energies of intoxication for the revolution. See his essay on "Surrealism," *Reflections: Essays, Aphorisms, Autobiographical Writings*, ed. with introduction, Peter Demetz, trans. Edmund Jephcott (New York, 1978), p. 189.

27. Ryan, p. 203.

28. *Ibid.*, p. 136.

29. To take just one other example, he argues against Althusser that "for Marx, at least, communism meant human control over human life" (p. 99), but elsewhere admits that "it is easy to see how [Derrida's] emphasis on the passivity of the subject could underwrite a conservative traditionalism" (p. 37). He tries to explain away what he admits is Derrida's exaggerated writing off of the subjective factor by saying it was an understandable reaction against the "excessively subjectivist humanism of the various phenomenologies and existentialisms" (p. 36) which preceded deconstruction on the French intellectual scene. The result is to trivialize the very fundamental challenge to humanism presented in Derrida's philosophy.

30. *Ibid.*, p. 8.

31. *Ibid*, p. 140.

32. Derrida, "The White Mythology: Metaphor in the Text of Philosophy," in *Margins of Philosophy*, trans. Alan Bass (Chicago, 1981).

33. Ryan, p. 121.

34. *Ibid.*, p. 172. Ryan is fond of these kinds of linkages. Thus, for example, he talks of "the circuit that leads from John Searle's reactionary philosophic study to David Rockefeller's bank office, to the torture chambers of Santiago de Chile" (p. 46).

35. Nolte, *Three Faces of Fascism*, trans. Leila Vennewitz (New York, 1969).

36. Ryan, p. 23.

37. *Ibid.*, p. 62.

38. *Ibid.*, p. 99. Yet another example of his conflation of two categories in his argument that the personal should be "seen as already being public, as a social text" (p. 220).

39. *Ibid.*, p. 221.

40. Arthur O. Lovejoy, *The Great Chain of Being: A Study of the History of an Idea* (New York, 1960), chap. II.

41. Emile Durkheim, *The Elementary Forms of the Religious Life*, trans. Joseph Ward Swain (New York, 1965).

42. Sigmund Freud, *Civilization and Its Discontents*, trans. James Strachey (New York, 1961), pp. 46–47.

43. Alfred Sohn-Rethel, *Intellectual and Manual Labor: A Critique of Epistemology* (Atlantic Highlands, N.J., 1977).

44. Michel Foucault, "The Discourse on Language," in *The Archaeology of Knowledge*, trans. A. M. Sheridan Smith (New York, 1972). For a discussion of Foucault's tacit emphasis on the trope of catechresis, which recognizes the ambiguous meanings of all signifiers, see Hayden White, "Michel Foucault," in *Structuralism and Since: From Lévi-Strauss to Derrida*, ed. John Sturrock (Oxford, 1979). In his more recent work, it should be noted, Foucault emphasized power relations more than linguisticality.

45. Louis Dumont, *Homo Hierarchicus: The Caste System and its Implications*, trans. Mark Sainsbury, Louis Dumont, and Basia Gulati (Chicago, 1980), p. 239. See also his

From Mandeville to Marx: The Genesis and Triumph of Economic Ideology (Chicago, 1977), which is the first installment of a projected series of books on *Homo aequalis*. Contrary to Ryan, Dumont argues that holism entails hierarchy, while individualism leads to equality.

46. Ryan, p. 10. See also his argument against Althusser that "the determination in the last instance of the economic is itself a determined effect of a metaphysical and patriarchal culture, which institutionalizes both philosophical and sociopolitical points of authority" (pp. 101–102). Whether or not this causal hierarchy is true, it demonstrates Ryan's inability to escape thinking in hierarchical terms.

47. That it may also lead to nihilism has been argued by Stanley Rosen, *Nihilism: A Philosophical Essay* (New Haven, 1969). Rosen's targets are Nietzsche, Heidegger, and, to some extent, Wittgenstein, but his arguments can just as easily be applied to post-structuralism.

48. An excellent example of Ryan's inability to grasp this possibility is his treatment of reason. "The homology, correspondence, adequation and compatibility between rational knowledge and the rationalized world is not likely to promote anything but an acceptance of that world as 'reasonable'" (pp. 149–150). He bases this argument on the belief that "logocentric reason . . . is by nature asocial. It privileges the individual mind and the individual actor" (p. 154). What Ryan thus ignores is the variety of rationalities that compete in the modern world: substantive, formal, instrumental, functionalist, communicative, etc. That some of these may be in tension with the way in which the world has been rationalized eludes him, as his inadequate discussion of Habermas illustrates. For the latter's distinction among forms of rationality, see *Theorie des kommunikativen Handelns*, 2 vols. (Frankfurt, 1981).

49. For a good summary of the debate, see Eugene Lunn, *Marxism and Modernism; An Historical Study of Lukács, Brecht, Benjamin and Adorno* (Berkeley, 1982).

50. Herbert Marcuse, *One-Dimensioal Man: Studies in the Ideology of Advanced Industrial Society (Boston, 1964)*.

51. Radnoti, "Mass Culture," *Telos*, 48 (Summer, 1981), p. 46.

4.   The Confessions of a Synoptic Intellectual Historian

1. Dominick LaCapra, "Rethinking Intellectual History and Reading Texts," in *Modern European Intellectual History: Reappraisals and New Perspectives*, ed. Dominick LaCapra and Steven L. Kaplan (Ithaca, 1982), p. 55.

2. Dominick LaCapra, *Rethinking Intellectual History: Texts, Contexts, Language* (Ithaca, 1983), pp. 116–17.

3. Martin Jay, "Should Intellectual History Take a Linguistic Turn? Reflections on the Habermas-Gadamer Debate," in LaCapra and Kaplan. Reprinted here as Chapter Two.

4. Michael Ryan, *Marxism and Deconstruction: A Critical Articulation* (Baltimore, 1982).

5. Jürgen Habermas, *Theory and Practice*, tr. John Viertel (London, 1974), p. 40.

6. Ryan discusses Habermas's model of communicative rationality in *Marxism and Deconstruction*, but gets it fundamentally wrong when he claims that "ideal speech is primary, original, and good, whereas distortion is secondary, derived, and bad. Politics must consist of restoring the original, removing distortion" (112). There is, in fact, no sense of an original undistorted discourse in Habermas that must be

restored. Instead, he posits it as a counter-factual telos in speech acts that has only a regulative and not constitutive function. To say, moreover, as Ryan does, that Habermas begins with the assumption of fully integrated egos who then communicate with one another is to miss the stress on the intersubjective construction of such egos in his work, which very deliberately abandoned the consciousness philosophy underlying traditional German Idealism. When Ryan asks "what if Habermas's starting point, the human subject conceived as the conscious, self-identical ego or cogito, is itself possible only as an *effect* of other structures, other networks of events and relations?" (113), he is merely repeating Habermas's own objection to monological theories of isolated consciousness. Although it is true that Habermas posits the ultimate formation of a strong ego as a concomitant of an emancipated society in ways that deconstructionists would not, he does not assume that such egos *precede* the socialization process, a process which in fact is not conducive under present circumstances to producing really mature egos. The inevitable deconstructionist riposte that even the goal is mistaken leaves its defenders with no real standard by which to distinguish between different forms of social relations, which tend to be reduced to variants of the same, unchangeable reality. Ryan's dubious attempt to derive a liberating politics from deconstruction is not a very encouraging sign of its power to generate anything that goes beyond a vague celebration of difference, marginality, and otherness for their own sakes.

7. Martin Heidegger, "The Age of the World View," in *The Question Concerning Technology: Heidegger's Critique of the Modern Age*, tr. William Lovitt (New York, 1977).

8. Martin Heidegger, "The Origin of the Work of Art," in *Poetry, Language, Thought*, tr. Albert Hofstadter (New York, 1975).

9. Galvano Della Volpe, *Critique of Taste*, tr. Michael Caesar (London, 1978), p. 22.

10. John Crowe Ransom, "Criticism, Inc.," in *20th-Century Literary Criticism: A Reader*, ed. David Lodge (London, 1972), p. 236.

11. Friedrich Nietzsche, "On Truth and Life in an Extra-Moral Sense," in *The Portable Nietzsche*, ed. Walter Kaufmann (New York, 1968), pp. 46–47.

12. Stanley Fish, *Is There a Text in This Class? The Authority of Interpretive Communities* (Cambridge, Mass., 1980), p. 48. For still other considerations of this issue, see Wolfgang Iser, *The Art of Reading: A Theory of Aesthetic Response* (Baltimore, 1978), esp. ch. 5.

13. Hans-Georg Gadamer, *Truth and Method*, tr. Garrett Barden and John Cumming (New York, 1975), p. 269.

14. It is, I would suggest, for this reason that a philosopher as linguistically oriented as Wittgenstein could call his own position synoptic, as in the remark from *Zettel*, tr. G. E. M. Anscombe (Berkeley, 1970), p. 83c, which is cited as the epigraph to this paper. For in interesting comparison of Wittgenstein's *Übersicht* with Heidegger's *Umsicht*, see Nicholas F. Gier, *Wittgenstein and Phenomenology: A Comparative Study of the Later Wittgenstein, Husserl, Heidegger, and Merleau-Ponty* (Albany, 1981), p. 80f.

15. Martin Jay, *Adorno* (London, 1984).

16. Theodor W. Adorno, "Subject-Object," in *The Essential Frankfurt School Reader*, ed. Andrew Arato and Eike Gebhardt (New York, 1978).

5. Vico and Western Marxism

1. *Capital*, trans. Samuel Moore and Edward Aveling (New York, 1906), p. 406.

2. Eugene Kamenka, "Vico and Marxism," in *Giambattista Vico: An International Symposium*, ed. Giorgio Tagliacozzo, co-ed., Hayden V. White (Baltimore, 1969). Kamenka's remarks are directed primarily against the introduction to the English translation of Vico's *Autobiography* (Ithaca and London, 1944), by Max Harold Fisch and Thomas Goddard Bergin.

3. Paul Lafargue, *Le Déterminisme économique de Karl Marx*, 3rd ed., (Paris, 1928); Antonio Labriola, *Essays on the Materialist Conception of History*, trans. Charles H. Herr (Chicago, 1963).

4. Max Adler, "Die Bedeutung Vicos für die Entwicklung des soziologischen Denken," *Grünbergs Archiv, XIV*, (1929). Kamenka neglects this important essay in his survey of Marxist writings on Vico.

5. Georges Sorel, "Etude sur Vico," *Devenir Social* (October-December, 1896). According to George Lichtheim, "Sorel came to Marxism by way of Vico." (*From Marx to Hegel* [New York, 1971], p. 101).

6. Many of these commentators were not Marxists themselves. See, for example, Isaiah Berlin, *Vico and Herder: Two Studies in the History of Ideas* (New York, 1976) for a number of these comparisons. Others may be found in Ernesto Grassi, "Marxism, Humanism, and the Problem of Imagination in Vico's Works," in Giorgio Tagliacozzo and Donald Phillip Verene, eds., *Giambattista Vico's Science of Humanity* (Baltimore and London, 1976), and in other essays in that collection.

7. The argument is, of course, elaborated throughout *The New Science of Giambattista Vico*, trans. from 3rd ed. (1744) Thomas Goddard Bergin and Max Harold Fisch (Garden City, New York, 1961).

8. For a history of the tradition, see Perry Anderson, *Considerations on Western Marxism* (London, 1976); see also Dick Howard and Karl E. Klare, *The Unknown Dimension: European Marxism Since Lenin* (New York, 1972).

9. *Adventures of the Dialectic*, trans. Joseph Bien (Evanston, 1973).

10. For a discussion of the validity of Anderson's broad definition see Martin Jay, "Further Considerations on Anderson's *Considerations on Western Marxism*," and Paul Piccone and Andrew Arato, "Rethinking Western Marxism: Reply to Jay," both in *Telos*, 32 (Summer, 1977).

11. Louis Althusser, *Essays in Self Criticism*, trans, Grahame Lock (London, 1976), p. 134–141. Althusser specifically dismisses the link between Marx and Vico on pages 41 and 55.

12. Martin Jay, "The Concept of Totality in Lukács and Adorno," *Telos* 32 (Summer, 1977).

13. Fredric Jameson, *Marxism and Form* (Princeton, 1971), p. 181.

14. Georg Lukács, *History and Class Consciousness*, trans. Rodney Livingstone (Cambridge, Mass., 1968), p. 112.

15. According to Berlin (p. 61), Vico explicitly anticipated the notion of reification which was so crucial to Lukács argument.

16. Georg Lukács, *Soul and Form*, trans. Anna Bostock (Cambridge, Mass., 1974).

17. Georg Lukács, *The Theory of the Novel*, trans. Anna Bostock (Cambridge, Mass., 1971), p. 41.

18. Georg Lukács, *The Young Hegel*, trans. Rodney Livingstone (London, 1975), p. 320 and 545.

19. H. Stuart Hughes, *Consciousness and Society* (New York, 1958), p. 208.

20. Kamenka, p. 141.

21. Max Horkheimer, *Die Anfänge der bürgerlichen Geschichtsphilosophie* (Stuttgart, 1930); for discussions of Horkheimer and Vico, see Eugenio Garin, "Max Horkheimer su Vico," *Bollettino del Centro di Studi Vichiani*, V (1975); Joseph Maier, "Vico and Critical Theory," *Social Research*, 43, 4 (Winter, 1976); and Fred R. Dallmayr, "'Natural History' and Social Evolution: Reflections on Vico's *Corsi e ricorsi*," *Social Research*, 43, 4 (Winter, 1976). Mayer's and Dallmayr's articles are reprinted in G. Tagliacozzo, M. Mooney, and D. Verene, eds., *Vico and Contemporary Thought* (Atlantic Highlands and London, 1980), Part II.

22. Ernst Bloch, *Vorlesungen zur Philosophie der Renaissance* (Frankfurt, 1982); see Giuseppe Cantilo, "Vico e la Filosofia del Rinascimento nella Lettura di Ernst Bloch," *Bollettino del Centro di Studi Vichiani, V* (1975).

23. Karel Kosik, *Dialectics of the Concrete*, trans. Karel Kovanda with James Schmidt (Dordrecht, Holland, 1976), p. 91.

24. Ibid., p. 137.

25. Max Horkheimer, "Zum Problem der Vorraussage in den Sozialwissenschaften," *Zeitschrift für Sozialforschung*, II, 3 (1933).

26. As Bergin and Fisch put it, for Vico, "The kind of making involved in the making of the world of nations by men was therefore not that of deliberate contrivance, but that conveyed by the term 'poet', which in Greek means maker; conveyed at least when once with Vico we have adopted a theory according to which the essence of poetry is imagination, passion, sense, rather than intellect." (Intro. to *The New Science of Giambattista Vico*, p. lii).

27. See note 21. The argument in *Dialectic of Enlightenment* is directed against the type of link between Vico and Marx forged by Berlin when he writes: "So begins the conception of the 'phenomenology' of human experience and activity, of men's history and life as determined by their own, at first unconscious, then progressively more conscious, creative molding, that is, *mastery of nature* both living and dead. In the forms given it by Hegel and Marx and their followers, this idea dominates the modern world." (p. 35, italics added).

28. Theodor W. Adorno, *Negative Dialectics*, trans. E. B. Ashton (New York, 1973), p. 304. In a recent article, one of Lukács's most talented students, Agnes Heller, has come to a similar conclusion: "Making history . . . does not simply mean creating objectifications, but also exercising control over them, i.e., actively participating in the creation of circumstances, conditions, social regulations, laws and events within which social wealth is produced. Conceived in this way, history is not made by men, but only by *some men*. The majority of human beings have the feeling of being mere means through which history acts not only by virtue of some false consciousness, but because *history has actually used them*." ("On the New Adventures of the Dialectic," *Telos*, 31 [Spring, 1977], p. 141, italics in original, translation somewhat improved).

29. *Negative Dialectics*, p. 376.

30. Ibid., p. 354f. For an acute discussion of the significance of the concept, see Dallmayr, op. cit. and Susan Buck-Morss, *The Origins of Negative Dialectics* (New York, 1977), p. 52–57.

31. Jürgen Habermas, *Theory and Practice*, trans. John Viertel (London, 1974). See Fulvio Tessitore, "Jürgen Habermas su Vico," in *Bollettino del Centro di Studi Vichiani*, IV (1974).

32. Habermas, p. 244.

33. Ibid.

34. Ibid., p. 251.

35. Ibid., p. 252.

36. Ibid., p. 303–4; see his *Zur Rekonstruktion des historischen Materialismus* (Frankfurt, 1976) for the most recent account of his communicative theory of society.

37. Hannah Arendt, *The Human Condition* (Chicago, 1958); see Habermas's review of it reprinted in *Kultur und Kritik* (Frankfurt, 1973).

38. See, for example, John Keane, "On Turning Theory Against Itself," *Theory and Society*, IV, 4 (Winter, 1977); and Herbert G. Reid and Ernest J. Yanarella, "Critical Political Theory and Moral Development: On Kohlberg, Hampden-Turner, and Habermas," *Theory and Society*, IV, 4 (Winter, 1977).

39. That Vico himself recognized a difficulty in transforming a philosophy of history into a theory of *praxis* is shown by his hesitation in publishing his so-called "Pratica" in the definitive 1744 edition of *The New Science*. For a discussion of its significance, see Max H. Fisch, "Vico's *Pratica*, and Alain Pons, "Prudence and Providence: the *Pratica della Scienza nuova* and the Problem of Theory and Practice in Vico," in Tagliacozzo and Verene, eds., *Giambattista Vico's Science of Humanity*.

6. The Debate Between Max Horkheimer and Siegfried Kracauer

1. Anthony Heilbut, *Exiled in Paradise: German Refugee Artists and Intellectuals in America from the 1930's to the Present* (New York, 1983), chap. VI.

2. See, for example, the account of Arnold Schoenberg's distaste for Los Angeles in Jarrell C. Jackman, "German Emigres in Southern California," *The Muses Flee Hitler: Cultural Transfer and Adaptation, 1930–1945* (Washington, D.C., 1983), p. 97.

3. Herbert Marcuse, *One-Dimensional Man: Studies in the Ideology of Advanced Industrial Society* (Boston, 1964).

4. John Willett, *Art and Politics in the Weimar Period: The New Sobriety 1917–1933* (New York, 1978); Anton Kaes, intro. to *Manifeste und Dokumente zur deutschen Literatur 1918–1933*, ed. Anton Kaes (Stuttgart, 1983).

5. John Zammito, "Simultaneous Futures and the Berlin Avant Garde," in *Literature and History*, eds. Leonard Schulze and Walter Wetzels (Lanham, Md., 1963), p. 145–156.

6. For accounts of SPD cultural policies in the Wilhelmian era, see Vernon L. Lidtke, "Naturalism and Socialism in Germany," *American Historical Review*, 79, 1 (February, 1974), 14–37; Frank Trommler, "Working-class Culture and Modern Mass Culture Before World War I," *New German Critique*, 29 (Spring/Summer, 1983), 57–70.

7. Helga Gallas, *Marxistische Literaturtheorie: Kontroversen im Bund proletarisch-revolutionärer Schriftsteller* (Neuwied, 1971).

8. For individual discussions of Horkheimer, see Helmut Gumnior and Rolf Ringguth, *Max Horkheimer in Selbstzeugnissen und Bilddokumenten* (Reinbek bei Hamburg, 1974); Franz Linert, *Theorie und Tradition: Zum Menschenbild in Werke Horkheimers* (Bern,

1977); and Anselm Skuhra, *Max Horkheimer: Eine Einführung in sein Denken* (Stuttgart, 1974). See also the general accounts of the Frankfurt School in Martin Jay, *The Dialectical Imagination: A History of the Frankfurt School and the Institute of Social Research, 1923–1950* (Boston, 1973) and David Held, *Introduction to Critical Theory: Horkheimer to Habermas* (Berkeley, 1980). Kracauer has been less well served by historians. For a general overview of his career, see Martin Jay, "The Extraterritorial Life of Siegfried Kracauer," *Salmagundi* 31–32 (Fall, 1975–Winter, 1976), 49–106. A list of other articles on him can be found in the special issue of *Text + Kritik*, 68 (October, 1980) devoted to him.

9. Peter Bürger, *Theory of the Avant-garde*, trans. Michael Shaw, foreword by Jochen Schulte-Sasse (Minneapolis, 1984).

10. *Aesthetics and Politics: Debates Between Bloch, Lukács, Brecht, Benjamin, Adorno*, ed. New Left Review, Afterword by Fredric Jameson (London, 1977); see also Eugene Lunn, *Marxism and Modernism: An Historical Study of Lukács, Brecht, Benjamin and Adorno* (Berkeley, 1982).

11. Conversation with Leo Lowenthal, Berkeley, September 18, 1973.

12. See the discussion in Martin Jay, "Adorno and Kracauer: Notes on a Troubled Friendship," *Salmagundi*, 40 (Winter, 1978), 50.

13. Kracauer was particularly upset by Adorno's editing of his manuscript on "Masses and Propaganda" in 1938; see the letters of Kracauer to Adorno, August 20, 1938 and Kracauer to Horkheimer, August 20, 1938 in the Kracauer *Nachlass*, Schiller Nationalmuseum, Marbach am Neckar.

14. Horkheimer is given the credit by Jörg Bundschuh, "Als dauere die Gegenwart eine Ewigkeit: Notizen zu Leben und Werk von Siegfried Kracauer," *Text + Kritik*, 68 (October, 1980), 8. From the evidence in the Kracauer archive and conversations with his old friends, it would seem that Adorno, Lowenthal, and Pollock at the Institute and Meyer Schapiro, the art historian, and Iris Barry of the Museum of Modern Art's Film Library were all more helpful than Horkheimer.

15. Wolfgang Schivelbusch, *Intellektuellendämmerung: Zur Lage der Frankfurter Intelligenz in den zwanziger Jahren* (Frankfurt, 1982), p. 50.

16. Reprinted in *Text + Kritik*, 68 (October, 1980), 1–3.

17. Heinrich Regius (pseud. for Horkheimer), *Dämmerung* (Zürich, 1934); reprinted in *Notizen 1950 bis 1969 und Dämmerung Notizen in Deutschland*, ed. Werner Bredel, intro. Alfred Schmidt (Frankfurt, 1974); partial English translation as *Dawn and Decline: Notes 1926–1931 and 1950–1969*, trans. Michael Shaw, afterword, Eike Gebhardt (New York, 1978).

18. Cited in Theodor W. Adorno, "Der wunderliche Realist," *Noten zur Literatur III* (Frankfurt, 1965), p. 86. Kracauer willingly accepted this title and in fact approvingly extended it to Benjamin in return. See his 1928 essay "Zu den Schriften Walter Benjamins," reprinted in *Das Ornament der Masse: Essays* (Frankfurt, 1963), p. 249–255.

19. Adorno, "Der wunderliche Realist," p. 94. A similar reproach is made by Heide Schlüpmann, "Kinosucht," *Frauen und Film*, 33 (October, 1982), 47.

20. Horkheimer, "Egoism and the Freedom Movement: On the Anthropology of the Bourgeois Era," *Telos*, 54 (Winter, 1982–83), 51. For an account of the importance of this essay, see my introduction to it in the same issue.

21. *Ibid.*

22. Herbert Marcuse, "The Affirmative Character of Culture," *Negations: Essays in Critical Theory*, trans. Jeremy J. Shapiro (Boston, 1968). Marcuse acknowledges the origin of the essay's title on p. 277.

23. See his early works in *Aus der Pubertät: Novellen und Tagebuchblatter*, ed. with an afterword, Alfred Schmidt (Munich, 1974). Schmidt stresses the importance of Pfemfert on p. 363. Significantly, Pfemfert was very hostile to the cinema during this time. See his "Kino als Erzieher," *Die Aktion*, 1 (June 19, 1911), reprinted in Anton Kaes, ed., *Kino-Debatte: Literatur und Film 1909–1929* (Tübingen, 1978), p. 59–62.

24. Lunn, *Marxism and Modernism*, p. 195–198, 261–267.

25. Horkheimer, "The New Objectivity" in *Dawn and Decline*, p. 97. Horkheimer did not explicitly attack the other avant-garde movements, as Adorno often did in the case of Surrealism. In fact, Leo Lowenthal recalls more ambivalence on his part than on Adorno's. (Conversation, Berkeley, June 1984).

26. Horkheimer, "Revolutionary Theater or 'Art Reconciles'," *Dawn and Decline*, p. 55.

27. Horkheimer, "Unlimited Possibilities," *Dawn and Decline*, p. 19.

28. For an account of Lukács's hostility towards the proletarian novels of the Weimar left, see Russell Berman, "Lukács' Critique of Bredel and Ottwalt: A Political Account of an Aesthetic Debate of 1931–1932," *New German Critique*, 10 (Winter, 1977), 155–178.

29. Adorno arrived in New York in February, 1938 and moved with Horkheimer to Los Angeles in 1941, where he and Horkheimer worked together on *Dialectic of Enlightenment*.

30. Horkheimer, "Art and Mass Culture," *Studies in Philosophy and Social Science*, IX, 2 (1941); reprinted in Horkheimer, *Critical Theory: Selected Essays* (New York, 1972) from which the following citations are quoted.

31. *Ibid.*, p. 273

32. *Ibid.*, p. 274–275.

33. *Ibid.*, p. 276.

34. *Ibid.*, p. 277.

35. *Ibid.*, p. 278.

36. *Ibid.*, p. 279.

37. *Ibid.*, p. 288.

38. Horkheimer and Adorno, *Dialectic of Enlightenment*, trans. John Cumming (New York, 1972), p. 126. (Translation corrected from original edition, p. 151.)

39. See his "Transparencies on Film," *New German Critique*, 24–25 (Fall/Winter, 1981–1982) with an excellent introduction by Miriam Hansen. Adorno did not relax his hostility to Kracauer's emphasis on the realistic nature of the film in this essay, which he claimed had its roots in the German *Jugendstil*'s hostility to subjectivity (p. 202), but he did acknowledge that the montage capacity of film and its ability to interact with other media give it a progressive potential.

40. Horkheimer, "Kunst und Kino," *Notizen 1950 bis 1969 und Dämmerung: Notizen in Deutschland*, p. 11; not included in the English translation.

41. Gary D. Stark, "Cinema, Society and the State: Policing the Film Industry in Imperial Germany," in Gary D. Stark and Bede Karl Lackner, eds. *Essays on Culture and Society in Modern Germany* (College Station, Texas, 1982).

42. Kracauer, *From Caligari to Hitler: A Psychological History of the German Film* (Princeton, 1947).

43. *Ibid.*, p. 10–11.

44. Kracauer, *Theory of Film: The Redemption of Physical Reality* (London, 1960), p. x–xi.

45. Kracauer, *From Caligari to Hitler*, p. 18.

46. Kracauer, *Jacques Offenbach und das Paris seiner Zeit* (Amsterdam, 1937), p. 219. The remark is cited in Karsten Witte, "Introduction to Siegfried Kraucauer's 'The Mass Ornament'," *New German Critique*, 5 (Spring, 1975), 63, where he notes that it is missing from the English translation.

47. Adorno, "Der wunderliche Realist," p. 107. For an account of Adorno's critique of Hegelian Marxism, see Martin Jay, *Marxism and Totality: The Adventures of a Concept from Lukács to Habermas* (Berkeley, 1984), chap. VIII.

48. Kracauer, "Über die Aufgabe des Filmkritikers," *Kino: Essays, Studien, Glossen zum Film*, ed. Karsten Witte (Frankfurte, 1974), p. 9.

49. Kracauer, *Die Angestellten* in *Schriften*, I (Frankfurt, 1971).

50. Kracauer, "Kult der Zerstreuung: Über die Berliner Lichtspielhäuser," *Das Ornament der Masse*, p. 313.

51. Helmut Lethen, *Neue Sachlichkeit 1924–1932: Studien zur Literatur des "Weißen Sozialismus"* (Stuttgart, 1970), p. 103.

52. See note 50.

53. Miriam Hansen, "Early Silent Cinema: Whose Public Sphere?," *New German Critique*, 29 (Spring/Summer, 1983), 180.

54. Walter Benjamin, "The Work of Art in the Age of Mechanical Reproduction," *Illuminations: Essays and Reflections*, ed. with intro. Hannah Arendt, trans. Harry Zohn (New York, 1968). Adorno's response appeared in "On the Fetish-Character in Music and the Regression of Listening," *The Essential Frankfurt School Reader*, ed. with intros. Andrew Arato and Eike Gebhardt (New York, 1978).

55. Kracauer, *Kino*, section II on Soviet Film; Benjamin, *Moskauer Tagebuch* (Frankfurt, 1980), p. 107 and 123.

56. Hugh Ridley, "Tretjakov in Berlin," in *Culture and Society in the Weimar Republic*, ed. Keith Bullivant (Manchester, 1977), p. 154 and 157.

57. Benjamin, *Gesammelte Schriften*, III (Frankfurt, 1977), p. 226–227; Gerwin Zohlen, "Text-Strassen," *Text + Kritik*, 68 (October, 1980), 71.

58. See for example, his critique in *Die Angestellten*, p. 287.

59. Kracauer, *Ginster* (Frankfurt, 1963); original published in 1928.

60. Quoted in Adorno, "Der wunderliche Realist," p.89.

61. Kracauer, "The Mass Ornament," *New German Critique*, 5 (Spring, 1975), 67.

62. *Ibid.*, p. 68.

63. Kracauer, "Masse und Propaganda. Eine Untersuchung über die faschistische Propaganda" (Paris, 1936) in the Kracauer archive. For a short summary, see Karstein Witte's introduction to "The Mass Ornament," p. 62. "Propaganda and the Nazi War Film," in *From Caligari to Hitler*, first written in 1942.

64. Benjamin, "The Work of Art in the Age of Mechanical Reproduction," p. 244. For an interesting account of the fascist aestheticization of technology, see Jeffrey Herf,

"Reactionary Modernism: Some Ideological Origins of the Primacy of Politics in the Third Reich," *Theory and Society*, 10, 6 (November, 1981).

65. Kracauer, "The Mass Ornament," p. 70.

66. *Ibid.*

67. *Ibid.*

68. *Ibid.*, p. 71.

69. *Ibid.*, p. 72.

70. *Ibid.*

71. *Ibid.*, p. 75.

72. *Ibid.*

73. *Ibid.*, p. 76.

74. See, for example, Rudolf Arnheim, "Melancholy Unshaped," in *Toward A Psychology of Art* (Berkeley, 1972).

75. Jay, "The Extraterritorial Life of Siegfried Kracauer," p. 79f.

76. See the critique of post-modernism by Fredric Jameson, "Postmodernism and Consumer Society," in *The Anti-Aesthetic: Essays on Postmodern Culture*, ed. Hal Foster (Port Townsend, Washington, 1983).

77. See, for example, Herbert Marcuse, *The Aesthetic Dimension: Toward a Critique of Marxist Aesthetics* (Boston, 1978).

78. Adorno, "Modern Music is Growing Old," *The Score*, 18 (December, 1956).

79. Horkheimer, "Mind, Art and the Bourgeoisie," *Dawn and Decline*, p. 180.

80. For an account of this turn, see Rudolf Siebert, "Horkheimer's Sociology of Religion," *Telos*, 30 (Winter, 1976–77).

81. Fredric Jameson, "Reification and Utopia in Mass Culture," *Social Text*, (1 (Winter, 1979); Stanley Aronowitz, *The Crisis in Historical Materialism: Class, Politics and Culture in Marxist Theory* (South Hadley, Mass., 1981); Douglas Kellner, "Critical Theory, Commodities and the Consumer Society," *Theory, Culture and Society*, I, 3 (1983).

82. Paul Piccone, "The Crisis of One-Dimensionality," *Telos*, 35 (Spring, 1978).

83. For a discussion of Habermas's attempt, see Martin Jay, "Habermas and Modernism," *Praxis International*, 4, 1 (April, 1984). Reprinted here as Chapter Nine.

7.   Reflections on an Outlaw Marxist

1. Göran Therborn, *Science, Class and Society: On the Formation of Sociology and Historical Materialism* (New Left Books, 1976), 32.

2. *Ibid.*, 31–32.

3. Alvin W. Gouldner, *The Coming Crisis of Western Sociology* (Basic Books, 1970), 504.

4. Therborn, 29.

5. See, for example, *ibid.*, 224.

6. Gouldner, *The Two Marxisms: Contradictions and Anomalies in the Development of a Theory* (Seabury Press, 1980), 374f.

7. Gouldner, *The Dialectic of Ideology and Technology: the Origins, Grammar, and Future of Ideology* (Seabury Press, 1976), xiv.

8. Gouldner, "Stalinism: A Study of Internal Colonialism," *Telos*, 34 (1977–78).

9. It might, of course, be argued that Gouldner's consideration of intellectuals as a "New Class" does represent just such an attempted replacement. There is something to this argument, but it must be remembered that his attitude towards it was extremely ambivalent. "No celebration," he wrote, "mine is a critique of the New Class which does not view its growing power as inevitable, which sees it as morally ambivalent, embodying the collective interest but partially and transiently, while simultaneously cultivating its own guild advantage." "The New Class Project, I,"*Theory and Society,* (1978), 159.

10. *The Dialectic of Ideology and Technology,* xii.

11. In *For Sociology: Renewal and Critique in Sociology Today* (Basic Books, 1973), he referred to it as "certainly the most creative school of social theorists in the twentieth century" (424). And in *The Dialectic of Ideology and Technology,* he remarked, "my relation to the first generation of the Frankfurt School, for and with whom I worked while they were in exile in the United States, has been a lasting, if hybridized influence" (22).

12. See the reminiscence of his former student, John Alt, "Alvin W. Gouldner (1920–1980)," *Telos,* 47 (1981), 200.

13. *For Sociology,* 116.

14. *Ibid.,* 117–118.

15. Gouldner, "Marxism and Social Theory," *Theory and Society,* 1/1 (1974), 23.

16. Gouldner, "Prologue to a Theory of Revolutionary Intellectuals," *Telos,* 26 (1975–76), 35.

17. Gouldner, "The Dark Side of the Dialectic: Toward a New Objectivity," the Seventh Geary Lecture, 1974; special reprint by The Economic and Social Research Institute, Dublin, 23. The lecture is also available in *Sociological Inquiry,* 46 (1975).

18. *For Sociology,* 420.

19. For Gouldner's critique of Habermas, see *The Dialectic of Ideology and Technology,* 138–152 and 157–260. For a spirited defense of Habermas against Gouldner's criticisms, see Ray Morrow's review in *Telos,* 32 (1977). For another critique of Habermas written under Gouldner's influence, see Cornelis Disco, "Critical Theory as Ideology of the New Class: Rereading Jürgen Habermas," *Theory and Society,* 82 (1979).

20. *The Two Marxisms,* 310. A similar point is made in *The Dialectic of Ideology and Technology,* 144.

21. *The Dialectic of Ideology and Technology* is dedicated to Demuth "who knew something of the dark side of the dialectic."

22. Therborn, and Robert N. Nisbet, *The Sociological Tradition* (New York, 1966).

23. *The Dialectic of Ideology and Technology,* 22.

24. *Ibid,* 44.

25. *The Two Marxisms,* 384. See also his article on "Emile Durkheim and the Critique of Socialism," in *For Sociology.*

26. *The Dialectic of Ideology and Technology,* 273.

27. *For Sociology,* 411.

28. For Gouldner's appropriation of their ideas, see especially *The Dialectic of Ideology and Technology,* 58–66. He always stressed that he filtered their ideas through the critiques of Dell Hymes and William Labov.

29. *The Dialectic of Ideology and Technology*, 224–226: and "The Metaphoricality of Marxism and the Context-Freeing Grammar of Socialism," *Theory and Society*, 14 (1974).

30. "The Metaphoricality of Marxism," 389.

31. *Ibid.*, 406.

32. *The Two Marxisms*, 118. It is because Gouldner saw the proletariat as metaphorically interchangeable with other terms that Douglas Kellner is not quite correct in arguing that he "never really examines the role of the proletariat within Marxian theory and the central significance Marx endowed to it in the revolutionary project." "Review of *The Two Marxisms*," in *Theory and Society*, 10/2 (1981), 274, Kellner goes on to quote Korsch's claim that the proletariat was the "empirical and historical foundation of marxian theory," but it was precisely Gouldner's intention to undermine such a literal reading of Marx's work.

33. *The Two Marxisms*, 24. See also his remarks in "Stalinism: A Study of Internal Colonialism," 7–8.

34. *The Two Marxisms*, 14. Gouldner, to be sure, was not the first to suggest that Marxism was internally contradictory or to attempt a classification of its different tendencies. See, for example, Henryk Skolimowski, "Open Marxism and Its Consequences," *Studies in Comparative Communism*, IV, 1 (January 1971), and the debate that followed in that issue and in VII, 3 (Autumn 1974).

35. Gouldner traced this process back to the period during and shortly after World War I, and cited Rodolfo Mondolfo's *Le Materialisme historique d'après F. Engels* of 1917 as the earliest example (*The Two Marxisms*, 250). Actually Mondolfo's work appeared in Italian in 1912, and if Leszek Kolakowski is right, an even earlier advocate of the differences between Marx and Engels was the Polish theorist Stanislaw Brzozowski, who died in 1911. See the discussion in Kolakowski, *Main Currents of Marxism*, vol. II, trans. P. S. Falla (Oxford: The Clarendon Press, 1978).

36. Gouldner's argument is similar to that made by Foucault in his 1969 essay "What Is an Author?," in *Language, Counter-Memory, Practice: Selected Essays and Interviews*, ed. with intro. Donald F. Bouchard, trans. Donald F. Bouchard and Sherry Simon (Cornell University Press, 1977). Gouldner perhaps too avidly practices the deconstruction of authorial property in one instance in *The Two Marxisms* (382), where he credits Marx with Engels's phrase (later quoted and made famous in Rosa Luxembourg's *Junius Pamphlet*) "socialism or barbarism."

37. Sebastiano Timpanaro, *On Materialism*, trans. Lawrence Garner (London, 1975), 129.

38. Engels, "The Role of Labor in the Ape's Evolution into Man," in *Dialectics: A Marxist Literary Journal*, 8 (n.d.), 10, quoted in *The Two Marxisms*, 264. Timpanaro, it might be noted, also praises Engels for the same insight (*On Materialism* 95–96). Interestingly, Timpanaro links Engels's ambivalent Prometheanism to a tradition of materialist pessimism he claims reached a high point in the writings of the nineteenth-century poet Leopardi. Whether or not the connection with Leopardi is important, Timpanaro suggests an earlier source of the pessimism in Western Marxism that Anderson traces to the failures of the post-World War I era and that Gouldner claims arose in the aftermath of the Great Depression of 1873–1896. That earlier source lies in the materialist tradition's anxiety about the domination of nature, which remained a check on the more idealist hubris generally characterizing Marxism's attitude towards the natural world.

39. Gouldner, "Romanticism and Classicism: Deep Structures in Social Science," in *For Sociology*.

40. *The Two Marxisms*, 14.

41. *Ibid.*, 109ff. Gouldner's discussion of the relationship between religion and Marxism is suggestive but underdeveloped. As Paul Breines points out in his review of *The Two Marxisms* in *Theory and Society*, 10/2 (1981), 255, he ignored the religious dimension of Critical Marxism, which was strongest in Lukács and Bloch, in favor of its importance for Scientific Marxism. One might also note that he never investigated the specifically Jewish component in the formulation of Marxism, preferring instead to emphasize with Alisdair McIntyre that it was a partially secularized version of Christianity (122). Surprisingly for someone with his interests in the sociology of knowledge, Gouldner neglected the interesting, if ultimately overdrawn, argument about the Jewish roots of Marxism in John Murray Cuddihy's *The Ordeal of Civility: Freud, Marx, Lévi-Strauss, and the Jewish Struggle with Modernity* (New York, 1974).

42. Alt, for example, claims that "throughout the book, he appropriated Critical Marxism's concern for culture and morality as a weapon against the economism of scientific Marxism" (202). This observation is true, but one-sidedly misses the ways in which Gouldner used certain of the insights of Scientific Marxism to point out the weakness of its Critical counterpart.

43. *The Two Marxisms*, 51.

44. *Ibid.*, 371.

45. *For Sociology*, 425.

46. "The Dark Side of the Dialectic," 24.

47. *The Dialectic of Ideology and Technology*, 294. Wolff's concept of "surrender and catch" has been elaborated in many of his works, for example, "Surrender, and Autonomy and Community," *Humanitas*, 1, 2 (1965). By "surrender," Wolff means a form of "cognitive love" entailing a total involvement with one's subject, a suspension of received notions in approaching it, a willingness to consider everything about it pertinent, an identification with it, and an openness to being hurt in the process. Its opposite, in Wolff's vocabulary "catch," emphasizes mastery, manipulation, and control.

48. *The Dialectic of Ideology and Technology*, 286ff.

49. *Ibid.*, 87–90.

50. *The Coming Crisis*, 111.

51. See note 38. Yet another dichotomy in his work was that between punishment and representative bureaucracies. See *Patterns of Industrial Bureaucracy* (Free Press, 1954).

52. *The Two Marxisms*, 162.

53. For Anderson's defense of the conceptual mediation of the "facts," see his critique of E. P. Thompson in *Arguments Within English Marxism* (London, 1980), chapter I. Anderson, to be sure, insists on Marxism's scientificity, but does so on the basis of Imre Lakatos's quasi-Popperian philosophy of Science. From the vantage point of a more Hegelian Marxism, both Anderson and Thompson may be seen as variants of an essentially "positivist" attitude towards the past. Still, it is questionable to lump all non-Hegelian Marxisms together and call them "empiricist."

54. *For Sociology*, 398.

55. *Ibid.*, 423.

56. Martin Jay, "Further Considerations on Western Marxism," and "The Concept of Totality in Lukács and Adorno," *Telos*, 32 (1977).

57. *The Two Marxisms*, 137ff.

58. Jürgen Habermas, *Theory and Practice*, trans. John Viertel (London, 1974), 40. It is hard to reconcile this statement with Disco's argument that "Habermas clearly casts mature cultural intellectuals, with Critical Theory as their guide, in the role of emancipatory saviours." Disco, "Critical Theory as Ideology of the New Class," *Theory and Society*, 8/2 (1979), 196.

59. Raymond Aron, *Marxism and the Existentialists*, trans. Helen Weaver, Robert Addis, and John Weightman (New York, 1969), 64.

60. In 1914, of course, nationalism showed itself to be the reality behind the internationalist rhetoric of most Western Scientific Marxists. Still, they never found a way to link their new-found nationalism with a revolutionary doctrine, as did their Eastern counterparts after the war.

61. *The Two Marxisms*, 316ff.

62. Interview with Andras Hegedüs (summer of 1980) in *Telos*, 47 (1981), 132–133.

63. *Ibid.*, 135.

64. Andrew Arato, "Civil Society Against the State: Poland 1980–1981," *Telos* 47 (1981).

65. Aside from a fleeting reference on p. 49 of *The Coming Crisis*, Gouldner seems not to have mentioned de Tocqueville in his work. The possible explanation is that conservative sociologists like Aron and Nisbet had been using de Tocqueville as a stick to beat Marxism for so long that Gouldner felt reluctant to join them. Or perhaps he was put off by de Tocqueville's disparaging remarks about the role of intellectuals in revolutionary movements. In any event, Gouldner's evocation of sociology's interest in civil society could have had no better example than de Tocqueville.

66. Paul Piccone, "Alvin Ward Gouldner: 1920–1980," *Theory and Society*, 10/2 (1981), 166.

8. Contradictions and Anomalies in the Development of Gouldner's Theory

1. Alvin W. Gouldner, *Against Fragmentation: The Origins of Marxism and the Sociology of Intellectuals* (New York, 1985), 299.

2. Martin Jay, *Marxism and Totality: The Adventures of a Concept from Lukács to Habermas* (Berkeley, 1984).

3. For a discussion of Gouldner's dualistic inclinations, see Martin Jay, "For Gouldner; Reflections on an Outlaw Marxist," *Theory and Society*, 11, 6 (1982). Reprinted here as Chapter Seven.

4. Gouldner, *Against Fragmentation*, 14.

5. Ibid, 26. Here, it might be noted, Gouldner neglects to distinguish between interests and needs. For a discussion of the difference, which sees the very idea of interest as still beholden to a bourgeois way of thinking, see Agnes Heller, *The Theory of Need in Marx* (London, 1974).

6. Gouldner's most extensive discussion of Bernstein's dichtomy comes in *The Dialectic of Ideology and Technology: The Origins, Grammar and Future of Ideology* (New York, 1976), 58ff.

7. Gouldner, *Against Fragmentation*, 46. Gouldner's assumption that material interests are somehow intrinsically outside of rational discussion is perhaps questionable. As Habermas has argued, it is possible to arrive at some sort of consensus about generalized interests through deliberation, even if these are not assumed to exist before the discussion merely to be recognized by superior insight. See his *Legitimation Crisis*, trans. Thomas McCarthy (Boston, 1973), 111ff.

8. Gouldner may have underestimated Marx's ambivalence toward the Jewish dimension of materialism. As Jerrold Seigel has shown, in works written after "On the Jewish Question," he favorably contrasted Jewish materialism with Christian spirituality. See Seigel's discussion of *The Holy Family* in his *Marx's Fate: The Shape of a Life* (Princeton, 1978), 144.

9. Dietzgen is incorrectly identified as Eugene on p. 13 of *Against Fragmentation,* one of the remarkably few errors in a book prepared by others for publication.

10. Gouldner, *Against Fragmentation,* 174.

11. Ibid., 169.

12. Ibid., 313.

13. Ibid., 158. In so arguing, Gouldner implicitly pits himself against the analysis of one of the people who prepared the text after his death, Cornelis Disco. See the latter's "Critical Theory as Ideology of the New Class: Reading Jürgen Habermas," *Theory and Society,* 8, 2 (September, 1979).

14. Gouldner, *Against Fragmentation,* 187.

15. Hayden White, *Metahistory: The Historical Imagination in Nineteenth-Century Europe* (Baltimore, 1973), chapter 8.

16. Ibid., 149.

17. For accounts of the anamnestic dimension in Marxism, see Christian Lenhardt, "Anamnestic Solidarity: The Proletariat and its *Manes,*" *Telos,* 25 (Fall, 1975), and Martin Jay, *Marxism and Totality,* chapter 7.

18. Gouldner, *Against Fragmentation,* 288.

19. Ibid., 279.

20. On p. 276, he writes, "Marx's analytic strategy for integrating the whole is, I have suggested, similar to Hegel's. Like Hegel, he focuses on a *single* sphere or substance which imposes a monistic integration on a societal whole seen as evolving via its internal contradictions." Here Gouldner identifies Marxism entirely with its expressive totalistic impulse, ignoring its no less important tendency toward a systemic analysis that leaves behind expressivism for a more decentered view of the whole.

21. Ibid., 261.

22. Gouldner, "The Politics of Mind," *For Sociology* (New York, 1973). In a footnote added to the final plea for holism in *Against Fragmentation,* Gouldner himself draws attention to this piece as an example of his preliminary thoughts on the problem.

9.   Habermas and Modernism

1. Shierry Weber, "Aesthetic Experience and Self-Reflection as Emancipatory Processes: Two Complementary Aspects of Critical Theory," in John O'Neill, ed., *On Critical Theory* (New York, 1976).

2. *Ibid.,* p. 79.

3. *Ibid.,* p. 81.

4. For a discussion of this issue in Marx and Critical Theory, see Jeremy J. Shapiro, "The Slime of History: Embeddedness in Nature and Critical Theory," in O'Neill.

5. Marcuse, *The Aesthetic Dimension: Toward a Critique of Marxist Aesthetics* (Boston, 1978), Adorno, *Aesthetische Theorie* (Frankfurt, 1970).

6. Weber, p. 80.

7. See, for example, the essays in John B. Thompson and David Held, eds., *Habermas: Critical Debates* (Cambridge, Mass., 1982), which contain only the most fleeting references to this aspect of his work.

8. Habermas, *Theory and Practice*, trans. John Viertel (London, 1974).

9. Habermas, "Consciousness-Raising or Redemptive Criticism: The Contemporaneity of Walter Benjamin," *New German Critique*, 17 (Spring, 1979); *Legitimation Crisis*, trans. Thomas McCarthy (Boston, 1975).

10. Habermas, *Legitimation Crisis*, p. 78. Much of the same paragraph appears in the Benjamin essay, p. 42.

11. Although this is not the place to launch a full-scale discussion of the relationship between artistic claims to autonomy and the auratic nature of art, it should be noted that rather than simply lengthening the distance between art and life, and thus strengthening the former's auratic quality, the increased focus on art's self-referentiality that grew out of the autonomy claim actually helped to shorten it. This paradoxical effect followed from the demystification of artistic illusion, that "baring of the device" so often emphasized by the Russian formalists, which accompanied the undermining of realistic or romantic aesthetics. In fact, the later argument of certain Marxist aestheticians, including Benjamin in his famous essay "The Author as Producer," that art was another form of production like all the rest, derived in part from this prior demystification. Thus the extreme 'art for art's sake' position led unexpectedly to its apparent opposite, the reintegration of art and life. The only way to reestablish the distance between the two and contend that autonomous art need not turn into its negation was to distinguish as rigorously as did Adorno between artistic productive techniques and their non-artistic counterparts. Benjamin's refusal to do so was at the heart of their dispute.

12. Habermas, *Legitimation Crisis*, p. 85. For Benjamin's appreciation of Surrealism, see his 1929 essay "Surrealism" in *Reflections: Essays, Aphorisms, Autobiographical Writings*, ed. with intro., Peter Demetz, trans. Edmund Jephcott (New York, 1978). There are other possible candidates for the same function, most notably the *Neue Sachlichkeit*. See the argument in John Willett, *Art and Politics in the Weimar Period: the New Sobriety 1917–1933* (New York, 1978).

13. Habermas, *Legitimation Crisis*, p. 86.

14. *Ibid.*

15. Bell's article "The Cultural Contradictions of Capitalism" had already been published in *Public Interest* (Fall, 1970) and was cited by Habermas. The book of the same name followed in 1976.

16. Habermas is careful to note that "redemption" for Benjamin never means "the empathy and identification with the past which historicism adopted from Romanticism" (p. 38).

17. In *The Aesthetic Dimension*, published after Marcuse had read Habermas's *Legitimation Crisis* and possibly the Benjamin article, he reversed his position and did consider these implications. See the discussion on p. 50f. which draws explicitly on Habermas.

18. Habermas, "Consciousness-Raising or Redemptive Criticism," p. 43.

19. *Ibid.*, p. 44.

20. *Ibid.* For a discussion of the shift in Benjamin's position, see Susan Buck-Morss, *The Origin of Negative Dialectics: Theodor W. Adorno, Walter Benjamin and the Frankfurt Institute* (New York, 1977), p. 160f.

21. Habermas, "Consciousness-Raising or Redemptive Criticism," p.46.

22. Philip Brewster and Carl Howard Buchner, "Language and Criticism: Jürgen Habermas on Walter Benjamin," *New German Critique*, 17 (Spring, 1979).

23. Habermas, *Theory and Practice*, p. 241.

24. Habermas, "Consciousness-Raising or Redemptive Criticism," p. 47. The major essays in which Benjamin developed his mimetic theory of language were "On the Mimetic Faculty," in *Reflections* and "Doctrine of the Similar," *New German Critique, 17 (Spring, 1979)*.

25. *Ibid.*, p. 48.

26. Habermas, "Consciousness-Raising or Redemptive Criticism," P. 48–49.

27. *Ibid.*, p. 57.

28. *Ibid.*, p. 50.

29. *Ibid.*, p. 51.

30. See, for example, his essay "History and Evolution," *Telos*, 39 (Spring, 1979).

31. Habermas, "Consciousness-Raising or Redemptive Criticism," p. 58. The full implications of this goal are spelled out in *Communication and the Evolution of Society*, trans. Thomas McCarthy (Boston, 1979) and *Theorie des kommunikativen Handelns*, 2 vols. (Frankfurt, 1981).

32. Habermas, "Consciousness-Raising or Redemptive Criticism," p.58.

33. *Ibid.*, p. 59.

34. Habermas, "Modernity versus Postmodernity," *New German Critique*, 22 (Winter, 1981); see fn. 31.

35. Habermas, "Modernity versus Postmodernity," p. 8.

36. *Ibid.*, p. 9.

37. *Ibid.*, p. 10–11.

38. *Ibid.*, p. 11.

39. Peter Weiss, *Aesthetik des Widerstands* (Frankfurt, 1975).

40. Brewster and Buchner, p. 23.

41. Anson Rabinbach, "Introduction to Walter Benjamin's 'Doctrine of the Similar'," *New German Critique*, 17 (Spring, 1979), p. 64.

42. Richard Wolin, *Walter Benjamin: An Aesthetic of Redemption* (New York, 1982), p. 246.

43. Benjamin, "Probleme der Sprachsoziologie: Ein Sammelreferat," *Zeitschrift für Sozialforschung*, IV, 3 (1935), p. 368.

44. Benjamin, "On the Mimetic Faculty," p. 335.

45. Lyotard, "Response à la question: qu'est-ce que le postmoderne?," *Critique*, 419 (April 1982), p. 358.

46. For Adorno's similar appreciation of the links between the sublime and modern art, see *Aesthetische Theorie*, p. 292.

47. Huyssen, "The Search for Tradition: Avant-garde and Postmodernism in the 1970's," *New German Critique*, 22 (Winter, 1981), p. 38.

48. *Ibid.*, p. 36.

49. Bürger, "Avant-garde and Contemporary Aesthetics: A Reply to Jürgen Habermas," *New German Critique*, 22 (Winter, 1981).

50. *Ibid.*, p. 20.

51. *Ibid.*, p. 21.

52. *Ibid.*, p. 22.

53. Bürger, *Theorie der Avantgarde* (Frankfurt, 1974).

54. Other deconstructionists who attack Habermas for his alleged belief in a rational utopia of perfect harmony include Dominick LaCapra, "Habermas and the Grounding of Critical Theory," *History and Theory*, 16 (1977); and Michael Ryan, *Marxism and Deconstruction: A Critical Articulation* (Baltimore, 1982). McCarthy and Ottmann, in contrast, criticize him for accepting an inevitable hostility between humans and nature. Although they do not suggest the perfect reconciliation that, say, Ernst Bloch would have wanted, they still advocate more of a harmonious unity than Habermas feels is possible. See their contributions to Thompson and Held.

55. Habermas, "A Reply to My Critics," in Thompson and Held, p. 235.

56. *Ibid.*, p. 249.

57. *Ibid.*

58. Habermas, "Modernity versus Postmodernity," p. 8.

59. Adorno, *Aesthetische Theorie*, p. 86f.

60. Wolin argues that "language is *rationalized mimesis*. In language the element of correspondence or similarity is wrested away from its primordial state of undifferentiated immediacy (submersion in nature) and raised to the status of *expression*" (p. 243). But why this transformation can be called rational is not very clear. Benjamin, in fact, was well aware of the Romantic roots of his onomatopoeic theory of language. See his remarks on Herder in "Probleme der Sprachsoziologie," p. 250. How such a Romantically derived theory can be harnessed for the Enlightenment intentions of Habermas is difficult to grasp. Habermas's conclusion that Benjamin's attempt to marry his mystically derived linguistic theory with his Marxism was a failure can perhaps be extended to Habermas's own attempt to do something similar.

61. Habermas, *Theorie des kommunikativen Handelns*, Vol. I, p. 512.

62. Gablik, *Progress in Art* (New York, 1977).

10.   Habermas and Postmodernism

1. Jürgen Habermas, *Der philosophische Diskurs der Moderne* (Frankfurt, 1985); *Die neue Unübersichtlichkeit* (Frankfurt, 1985); "Questions and Counterquestions," in Richard Bernstein, ed., *Habermas and Modernity* (Cambridge, Mass., 1985).

2. Jürgen Habermas, "Modernity versus Postmodernity," *New German Critique*, 22 (Winter, 1981); "The Entwinement of Myth and Enlightenment: Re-reading *Dialectic of Enlightenment*," *New German Critique*, 26 (Spring–Summer, 1982).

3. Andreas Huyssen, "Mapping the Postmodern," *New German Critique*, 33 (Fall, 1984), p. 30.

4. Jacques Derrida, "Differance," in *Speech and Phenomena and Other Essays on Husserl's Theory of Signs*, trans. David Allison (Evanston, 1973), p. 143.

5. See, for example, Naomi Schor and Henry F. Majewski, eds., *Flaubert and Postmodernism* (Lincoln, 1984).

6. Jean-François Lyotard, *The Post Modern Condition: A Report on Knowledge*, trans. Geoff Bennington and Brian Massumi (Minneapolis, 1984), p. 36.

7. *Les Immatériaux* was presented at the Centre Pompidou from March 28 to July 15, 1985. For a selection of texts reflecting on it, see the simultaneously published *Modernes et Après: Les Immatériaux*, ed. Élie Théofilakis (Paris, 1985).

   It should be acknowledged that in certain of his writings, Lyotard himself emphasizes the impermeability of boundaries between radically incommensurable spheres. See, for example, his dialogue with Jean-Loup Thébaud, *Just Gaming*, trans. Wlad Godzich (Minneapolis, 1985). In the Afterword to the volume by Samuel Weber, Lyotard is in fact criticized from a more rigorously Derridean perspective for being too obsessed with the purity and specificity of discrete language games. Instead, Weber asks him to be aware of their ambiguous interpenetration, that is, of the very ubiquity of *différance*, which is privileged by the postmodern temper.

8. Jacques Bouveresse, *Rationalité et Cynisme* (Paris, 1984), p. 163.

9. Suzi Gablik, *Has Modernism Failed?* (New York, 1984), p. 48.

10. Peter Bürger, *Theory of the Avant-garde*, trans. Michael Shaw (Minneapolis, 1984).

11. Charles Jencks, *The Language of Post-modern Architecture* (New York, 1984), p. 127f.

12. Robert Venturi et al., *Learning from Las Vegas* (Cambridge, 1977).

13. Craig Owens, "The Discourse of Others: Feminists and Postmodernism," in Hal Foster, ed., *The Anti-Aesthetic: Essays on Postmodern Culture* (Port Townsend, Washington, 1983).

14. For a feminist-deconstructionist critique of Habermas, see Gayatri Chakravorty Spivak, "Three Feminist Readings: McCullers, Drabble, Habermas," *Union Seminary Quarterly Review*, 35, 1–2 (Fall, 1979–Winter, 1980). For a feminist critique closer to his own position, see Nancy Fraser, "What's Critical about Critical Theory? The Case of Habermas and Gender," *New German Critique*, 35 (Spring/Summer, 1985).

15. Lyotard, *The Postmodern Condition*, p. 72. This characterization of Habermas is also taken for granted by Philippe Lacoue-Labarthe in his 1982 discussion with Lyotard at Cerisy-la-Salle. See the transcript, "Talks," in *Diacritics*, 14, 3 (Fall, 1984), p. 26.

16. *Ibid.*, p. 66.

17. Dominick LaCapra, *Rethinking Intellectual History: Texts, Contexts, Language* (Ithaca, 1983), pp. 178–179.

18. Michael Ryan, *Marxism and Deconstruction: A Critical Articulation* (Baltimore, 1982), p. 112f; Jonathan Culler, "Communicative Competence and Normative Force," *New German Critique*, 35 (Spring/Summer, 1985).

19. For an account of Habermas's break with the idea of a meta-subject, see Martin Jay, *Marxism and Totality: The Adventures of a Concept from Lukács to Habermas* (Berkeley, 1984), chapter XV.

20. Thomas McCarthy, "Rationality and Relativism: Habermas's 'Overcoming' of Hermeneutics," in John B. Thompson and David Held, eds., *Habermas: Critical Debates* (Cambridge, Mass., 1982); Joel Whitebook, "The Problem of Nature in Habermas," *Telos*, 40 (Summer, 1979); Henning Ottmann, "Cognitive Interests and Self-Reflection," in Thompson and Held, *Habermas: Critical Debates*.

21. Jürgen Habermas, *Theory of Communicative Action*, trans. Thomas McCarthy, 2 vols. (Cambridge, Mass., 1985).

22. Anthony Giddens, "Reason Without Revolution? Habermas's *Theorie des kommunikativen Handelns*," in Bernstein, *Habermas and Modernity*.

23. Martin Jay, *Marxism and Totality*.

24. Jürgen Habermas, *Communication and the Evolution of Society*, trans. Thomas McCarthy (Boston, 1979), p. 130f.

25. Jürgen Habermas, *Der Philosophische Diskurs der Moderne*, p. 361.

26. Jürgen Habermas, "Modernity versus Postmodernity," *New German Critique*, 22 (Winter, 1981), p. 9. Translation amended.

27. Martin Jay, "Habermas and Modernism," in Bernstein, *Habermas and Modernity*; reprinted here as Chapter Nine.

28. Jürgen Habermas, "Questions and Counterquestions," p. 200.

29. *Ibid*.

30. *Ibid.*, p. 201.

31. *Ibid*. For another recent consideration of the issue of aesthetic rationality that draws in part on Habermas, see Martin Seel, *Die Kunst der Entzweiung: Zum Begriff der Ästhetischen Rationalität* (Frankfurt, 1985). Ironically, the inflationary expansion of different aesthetic experiences has itself been connected to postmodernism by Charles Newman. See his *The Post-Modern Aura: The Act of Fiction in an Age of Inflation* (Evanston, 1985). Quantitative increase may not in fact be a fully satisfactory criterion of rationalization.

32. Ironically, despite his opposition to Habermas, Lyotard can perhaps be read against the grain as expressing hope for something similar. Thus, Cecile Lindsay recently writes, "By meticulously unmasking the operations of the various types of metanarratives, by turning the conditions of any narrative back upon itself, Lyotard's work points to a powerful potential for a dialogic situation among genres of discourse that have been kept separate and hierarchized." See her "Experiments in Postmodern Dialogue," *Diacritics*, 14, 3 (Fall, 1984), p. 61. It is of course in a similar direction—without the overly intersubjectivist notion of dialogue—that Weber wants to turn Lyotard in the Afterword to *Just Gaming* cited above. But because Lyotard, like Habermas, is interested in preserving boundary maintenance to a greater extent than the more rabid deconstructionists, he preserves the hope for some sort of actual dialogue. For unless there is a sense of relatively autonomous language games capable of interacting, then all we have is an undifferentiated soup of homogeneous heterogenity, a kind of absolute concreteness that paradoxically turns itself into pure abstraction.

33. Jürgen Habermas, "Modern and Postmodern Architecture" in John Forester, ed., *Critical Theory and Public Life* (Cambridge, Mass.).

34. *Ibid.*, p. 328.

35. See Frampton's "Toward a Critical Regionalism: Six Points for an Architecture of Resistance," in Hal Foster, *The Anti-Aesthetic*. Frampton, to be sure, is no friend of postmodernism and acknowledged a debt to the Frankfurt School, as well as to Heidegger and Hannah Arendt.

36. Jürgen Habermas, *Der Philosophische Diskurs der Moderne*, p. 392.

37. *Ibid.*, p. 393.

38. Jonathan Culler, in the essay cited in note 18, chides Habermas for marginalizing literature and rhetoric in the name of philosophy. One might reply that the deconstructionist impulse in postmodernism is open to the reverse charge.

39. Habermas, *Der Philosophische Diskurs der Moderne*, p. 240.

40. Albrecht Wellmer, "Reason, Utopia and the *Dialectic of Enlightenment*," in Bernstein, *Habermas and Modernity*, p. 62–63.

41. Thomas McCarthy, "Complexity and Democracy, or the Seducements of Systems Theory," *New German Critique*, 35 (Spring/Summer, 1985), p. 50.

42. Peter Uwe Hohendahl, "The Dialectic of Enlightenment Revisited: Habermas' Critique of the Frankfurt School," *New German Critique*, 35 (Spring/Summer, 1985), p. 25.

11. A reflection on *The Legitimacy of the Modern Age*

1. Jean-François Lyotard, *The Postmodern Condition: A Report on Knowledge*, transl. Geoff Bennington and Brian Massumi, foreword by Fredric Jameson (Minneapolis, 1984).

2. I borrow this felicitous phrase from a paper given by Rainer Röchlitz to the colloquium on "Modernité et Post-modernité" at the Maison des Sciences de l'Homme in Paris in March, 1984.

3. (Cambridge, Ma., 1983). The translation is by Robert M. Wallace, who provides a very useful introduction. Although it would be too generous to call it a really graceful and transparent rendering of Blumenberg's cumbersome prose, we are nonetheless deeply in his debt for taking on such a daunting task.

4. It should, however, be noted that post-modernists also sometimes employ the same strategy of debunking the modern by showing that it was "always, already" in existence. Thus, for example, Derrida's critique of the logocentricity of Western thought makes no real distinction between modernity and its predecessor.

5. Michael Foucault, "What is an Author?, *Language, Counter-Memory, Practice: Selected Essays and Interviews*, ed. with intro. Donald F. Bouchard, transl. Donald F. Bouchard and Sherry Simon (Ithaca, 1977). Roland Barthes, "The Death of the Author," *Image, Music, Text, transl. Stephen Heath (New York, 1977)*.

6. For accounts of the role of memory in recent Western Marxist thought, see Christian Lenhardt, "Anamnestic Solidarity: The Proletariat and its Manes," *Telos* 25 (Fall, 1975) and Martin Jay, *Marxism and Totality: The Adventures of a Concept from Lukács to Habermas* (Berkeley, 1984), chap. VII, Bloch's stress was more on *anagnorisis*, the recognition of prefigurative traces of the future in the past, than on *anamnesis* in the Platonic sense.

7. Carl Schmitt, *Politische Romantik* (Munich, 1925). Schmitt argued that Romanticism was a subjective version of occasionalism, the doctrine devised by Malebranche to explain the way in which mind could influence matter. For Malebranche, the explanation was God's intervention; for the Romantics, according to Schmitt, it was the subjective will of the artist.

8. Hans Jonas, "Gnosticism, Existentialism and Nihilism," *The Phenomenon of Life: Toward a Philosophical Biology* (Chicago, 1966).

12.   Concluding Unhistorical Postscript

1. Wlad Godzich, Foreword to Paul de Man, *The Resistance to Theory* (Minneapolis, 1986), p. ix. For de Man's own, somewhat less positive thoughts on this issue, see the Preface to *The Rhetoric of Romanticism* (New York, 1984).

2. Martin Jay, *Marxism and Totality: The Adventures of a Concept from Lukács to Habermas* (Berkeley, 1984).

3. Godzich, p. ix.

4. Georg Lukács, "On the Nature and Form of the Essay," *Soul and Form*, trans. Anna Bostock (Cambridge, Mass., 1974); Theodor W. Adorno, "Der Essay als Form," *Gesammelte Schriften 11: Noten zur Literatur I* (Frankfurt, 1958).

5. The conference proceedings appeared as *Vico: Past and Present*, ed. Giorgio Tagliacozzo (Atlantic Highlands, N.J., 1981).

6. The initial essay was composed as a contribution to the memorial session of the American Sociological Association meetings in Toronto in August, 1981, and then published in the special issue edited by Charles Lemert of the journal Gouldner founded, *Theory and Society*, 11, 6 (November 1982). The second essay appeared in *Theory and Society*, 15, 4 (1986), alongside another consideration of *Against Fragmentation* by Paul Breines.

7. The conference proceedings have been published as *Exil, Wissenschaft, Identität: Deutschsprachige sozialwissenschaftliches Emigration 1933–1945 und ihre Wirkung*, ed. Ilja Srubar (Frankfurt, 1988). The German version has a slightly different opening section.

8. Herbert Marcuse, *The Aesthetic Dimension: Toward a Critique of Marxist Aesthetics* (Boston, 1978).

9. The conference proceedings will be published in Dutch, in a volume edited by Lolla Nauta, the organizer of the symposium. An English version appeared in *Praxis International*, 8, 1 (April, 1988).

10. The papers of the National Symposium on the Humanities, which took place at Simon Fraser University, were published in a volume called *Tradition and Modernity: Contemporary Perspectives on the Humanities*, ed. David Wallace (Burnaby, B.C., n.d.). My talk also appeared in *Telos*, 62 (Winter, 1984–85) and in a shortened version in *The London Times Higher Educational Supplement* (September 16, 1983).

11. It appeared in *History and Theory*, XXIV, 2 (1985).

12. Jürgen Habermas, *Die neue Unübersichtlichkeit* (Frankfurt, 1985).

13. For a discussion of Kant's belief that reason was ultimately one, see Ernst Cassirer, *Kant's Life and Thought*, trans. James Haden, intro. Stephan Körner (New Haven, 1981), p. 246.

14. Jürgen Habermas, "Questions and Counterquestions," in *Habermas and Modernity*, ed. Richard J. Bernstein (Cambridge, Mass., 1985).

15. To be fair, one should warn as well against the same temptation in dealing with bodies of thought such as deconstruction that are too easily dismissed by assailing their weakest versions. Defenders of deconstruction have a point when they react indignantly to my focus on certain American interpreters of Derridean thought rather than on Derrida himself in certain of the essays in this collection.

16. Hans Blumenberg, "An Anthropological Approach to the Contemporary Significance of Rhetoric," in *After Philosophy: End or Transformation?*, eds. Kenneth Baynes, James Bohman, Thomas McCarthy (Cambridge, Mass., 1987).

17. *Ibid.*, p. 447.

18. *Ibid.*, p. 448.

19. For a discussion of Habermas's relation to Schmitt, see the essays by Ellen Kennedy, Alfons Söllner, Ulrich Preuss, and the author in *Telos*, 71 (Spring, 1987).

20. Blumenberg, p. 452.

21. *Ibid.*, p. 451. "Vico and Western Marxism" is aimed at calling into question this claim.

22. Cited in Karl Korsch, *Three Essays on Marxism*, intro. Paul Breines (New York, 1972), p. 58.

23. *Philosophy and History*, eds. Richard Rorty, J. B. Schneewind, and Quentin Skinner (Cambridge, 1984).

24. The difference in attitude toward the status of intellectual history can be discerned by comparing two collections from conferences only three years apart: *New Directions in American Intellectual History*, eds. John Higham and Paul K. Conkin (Baltimore, 1979) and *Modern European Intellectual History: Reappraisals and New Perspectives*, eds. Dominick LaCapra and Steven L. Kaplan (Ithaca, 1982). The former is much more defensive and anxious than the latter. For a recent survey of the field as a whole, see Donald R. Kelley, "Horizons of Intellectual History: Retrospect, Circumspect and Prospect," *Journal of the History of Ideas*, XLVIII, 1 (January–March, 1987).

Index